Heroic Defeats is a comparative investigation of how unions and firms interact when economic circumstances require substantial job loss. Using simple game theory to generate testable propositions about when these situations will result in industrial conflict, Professor Golden illustrates the theory in a range of situations between 1950 and 1985 in Japan, Italy, and Britain. Additionally, the author shows how the theory explains why strikes over job loss almost never occur in postwar unionized firms in the United States. While these four countries exhibit substantial historical, cultural, and political differences – as well as marked variations in their industrial and economic structures – this book shows that unions' responses to job loss can be analyzed within the same theoretical framework in all cases.

With its blend of rational choice and comparative politics, *Heroic Defeats* is the first systematic attempt to account for industrial conflict or its absence in situations of mass job loss. This book should be of interest to political scientists, sociologists, economists, and students of labor and industrial relations, as well as specialists in European and Japanese history.

HEROIC DEFEATS

CAMBRIDGE STUDIES IN COMPARATIVE POLITICS

General Editor
PETER LANGE   Duke University

Associate Editors
ELLEN COMISSO   University of California, San Diego
PETER HALL   Harvard University
JOEL MIGDAL   University of Washington
HELEN MILNER   Columbia University
RONALD ROGOWSKI   University of California, Los Angeles
SIDNEY TARROW   Cornell University

OTHER BOOKS IN THE SERIES

HEROIC DEFEATS

The Politics of Job Loss

MIRIAM A. GOLDEN

University of California, Los Angeles

CAMBRIDGE
UNIVERSITY PRESS

PUBLISHED BY THE PRESS SYNDICATE OF THE UNIVERSITY OF CAMBRIDGE
The Pitt Building, Trumpington Street, Cambridge CB2 1RP, United Kingdom

CAMBRIDGE UNIVERSITY PRESS
The Edinburgh Building, Cambridge CB2 2RU, United Kingdom
40 West 20th Street, New York, NY 10011-4211, USA
10 Stamford Road, Oakleigh, Melbourne 3166, Australia

First published 1997

Printed in the United States of America

Typeset in Garamond #3

Library of Congress Cataloging-in-Publication Data
Golden, Miriam, 1954-
Heroic defeats : the politics of job loss / Miriam A. Golden.
p. cm. – (Cambridge studies in comparative politics)
Includes bibliographical references.
ISBN 0-521-48209-7 (hc). – ISBN 0-521-48432-4 (pb)
1. Downsizing of organizations – Case studies. 2. Trade-unions –
Case studies. 3. Labor disputes – Case studies. I. Title.
II. Series.
HD5708.5.G65 1997
331.25–dc20   96-12296
                                                                CIP

A catalog record for this book is available from the British Library.

ISBN 0-521-48209-7 hardback
ISBN 0-521-48432-4 paperback

For three generations of my family
Joan, Abe, George, and Alexander

CONTENTS

PREFACE

This is a study of how trade unions and firms interact during periods of large-scale job loss. It uses some simple game-theoretic models to delineate the conditions under which these interactions will or will not engender industrial conflict. It explores the utility of these models with empirical analyses of strikes over workforce reductions in two industries – automobile production and coal mining – and in three countries: Britain, Italy, and Japan. Since the same models prove useful in explaining why workforce reductions typically fail to generate industrial conflict in many other countries, I also look at mass job loss in the United States. In the United States, fluctuations in employment are chronic, but rarely do they engender organized union resistance.

The main claim of this study is that unions resist job loss only when the latter presents a severe threat to the union organization itself. This argument is quite general and could in principle be extended across the advanced capitalist countries. I have limited the empirical analysis to four countries in order to examine specific industrial disputes in detail, since the usual constraints of time and access to relevant secondary materials limited my efforts. At the same time, the four countries investigated in this study exhibit substantial historical, cultural, and political differences, as well as marked variations in their industrial and economic structures. Despite this, I show that unions' responses to job loss can be analyzed within the same theoretical framework for all four cases. Regardless of national context, unions and firms in modern capitalism interact in similar and predictable ways when economic pressures induce firms to downsize.

In writing this book, I have had both substantive and methodological aims. Substantively, the original impetus for the study came out of my personal observation of a lengthy and bitter dispute at the Fiat works in 1980, when the Italian union movement undertook a dramatic and fruitless strike for 35 days in an apparent attempt to resist workforce reductions. The dispute was puzzling in at least two regards. First, it seemed so obviously hopeless from the outset as to throw into doubt the very rationality of the union actors involved. Second, even as events were unfolding at Fiat, trade unionists there were reading newspaper accounts of similar situations at British Leyland and Chrysler. But in these latter two cases, industrial action to resist workforce reductions did not occur. Why such ostensibly similar situations should provoke such dramatically different responses was an analytic problem that seemed to warrant additional investigation.

Methodologically, my goal has been to integrate some microeconomics and simple game theory into the study of comparative labor politics and comparative political economy more generally. Whereas formal methods drawn from economics have produced an impressive body of work in the field of American politics, considerably less has been done in the comparative field. Rather surprisingly, political scientists who study labor politics, industrial relations, and trade unions have drawn little from the field of microeconomics, although the two would seem to display a natural affinity. Opening a dialogue between these two areas seemed worthy of effort, especially once I realized — as was quickly the case — that the standard methods of comparative case analysis were inadequate for the problem at hand.

This research was initially inspired by my observations of the 1980 Fiat strike, while I was undertaking research for an earlier book. Nonetheless, I have tried not to privilege the Fiat case in this study. This work is not based primarily on field research. Instead, it largely uses readily available secondary and primary sources to work through an argument that has been deductively derived.

In conducting research on the Fiat strike, I wish to acknowledge the assistance of the Federazione Lavoratori Metalmeccanici in Turin. Giuseppe Bonazzi and Fabrizio Carmignani generously granted access to their interviews with participants in the events at Fiat, and I am grateful to them. Helpful comments on the Italian case (and a lot of early inspiration) came from Aris Accornero, Giuseppe Bonazzi, Fabrizio Carmignani, and Gian Primo Cella.

Research on British Leyland was aided by documents and reference help from the Modern Records Center at the University of Warwick and by a small number of interviews at the Austin Rover Group (formerly

British Leyland), where company officials generously provided helpful information and historical documentation. I would also like to thank Harry Scarbrough for comments on this case.

For the research on the British coal industry, British Coal (formerly the National Coal Board) as well as the National Union of Mineworkers each provided access to materials and helpful discussions with senior officials. I am grateful to Peggy Kahn and Jonathan Winterton for guidance in researching the industry.

The research on Japan, finally, was conducted entirely from the United States and entirely in English, with the exception of a few critical articles for whose translation I am grateful to Toshio Nagahisa. Helpful comments on a draft of the Japanese case came from Andrew Gordon, Peter Katzenstein, Ikuo Kume, and T. J. Pempel.

Various drafts of materials eventually included in this study received useful comments from Stephen Amberg, David Laitin, Susanne Lohmann, Carol Mershon, Volker Schmidt, Stephen Silvia, Wolfgang Streeck, George Tsebelis, and Adam Przeworski. I received guidance developing the models presented in the first two chapters from George Tsebelis and Barry Weingast. A penultimate draft of the whole manuscript received careful readings and useful suggestions from Richard Hyman, John Kelly, Gary Marks, Andrew Oswald, Jonas Pontusson, Marsha Posusney, Peter Swenson, Sidney Tarrow, and Michael Wallerstein.

Earlier versions of materials incorporated here were presented at the 1989 annual meetings of the Canadian Political Science Association, the 1988 and the 1990 annual meetings of the American Political Science Association, and the 1993 meetings of the Midwest Political Science Association. In addition, preliminary findings were presented at Cornell University, the University of Pittsburgh, the University of California at Davis, the University of California at Los Angeles, the University of Chicago, the University of Uppsala, Washington University in St. Louis, and the Swedish Collegium for Advanced Study in the Social Sciences. In all these cases, discussants and members of the audience offered probing remarks to which I hope I have been able to respond.

Research assistance was provided by Bronwyn Dylla, Bernadette Kilroy, Jonathan Moses, and Roland Stephen. I would especially like to thank Robert Carrico for extensive assistance, including outstanding work on the Japanese case. Danise Kimball and Terri Givens helped with the graphics. In addition, Wiley Hodges of Lighthouse Design assisted in designing the game trees.

Some of the material presented here has been revised from *A Rational Choice Analysis of Union Militancy with Application to the Cases of British Coal and Fiat* (Ithaca, N.Y.: Center for International Studies, Cornell University, 1990), from "The Politics of Job Loss," *American Journal of Political Science*, 36 (May 1992), pp. 408–30, and from "Le sconfitte eroiche della classe operaia," *Politica ed Economia*, 19 (January 1989), pp. 33–44.

I wish to acknowledge the sponsors that made the original research on Fiat possible, namely the Social Science Research Council in conjunction with the American Council of Learned Societies, the Danforth Foundation, and the Fulbright-Hays Commission.

Financial support specifically for this project was provided by the German Marshall Fund of the United States and the National Endowment for the Humanities. At the University of California at Los Angeles, assistance was given by the Institute of Industrial Relations, the Center for International Business Education and Research, the International Studies and Overseas Programs, and the Committee on Research of the Academic Senate. The Political Science Departments at Yale University, at UCLA, and at Stanford University all extended hospitality when the author was on research leave, as did the Government Department at the University of Uppsala. Finally, a large part of the manuscript was written while working under grant number SES-9108513 of the National Science Foundation. None of these organizations bears any responsibility for the work that follows.

Los Angeles
July 1995

ABBREVIATIONS

AEU	Amalgamated Engineering Union
AUEW	Amalgamated Union of Engineering Workers
AUEW-TASS	Amalgamated Union of Engineering Workers – Technical, Administrative and Supervisory Section
BACM	British Association of Colliery Management
BL	British Leyland
BMC	British Motor Corporation
BSC	British Steel Corporation
CEGB	Central Energy Generating Board
CGIL	Confederazione Generale Italiana del Lavoro
CIG	Cassa Integrazione Guadagni
CISL	Confederazione Italiana Sindacati Lavoratori
CLRC	Central Labor Relations Committee
CSEU	Confederation of Shipbuilding and Engineering Unions
EC	European Community
EEF	Engineering Employers' Federation
FIM-CISL	Federazione Italiana Metallurgici
FIOM-CGIL	Federazione Impiegati Operai Metallurgici
FLM	Federazione Lavoratori Metalmeccanici
JSP	Japan Socialist Party
LIFO	last in/first out
MDW	measured day-work
MFGB	Mineworkers' Federation of Great Britain

MMC	Monopolies and Mergers Commission
NACODS	National Association of Colliery Overman Deputies and Shotfirers
NCB	National Coal Board
NEB	National Enterprise Board
NEC	National Executive Committee
Nihon Keieisha Dantai Renmei	Neikkeiren
NPLA	National Power Loading Agreement
NUM	National Union of Mineworkers
NUVB	National Union of Vehicle Builders
OECD	Organization for Economic Cooperation and Development
PCI	Partito Comunista Italiano
RMPS	Redundant Mineworkers (Payment Scheme) Order
TGWU	Transport and General Workers' Union
TUC	Trades Union Congress
UDM	Union of Democratic Mineworkers
UIL	Unione Italiana del Lavoro
UILM-UIL	Unione Italiana dei Lavoratori-Metallurgici

THE PUZZLE OF
UNION RESPONSES TO
WORKFORCE REDUCTIONS

Threatened with the bankruptcy of their employer in 1979, a majority of workers in Chrysler plants in the United States voted for major concessions in wages and benefits in an attempt to reduce the company's need for workforce reductions. Nonetheless, by so doing, employees tacitly endorsed the subsequent firings of thousands of their fellows. Faced with a similar situation a year later, autoworkers in Turin, rather than negotiating concessions, held out for 35 days in a strike against Italy's largest private employer, Fiat, a strike that paradoxically only intensified after the firm retracted its threat to effect forced dismissals and proposed temporary layoffs in their place. At the same time, neighboring Olivetti plants were laying off thousands of employees with the active cooperation of the very same union that was making national headlines with its dramatic industrial action at Fiat.

A year earlier, British autoworkers had already conceded that large-scale workforce reductions would be required were British Leyland to recover profitability and competitiveness. Just a few years later, by contrast, British coal miners decided to battle pit closures in a year-long strike that opened in 1984, a strike garnering international attention as the country's most severe and bitter since the General Strike of 1926. Paradoxically in this case too, the 1984–85 miners' strike occurred despite repeated assurances from the National Coal Board that no miner would suffer involuntary job loss. Equally ironic was the fact that many thousands more British miners had lost their jobs over the course of the large-scale decline, or "rundown," of the industry that had taken place in the 1950s and 1960s than were under threat of job loss in 1984, and the National Union of Mineworkers had at that time hardly protested. Its acquiescence in that earlier period was also striking compared with the 262-day strike undertaken in 1960 by its Japanese counterpart in the Miike mines, when rationalization in response to the shift from coal to imported oil eradicated the jobs of more than a 100,000 miners.

Why, confronting apparently identical threats, do workers and trade unions in advanced capitalist democracies respond so differently? Why do unions sometimes endorse job loss for hundreds of thousands of their members, whereas on other occasions unions wage pitched battles over the mere threat of temporary layoffs involving only a few thousand? How do we explain variations in the responses of organized labor to large-scale personnel reductions?

This study examines the interactions that occur between firms and trade unions in situations of mass workforce reductions. Since the terminology associated with mass workforce reductions is inconsistent cross-nationally (British and American usage differ, for instance), historically, and even in one country in one period, some initial terminological clarification is in order. American usage is especially confusing and ambiguous (Oaklander 1982: 187). British usage is superior, because it distinguishes temporary layoffs from permanent workforce reductions, which are referred to as redundancies (Gennard 1982: 107; Lee 1987: 20). I will consistently use the term "layoff" to refer to a temporary separation of the employee from the workplace, one carrying with it the likelihood of recall. "Firing," "dismissal," or "redundancy," will all be used to refer to permanent, forced dismissal, one where the worker's job has ceased to exist. In speaking generally of "workforce reductions," I deliberately fail to specify how these reductions will occur. Options include layoffs, firings, natural wastage and attrition, incentives to encourage workers to retire early, and so forth. I define mass workforce reductions as those involving at least 10 percent of the workforce (specified at the plant, division, or company level), although the particular threshold is only a matter of convenience.

Strikes over job loss are often of considerable political importance, and even when they are not, they are inevitably quite dramatic. They may subsequently entail innovations in public policy; in the meantime, they are usually extremely costly, highly visible, and terribly polarizing of public opinion. As the first section of this chapter will argue in greater detail, some of the disputes investigated in this book constituted turning points for labor politics – indeed, for national politics *tout court* – in the histories of the countries in which they occurred.

Behind the drama of the occasional outbreak of intense conflict over reductions in force lies the ongoing tragedy of persistent unemployment in the years since the two oil shocks. Unemployment rates in the 24 member states of the Organization for Economic Cooperation and Development (OECD) averaged 8.2 percent in 1984, for instance, compared with 2.6 percent in 1969 (Sinclair 1987: 17). By the fourth quarter of 1992 unemployment in member states of the European Community (EC) – by then much more deeply affected by joblessness than the United States and Japan – was 9.7 percent, while it was 7.6 percent in the OECD as a whole (OECD 1993: 82).

Although especially dramatic in recent decades, unemployment has long been of central concern to workers and hence to trade unions, certainly since the rise of modern industrial capitalism in the late nineteenth century (Garraty 1978; Harris 1972; Keyssar 1986). This concern has made unemployment a major policy issue in modern societies. Most social policies – and hence a large fraction of public spending – originally emerged as responses to joblessness, whether thanks to actual job loss itself or to those periods in the life cycle (mainly childhood and old age) when people are unable to participate in the active labor market. To be without work in modern society is generally to be without means. Accordingly, in his analysis of the history of the welfare state, Asa Briggs (1961: 229) argues that "it is unemployment more than any other social contingency which has determined the shape and timing of modern 'welfare' legislation."

Not surprisingly, given its history, those aspects of unemployment that have tended to interest political scientists most have been connected to national politics and public policy. Do governments manipulate the unemployment rate for partisan reasons? Under what kinds of political conditions are unemployment rates kept low? What are the effects of unemployment on social policy and government spending? Pitched at the macrolevel, questions such as these typically generate aggregate cross-national statistical analyses.

This study, by contrast, concerns unemployment at the microlevel. For individual citizens, the most direct manifestation of unemployment often takes the form of layoffs, redundancies, downsizing, and plant closures. Job loss has been a widespread and important phenomenon in the 1970s and 1980s. Between January 1981 and January 1986 more than 10 million U.S. workers above the age of 20 were displaced from their jobs (Horvath 1987: 3), for instance. Yet the politics of workforce reductions and job loss has received little systematic analysis. In particular, little has been done to understand how trade unions and employers interact during situations of workforce reductions and when these interactions will or will not engender industrial conflict. The issue of workforce reductions has sometimes figured as one of incidental importance in comparative analyses of industrial restructuring (e.g. Rhodes and Wright 1988). But it is telling that a recent study of restructuring in the European steel industry across seven major producing nations hardly mentions unions as independent actors (Houseman 1991).

The intrinsic political and economic importance of the disputes that may arise during personnel reductions is not the only reason to study them, however. Strikes over job loss are also theoretically interesting in at least three separate ways. First, they often give the appearance of irrationality, in the sense of claiming ends that seem inherently unattainable.[1] Often these disputes appear to revolve around preventing workforce reductions from taking place. But the out and out prevention of job loss in a modern market economy is hardly a realistic goal. Indeed, the ability to adjust the size of the labor force is an essential and intrinsic component of market behavior for the firm.

This is not to say that various restrictions on how firms go about downsizing do not exist. In most advanced capitalist countries, enterprises find their discretion in effecting large-scale layoffs curtailed by national legislation, collective agreements, or both.[2] Given this, it is generally entirely realistic for unions to seek to negotiate the numbers, terms, and conditions of job loss. This is precisely what occurs with what in the United States is commonly referred to as concession bargaining. In other countries, firms may be required (by law or agreement) to undertake such negotiations or consultations (for details, see OECD 1986a). But when industrial action over workforce reductions ignites, concession bargaining has by definition failed. Strikes that mobilize workers with the purported aim of preventing workforce reductions are puzzling because less ambitious but more realistically attainable goals could be deployed instead.

The argument I seek to demonstrate in this study is that strikes that occur during large-scale workforce reductions are not – whatever their slogans may suggest – aimed at *preventing* job loss. Rather, they seek to *defend the trade union organization* during the course of downsizing. I contend that even unions that appear radically to resist market forces accept that there are circumstances in which the enterprise must reduce the size of its labor force. But what no union can accept, I argue, is that the firm take advantage of such a situation to break the union itself. If too many shopfloor union representatives are included among those to be let go, or if so much of the union's membership is slotted for expulsion as to jeopardize the very future of the union as an organization, or if management is using workforce reductions as part of a larger national strategy of realigning industrial relations against organized labor, the union responds with industrial action. The aim of such action is to restore the union organization, not to prevent job loss. Strikes over workforce reductions are not, therefore, waged over their ostensible goal. Rather, they are rational, self-interested responses on the part of labor organizations to threats to trade unionism, not threats to workers.

In addition to the substantive puzzle of industrial action during workforce reductions, there are two other theoretical reasons to study strikes. Both arise naturally out of the microeconomic framework adopted in this study. The first concerns the general difficulties in studying industrial relations as rational action; the second, the particular difficulties in studying strikes.

Industrial action and collective bargaining more broadly constitute hard tests for rational choice theory, thereby posing just the sort of problem that rational choice should take on. Jon Elster (1989) has argued that collective bargaining is too complex a phenomenon to be studied exclusively using the tools of rational choice. One goal of the present study is to show, by contrast, that if we properly delineate the problem to be investigated, the tools of rational choice can be used to produce new and intellectually compelling solutions. It is true that the problem must be narrowly focused to achieve such results but, as William Riker has suggested (1990), a narrow focus to attain a proper solution is a better research strategy than a broad focus that fails to generate conclusive results. Indeed, if Riker is correct, scientific inquiry is more likely to proceed through investigation of what he labels "small events" than those classes of phenomena given by common language ("capitalism," "social democracy," "civilization"). Defensive strikes against job loss certainly fall into the camp of "small events," and by studying some specific instances, I hope to show that these apparently complex, irrational, and self-defeating actions can be analyzed within the parameters of a rational choice framework.

Finally, strikes are theoretically interesting because, until recently, economic theory could not offer much guidance for understanding how interactions between labor and capital *ever* resulted in industrial conflict. If labor and capital are fully rational, and if they have complete information about each other's preferences, they can settle on the agreement that would result from a strike – without having to strike at all. The paradox of strikes is that, if they can be anticipated, they need not occur (Hicks 1966; for a review, see Kennan 1986). As John Hicks (1966: 147) puts it, strikes often arise "from the divergence of estimates" between union and employer over how long the union can hold out, on the one hand, and the wage concessions the firm is able to make, on the other. Strikes, in other words, arise because of problems in communication between the parties, not as a necessary result of the conflicts of interest characterizing their relations.

Recent advances in game theory have developed this line of argument formally, thereby solving what is called the Hicks Paradox with the introduction of incomplete information (e.g. Hayes 1984). As Hicks's remark just quoted suggests, strikes may occur even if both parties are fully rational if one or the other lacks complete information. In wage bargaining, for instance, labor may not know exactly how profitable the firm is, and may strike to find out just how much the firm can afford to pay in wages. This line of reasoning allows that industrial action is a mechanism with which to acquire new information about the other party. It contends that, because labor and capital may have strategic reasons to withhold pertinent information, the negotiating process may break down, resulting in industrial conflict, even if both labor and the firm are fully rational.[3]

The models of strikes that have been developed using the theory of incomplete information are often technically highly complex, while nonetheless based on radically simplified assumptions about the situation and the actors. This combination of mathematical complexity and conceptual simplicity tends to make these models difficult to use in empirical investigations.[4] The assumptions bear only a vague approximation to real-world situations, the results are difficult to interpret, and critical variables almost impossible to operationalize.

This study employs a different approach. The models I develop are technically extremely simple, but highly tailored to the specifics of the problem to be investigated. Because they have been deliberately designed exclusively to study situations of workforce reduction,[5] technical simplicity becomes a virtue: it generates results that are relatively easy to interpret, and hence easily applicable empirically.

In the present chapter, I discuss the assumptions that underlie the games used in this study, and I present a small number of testable hypotheses that guide the empirical inquiry to follow. Chapter 2 presents some simple game-theoretic models of the interactions between labor and capital in situations of mass job loss. Armed with this theoretical ammunition, the book as a whole investigates a series of real-world cases of workforce reductions drawn from various countries and a range of industries. Often the case studies are already relatively well known. The theoretical materials developed in the first two chapters, however, allow new interpretations even of previously well-researched cases of mass job loss.

The current chapter proceeds as follows. The next section gives an overview of the cases to be explored in depth in this study, highlighting their intrinsic political importance. Following that, I present the reasoning that underlies the use of game theory in this study and I detail the testable propositions derived from it that will guide investigation in the book as a whole. A third section offers an initial empirical test of some of the major hypotheses advanced, by examining the extent of strikes over job loss in the four countries for which later case materials are offered – Britain, Italy, Japan, and the United States.

A PREVIEW OF THE CASES
TO BE INVESTIGATED

As I show later in this chapter, disputes over workforce reductions may sometimes constitute as many as a quarter of all strikes in a nation in a single year. Nonetheless, the number of such strikes is inevitably far less than the number of strikes that occurs over issues affecting wages. The latter almost always constitute the vast majority of industrial conflicts in any given year. Despite this, industrial action over job loss often attains a political importance well beyond what the quantitative record alone suggests. Indeed, it would hardly be an exaggeration to claim that politically the most important strikes to have affected the advanced industrial countries in the years since World War II – the strikes whose names are familiar even to the casual observer of industrial conflict and political economy – have been strikes over job loss, not strikes over wages.

Some of the cases of industrial strife selected for intensive investigation in this study constituted turning points in the politics of their countries. (A more thorough discussion of case selection is found in Chapter 2.) They will therefore undoubtedly be familiar even to readers who attend but little to matters involving industrial relations. These strikes occupied the front pages of national newspapers throughout their relatively long durations; they polarized public opinion and threatened premature death to the government in office; they mobilized hundreds of thousands of workers and often almost equally many police; and they entailed subsequent innovations in national public policy. For the unions that fought them, these strikes almost always ended in crushing defeats, and these defeats marked more general setbacks for the labor movement nationally, setbacks that in all three relevant cases affect the strength, militancy, and legitimacy of the labor movements of these countries even today. A more detailed assessment of the impact of the various strikes considered here on the industrial relations of their respective countries is found in Chapter 7.

In the chapters to follow this one, I examine interactions between firms and trade unions in situations of mass workforce reductions in Japan, Britain, Italy, and the United States. In Japan, I investigate two disputes in the mining industry, both at the Miike mines owned by the Mitsui company. The first, which resulted in a short-lived and partial victory for organized labor, occurred in 1953; the second, which ended in a dramatic defeat, lasted from 1959 to 1960. In Britain, I examine three specific cases: a strike at British Leyland in 1956, again resulting in a partial victory for the trade unions involved, another series of events at the same firm in 1979 and 1980 – events that, however, did not engender industrial conflict – and the strike of British mineworkers in 1984 and 1985, which ended in defeat for the National Union of Mineworkers (NUM). In Italy, I concentrate on a strike at the Fiat works in 1980, which labor lost. Finally, I survey historical materials relevant to showing why strikes over workforce reductions are exceedingly rare in the United States, and why the massive job loss that has regularly affected U.S. industry in the years since World War II has almost always been handled with the acquiescence of organized labor.

Many of the disputes investigated here proved to be of lasting historical significance. The two Japanese Miike strikes were among the longest and most important labor conflicts to have occurred in that country in the postwar era. The second dispute, which ended with defeat for the union movement, also marked the end of the hope for anything other than the enterprise union system that characterizes Japan today. With it, organized labor lost its attempt to secure the recognition of bargaining agents other than employees of the particular firm. If only employees of the firm can act as collective bargaining agents, trade union representation is by definition confined to the level of the enterprise. The aspiration to establish national industrial unions along the lines of those found in continental Europe was thereby stifled after the Miike defeat of 1960. Indeed, as we see in more detail in Chapter 6, the national mining federation as well as the country's major union confederation became involved in the Miike dispute precisely because of the interest they shared in acquiring recognition and legitimacy for national trade unionism generally. The defeat in the Miike mines constituted the final blow to a union movement that subsequently developed along the unique and extremely fragmented enterprise lines with which we are familiar today.

Nonetheless, the events that occurred also heralded important political gains for the Japanese working classes. The plight of the Miike miners catalyzed public opinion, and even though the campaign was orchestrated by the leftwing parties, Japan's conservative government subsequently endorsed new welfare legislation that was, by international standards, quite progressive. Even today, the Japanese welfare state remains, by most comparative measures, relatively underdeveloped. But it took an important step forward in the early 1960s with the passage of new legislation to help displaced miners in particular and later displaced workers more generally. The active labor market policy adopted for coal has since been used for other industries. Active manpower policy has, moreover, proved an important component in maintaining Japan's low unemployment rate even as most of the rest of the advanced capitalist countries faced increasingly high unemployment in the 1970s and 1980s.[6]

The strike of autoworkers at British Leyland in 1956 also helped catalyze innovations in public policy, although these were somewhat slower in coming than those that followed the great Miike strike of 1959–60. Not until 1965 did the British Parliament pass the Redundancy Payments Act, whose main goal was the prevention of industrial disputes over redundancy, largely through the provision of severance payments. At the same time, the 1956 strike had been only one of a series of disputes over workforce reductions that had swept the British automobile industry, a series that eventually led the industry as a whole to adopt methods to handle job loss that were less likely to engender industrial conflict. Although automobiles remained an industry that was relatively strike prone, disputes increasingly concentrated on wages, and workforce reductions became less provocative an issue.

Even more important to British history was the miners' strike of 1984–85, the country's largest and most serious industrial conflict since the General Strike of 1926. The strike represented a showdown between organized labor and the newly ideological Conservative Party under Prime Minister Margaret Thatcher, and it was a showdown that the union movement lost. Organized opposition to Thatcher's plans for the nationalized industries, to her new industrial relations policies, and more generally to the new Conservative political agenda largely ceased after the defeat of the miners. The British labor movement found itself in retreat thereafter. In the decade following the strike, the trade union movement increasingly adopted policies labeled "the new realism," policies that represented an accommodation to Tory power and to management's newly claimed authority. In the mining industry, too, the strike represented the last (and indeed the only) attempt to use industrial action to prevent the government from moving Britain largely out of the production of coal altogether.

The defeat of autoworkers at Fiat in 1980 also signaled a more general weakening of Italian union militancy. (For a more qualified assessment, see Chapter 7.) Like the British union movement, in the 1970s the Italian had been highly aggressive, relatively strike-prone, and extremely powerful on the shopfloor. Indeed, prior to 1980, the Italian labor movement had arguably been Europe's strongest on the shopfloor, as the shop steward movement that had arisen at the end of the 1960s in the wave of militancy known as the Hot Autumn acquired extensive influence over all matters of industrial organization and wage setting. After the Fiat strike, however, organized labor was forced onto the defensive, seeking as best it could to accommodate the economic turmoil of the 1980s. On the shopfloor, union influence was undermined as firms sought to regain the authority they had ceded shop stewards. Europe's strongest factory-based union movement thus found its influence enervated. The Fiat strike was considered a turning point for organized labor, and indeed for the left more generally, one that signaled an overall political shift to the right in the country. Just as the Miike strike of 1959–60 represented the end of the attempt by Japanese unions to construct a European-style nationally based labor movement, the Fiat strike of 1980 represented the end of the attempt by Italian unions to construct a radical, shopfloor-based labor movement.

THE CONTEXT: WHEN FIRMS SHED LABOR

However dramatic and important politically, the industrial disputes studied here are unusual events. Only rarely do firms ignite major displays of labor militancy in the course of workforce reductions. In all the cases reviewed in this book, unexpected exogenous shocks in the energy sector form the backdrop for the events described. Dramatic changes in energy prices threw into turmoil the various enterprises studied. Their abilities to control their costs of production were shaken; competition greatly intensified in the product markets in which they operated.

In the mid- to late 1950s, when the disputes in the British automobile industry and the Japanese coal industry transpired, the world's coal industry was undergoing early exposure to competition from oil. Coal companies everywhere were forced to close mines and develop ways to cut the costs of production for those that remained open. At the same time, the British automobile industry underwent a short-term but severe recession due to the Suez crisis. In all these cases, changes in the price of raw materials and related changes in the nature of product demand put the various enterprises under enormous pressures to lower their costs.

Likewise, events in the 1980s in the Italian, British, and Japanese automobile and coal sectors occurred shortly after the dramatic increases in world oil prices in 1973–74 and then again in 1979. For automobile firms worldwide, these changes entailed both recession and restructuring (Altshuler et al. 1984). Workforce reductions were common. For coal, which was initially expected to benefit from the increase in oil prices, competition from low-cost producers, especially countries such as South Africa, actually meant intensified competition and pressure on prices. As in the 1950s, another global round of mine closures occurred (see Rutledge and Wright 1985).

Not surprisingly, the responses to changes in energy prices by all the firms in question included increased attention to labor costs. In theory, workforce reductions would have been unnecessary if wages could have been sufficiently reduced instead. For various reasons, however, postwar capitalism is characterized by the feature that firms generally *cannot* quickly adjust wages with complete discretion, or often even with much discretion at all. Even in a context of excess labor – and relatively high levels of unemployment were evident in all the cases discussed in this study – wage rates are difficult to lower.[7] They are, as economists put it, downwardly rigid, or sticky. Economists are unsure of the underlying causes of the persistent unemployment affecting the European Community countries in the 1980s and 1990s, but most agree that rigidity of real wages is at least part of the story (Bean 1994: 614). While they have various ways of interpreting this phenomenon (for instance, see the collection available in Akerlof and Yellen 1986), for our purposes the important point is simply that if production costs increase due to an exogenous shock, and if wage costs cannot be adequately adjusted, the firm will necessarily seek to reduce the size of its labor force.

When this adjustment engenders industrial conflict is the main question this study seeks to answer. Various possible responses that may seem intuitively obvious turn out simply to be wrong. In the chapters that follow I show, for instance, that unions do not necessarily accommodate temporary layoffs but resist permanent downsizing. Similarly, the nature of the options workers would enjoy were they let go (including alternative employment prospects or the level of unemployment benefits available) does not systematically correspond to union responses to workforce reductions. Likewise, the number of workers threatened by downsizing is irrelevant to predicting industrial conflict. More generally, as all these examples illustrate, I show that union responses cannot be predicted on the basis of a *median voter* model of union behavior. That is, the decisions of union leaders facing workforce reductions cannot be accurately predicted on the basis of what the average union member seems likely to want. Such an approach is typically taken by economists who study trade union behavior. But it is, I argue, misleading to study unions in this way, at least in situations of mass workforce reductions, and possibly more generally.

What we might call *structural models* of union behavior and industrial relations are also inadequate in the face of the problem at hand. These models, which are used by both political scientists and economists, examine the impact of structural features of trade unions and the bargaining system – such as the degree of internal union centralization, the extent of union concentration, the level of wage bargaining, and the degree of cohesion among employers – on macroeconomic outcomes, such as the extent of

unemployment, inflation, and economic growth (for an example, see Calmfors and Driffill 1988). This general line of argument suggests that where
unions, employers, and/or wage bargaining are relatively encompassing
nationally, industrial action will in general be less common (by extension,
Hibbs 1978; Olson 1982). Accommodations between unions and employers
over workforce reductions should be more likely to characterize such settings.
Conversely, all the countries examined in this study exhibit comparatively
decentralized and fragmented industrial relations systems, where industrial
conflict occurs with relative frequency and where accommodations over
workforce reductions would be less often expected. As a general rule, a
structural approach would expect relatively frequent industrial conflict over
workforce reductions (and other issues) in all four countries studied in this
book. This, however, is not the case. In what follows, we see that system-
level structural characteristics do a poor job accounting for the outcomes
observed both within and across countries. While the former is hardly
surprising – no cluster of system-level characteristics could be expected to
account for all the sub-system-level variation observed – the latter is far
more damaging analytically. I show that some countries with relatively
decentralized union movements and fragmented industrial relations systems
experience conflict over job loss only rarely, whereas other, structurally
similar countries experience such conflict relatively often. Because a structural approach groups such cases together, it does a poor job accounting
for the apparently systematic differences among some of these countries.

The inadequacies of conventional approaches in explaining the outcomes
characterizing the interactions of firms and unions when workforce reductions take place call for developing an alternative approach. This study uses
a simple game-theoretic framework. Some reasons for using game theory
and some assumptions that underlie it are spelled out in the next two
sections. The framework is then used to generate testable propositions,
which are examined in a preliminary fashion in the present chapter.

PRELIMINARY METHODOLOGICAL
OBSERVATIONS ABOUT APPLIED
GAME THEORY

The use of deductive game-theoretic models for empirical comparative
analysis, especially case study analysis, is relatively undeveloped. Hence,
there is no body of research to call on that has developed rules (or even
norms) in how to apply rational choice in empirical settings. Rules of
evidence for assessing causal statements are generally consolidated across

the (social) sciences (for application in political science, see King, Keohane, and Verba 1994). But issues arise in game theory that are peculiar to the study of behavior as strategic interaction involving actors' preferences. In particular, since different conclusions follow from different assumptions about what actors' goals are (their preferences), determining preferences is obviously a crucial and sensitive endeavor. In this section, I argue that *asking* actors what their intentions are is a poor research strategy, and that we should instead rely on strong theoretical propositions combined with good case selection to *infer* preferences.

In the study that follows, I begin by making assumptions about what trade unions and firms want during the course of workforce reductions. I assume unions aim first and foremost at protecting themselves organizationally, whereas firms, at least in their interactions with organized labor, aim at taking advantage of the situation to threaten trade union organization. This study both explores some implications of these assumptions, especially implications having to do with whether industrial conflict will ensue, and by the same token tests the accuracy of the assumptions themselves. If outcomes correspond empirically to what theoretical models based on these assumptions predict, some claims can be made for the accuracy of the assumptions about the actors' preferences. As a result, we can gain some confidence in our assumptions about actors' goals without necessarily investigating these goals empirically.

It may be surprising that the kind of intentional analysis entailed by game theory (see Elster 1983) does not require actual empirical investigation into the intentions of agents. If anything, in most circumstances, direct empirical investigation is both unnecessary and undesirable. The reason, as we shall see in more detail in a moment, is that participants have strong incentives to misrepresent their goals in these situations. Hence, asking them why they did things is likely to confuse and mislead the observer. Instead, a strong research design and proper case selection allow for testing intentional propositions by examining whether the pattern of outcomes across cases is that predicted by the models. At the same time, examining the actual behavior of participants during the course of events is also often an illuminating way to assess their motives.

For the problem at hand, direct examination of the intentions expressed by trade union officials and company managers is likely to produce misleading information. Both groups have strong incentives to describe their goals in ways that render it difficult to assess them. In this study, I contend that unions that engage in industrial action over job loss are really aiming at protecting their own militants from job loss, not ordinary workers. But it would be extremely difficult to validate this argument by asking union officials if it were true. There are many reasons why union leaders cannot necessarily define industrial action as directed specifically and exclusively at protecting the union's own militants. Such a goal may strike potential participants as unworthy of the sacrifices required. Similarly, the managers of an enterprise may wish to target shopfloor union representatives during workforce reductions but may find it politically inopportune to admit this publicly.

More generally, students of strikes and industrial conflict have observed that a number of features render strikes problematic to analyze through the expressed decisions and ostensible goals of the actors involved. First, it is usually difficult to describe in any detail the nature of decision making during situations of industrial conflict. Observers of a major industrial conflict in Britain explain:

> Decisions 'emerge' or are determined almost by default over quite long periods of time. The gradual nature of decision-making which converges on a consensus makes it quite difficult to observe and identify a clearly delineated choice point which could be described as a decision. Furthermore, the decision-making may be subject to continuing adjustment as the circumstances surrounding the issue change or develop, such that a final decision is in any case sometimes not possible. (Hartley, Kelly, and Nicholson 1983: 104–5)

Even in the best of circumstances, it is often difficult to know who decided what, when they did so, or what they sought to gain in situations of industrial conflict.

There is, in addition, the fact that industrial conflict is inevitably experienced by participants as a complex phenomenon, one with multiple goals. This is in part because of the multifaceted relationship that obtains between union leaders (shopfloor representatives in particular, but also full-time external officials) and the rank and file (see Batstone, Boraston, and Frenkel 1977). Leaders themselves are a diverse group, and their goals coincide only imperfectly with the goals of the organization generally. Strikes are especially complex phenomena, because they require an unusually high level of leadership; the coordinated, effective sacrifice of pay by a large number of persons is hardly a spontaneous event. As a result, it is often in the interest of leaders to represent the strike situation to the rank and file in ways that may not entirely correspond to the leaders' own views, or to other objective aspects of the situation. This makes it difficult to evaluate directly available empirical evidence regarding the reasons for strikes.

Finally, there are specific problems associated with the study of strikes that end in what participants define as defeat, an outcome common to the situations considered here where union acquiescence to both workforce reductions and to the dismissal of shopfloor activists usually ensued. "It is common," as one study notes, "in situations of failure or defeat, for groups and individuals to attribute blame to sources external to themselves . . . " (Hartley et al. 1983: 156). Such circumstances render attempts to collect interview evidence after the fact highly problematic. Even where researchers have established trust with participants, information gathered in this fashion will be contaminated by a genuine inability on the part of participants to recall events truthfully.

For all these reasons, in the case studies that follow I rely only occasionally on direct testimony from participants. More frequently, I assess evidence regarding patterns of behavior during the course of events and across cases, the sequencing of particular events, and the patterns of outcomes found across numbers of cases. Sometimes these correspond to the professed intentions of agents; but when they do not, I take what organizations and officials did over what they said as evidence of their intentions.

THE JOB LOSS GAME

A game-theoretic model is a simple depiction of an interaction between two or more agents, known as players. Every game has three elements: a set of players, a strategy space, and payoff functions.[8] In any game players are assumed to be rational. This simply means that they will try to do the best they can given the circumstances in which they find themselves. What this exactly is, in turn, depends on the preferences each actor holds.

In Chapter 2, we examine interactions between the institutional representative of the firm's employees – the trade union – and the firm's management. Here I lay out the assumptions that drive the models. All the games we examine begin when the firm, confronting some exogenous shock (such as a change in energy prices), announces that large-scale personnel reductions are required. The game thus begins with the decision by the firm to expel workers.

ASSUMPTIONS OF THE MODELS

In order to calculate payoff functions in the games presented in the next chapter, we initially make three simple assumptions. These are: that strikes are costly; that firms want to target shopfloor trade union activists during workforce reductions; and that unions in turn want to protect their activists.[9] I discuss each in turn.

First, assume that a strike, were it to occur, would be costly to both sides. For the union, a strike is costly because workers lose wages and may need or expect strike funds to be paid, or because the union may lose members if scabs enter the enterprise and work in place of striking employees. For a firm, a strike is costly because it stops or disorganizes production.[10] Firms prefer that industrial relations go smoothly, and that open conflict be avoided. The assumption that industrial action carries costs to both the union and the firm is intuitively obvious and empirically plausible in most circumstances.

Second, assume that when personnel reductions occur, the firm prefers to target union representatives among those to be let go. (In what follows, I interchangeably refer to these persons as shop stewards, union representatives, activists, and organizers.) This assumption is more unusual, and accordingly requires a more elaborate justification. One way for the reader to consider the matter is to imagine how a firm and its employees would confront each other in a kind of preorganizational state of nature – a situation in which worker organization (both in the particular firm in question as well as in its competitors) did not already exist and in which protective and enabling legislation was absent. In such a context, the firm would prefer to continue dealing with its employees as single individuals rather than an organized entity. The history of early industrial capitalism largely corroborates that the primitive preferences of the firm involve avoiding trade unionism, in that firms in this early period typically tried to discourage the formation of unions.

History, of course, only serves as a metaphor for the game-theoretic situation analyzed here. Nonetheless, trade unionism is undeniably costly to a profit-maximizing firm. Just how costly is variable empirically. Using data from the United States, Richard B. Freeman and James L. Medoff (1984: ch. 12) show that where workers are organized into unions, profitability falls. To some extent, this is offset by the contribution union organization makes to the firm's productivity, but whether the losses or the gains associated with trade unionism are larger is not predetermined. The main advantage to the firm in dealing with employees as individuals rather than as a collectively organized body is that organization entails the capacity to engage in collective action (cf. Pizzorno 1978: 278). Without organization, individual workers can disrupt or sabotage production, but strikes as such do not occur, for instance.[11] Incapable of an organized withdrawal of labor power, workers are not collectively able to raise their wages or extract other costly improvements in their benefits and working conditions.

But the most compelling evidence that firms – or at least some firms – would prefer a nonunion environment comes from the myriad legislation found across OECD countries protecting trade unions from employer discrimination.[12] OECD countries generally have legislation against unfair dismissal, legislation preventing firms from firing union activists purely and simply because of their union activities (OECD 1986b: 94). In the United States, the Wagner Act provides the right to organize, thereby protecting union activists (Meyers 1964). Such protections for union activists require that firms that remain intent on union busting employ subtler means than firing individual union organizers for no reason other than their union activities.

Mass workforce reductions provide just such a convenient cover for picking off union representatives. When large numbers of workers are let go for justifiable economic reasons, who is to say how many union activists can legitimately be included? Precisely because of the extreme vulnerability of the union during the course of personnel reductions, legislation or collective agreements specifically protecting the organization during downsizing exist in many countries. In fact, the analysis of the development of seniority rules for layoffs in the United States that appears in Chapter 7 illustrates that such rules develop endogenously: that is, they develop out of the need to provide institutional protections for trade unions in a context in which picking off union organizers is endemic. Once such rules exist, union busting during large-scale workforce reductions is no longer a viable option for firms. Thus, where protective legislation or collective agreements exist, we no longer observe firms attempting to discriminate against union organizers when workforce reductions transpire. That we do not observe such behavior does not mean that the firm would not prefer to target activists. The preference remains, but the evidence for it now lies in the rules that prevent it being acted upon. This argument may seem a slight of hand, but in fact it can be assessed empirically. Cross-national evidence for it, and thus for the realism of the assumption that firms prefer to target union activists in the absence of restrictions on doing so, is provided later in this chapter.

In the absence of institutional protections preventing such a move, we thus assume that management would always prefer to take advantage of situations involving mass personnel reductions to try to disrupt and even to break trade unionism, unless there is too high a cost to doing so. The cost incorporated into the models that are developed in Chapter 2 is that of industrial action itself. Strikes themselves are sufficiently costly to the firm such that we assume – in most of the models – that the firm would refrain from targeting union activists for dismissal if it knew industrial action would ensue as a result.

The third assumption in the models to follow is that the union wants to protect its activists on the shopfloor from expulsion from the enterprise.

Ordinary workers have only to pursue their individual interests, but union leaders have to pursue the interests of the organization itself; that is, they have to act as caretakers for the union or risk its demise. Union officials are the guardians of the institutional needs of the union itself, of which self-preservation is a prime example. Just as the managers of the firm must worry about profits in the competitive market environment, managers of the union must worry about *organizational survival*, or *organizational maintenance*, in their constant struggle against capital. Indeed, organizational survival may well be thought of as "the central aim of the leadership" (Ross 1948: 16).

An important reason is that, in a democratic context, unions are voluntary associations. Because of this, they are inherently vulnerable to catastrophic losses of power. Members may resign; the firm may refuse to negotiate; the government may withdraw legal recognition of the union or the contracts it underwrites. There is no democratic country in which such threats do not constitute concerns for organized labor. Even where recognition seems secure, a precipitous drop in membership levels or some exogenous change may trigger unexpected aggression on the part of firms that had previously seemed reconciled to dealing with a powerful labor movement.[13] At bottom, capital only tolerates organized labor when constrained to do so, and labor is never entirely immune to organizational threats.

For modeling purposes, we need to translate labor's concern with organizational survival into a maximand – something that unions seek to maximize and that drives their behavior. In its struggle for survival the union seeks to maximize the number of shopfloor activists it deploys.[14] Perhaps this is a function of the number of members the organization seeks, the revenues it thereby collects, and thus the potential income of union leaders.[15] Nothing so crudely cynical need be the case, however. Shopfloor activists are essential for trade unions to survive and to thrive. "The union participant," a study of shopfloor unionism has explained, "is a necessary ingredient without which most local unions could not operate. There must be personnel to fill posts, opinion leaders to inform and stimulate, a cadre to mobilize for the various modes of latent and overt combat" (Spinrad 1960: 244). Seconding this view while speaking directly to the occurrence of mass workforce reductions, another scholar has argued:

> If the management had complete discretion in making the selection [of those to be made redundant], the labour union would be vulnerable insofar as its shop stewards could be made redundant. Shopfloor workers would, therefore, become reluctant to become shop stewards. Even though the union structure of officials and members might still be maintained, the activities of shop stewards in looking after the interests of their fellow

workers, which is the basis of the union's existence, would tend to diminish. (Koike 1988: 88)

Activists, finally, are hard to find; perhaps the single most common characterization of local unions is the chronic difficulty they experience in stimulating activism and the reluctance of ordinary workers to serve as union representatives (Lipset 1981: ch. 12). Except in extraordinary periods of mass enthusiasm for trade unionism, union organizations are usually hard pressed to recruit shopfloor representatives.

Some comparative data corroborating the rarity of union activism comes from the World Values Surveys, conducted in 1981–84 and again in 1990–93.[16] These surveys report values for active union participation among union members in numerous countries, including those under investigation in this book. According to the data, in 1980 only 5 percent of British union members reported volunteering for their organizations[17]; in Japan, the equivalent figure was 20 percent; in the United States, only 7 percent; and in Italy, a remarkable 48 percent (World Values Study Group 1994; author's computer analysis).[18] Leaving aside the Italian figure, the other results seem as one would have expected. Union activism among union members is relatively infrequent in the United States, Britain, and Japan. Hence, replacing union representatives would not be easy, since the pool of activists from which they are drawn is so small.

Unions, therefore, value their activists and when mass job loss threatens, their primary concern is to protect their own shopfloor organizations despite the workforce reductions that may occur.[19] Nonetheless, most of the models I develop assume that however much they value their activists, unions do not resort to industrial action to protect their activists from job loss.[20] Like the firm, the union is aware of the heavy costs of a strike and will avoid incurring them even to protect its shopfloor organization.

The three assumptions just spelled out underlie the game-theoretic models presented in the next chapter. The models themselves use simple technical reasoning, and rather than interrupt the presentation of the book's major assumptions and arguments, a full presentation is postponed for the next chapter. In the next sections I present the results of the models, results that serve as the hypotheses guiding empirical inquiry through the book as a whole.

TESTABLE PROPOSITIONS GENERATED BY THE MODELS

The games that are presented in detail in the next chapter generate a number of simple, easily testable propositions regarding the circumstances in which strikes over job loss do or do not occur. The circumstances in which strikes over job loss do occur are:

- when the firm does not know the union's threshold for tolerating the dismissal of activists during workforce reductions or, alternatively, when the firm does not know if the union would enjoy substantial externally provided resources were industrial action to occur;
- when both parties prefer a strike over nonengagement despite the costs of striking, typically because each knows some third party will help subsidize the costs of a dispute.

Conversely, strikes over workforce reductions will never occur in certain circumstances. These circumstances are:

- when, for reasons exogenous to the immediate situation (such as statutory requirements or legally enforceable collective agreements), the firm is prevented from targeting union activists during the course of workforce reductions;
- when the union's reputation for toughness is sufficiently secure such that the firm refrains from targeting activists, typically because the union enjoys the protection of a well-organized, well-financed national organization.

The case studies constituting the bulk of this work demonstrate these four propositions. Indeed, this is their main task. They do not test them statistically, for which information on far more cases would be required. Instead, they look at whether the propositions are empirically convincing: whether, that is, they illuminate the cases in powerful ways and whether, even with a limited number of cases, they make sense across time and space. Even without information on enough cases for statistical analysis, it is possible for research to use the same underlying rules of inference, thereby generating plausible and believable conclusions (King et al. 1994). In the next section, I offer an initial empirical assessment of the basic theory presented here.

A PRELIMINARY COMPARATIVE TEST OF THE MODEL

Considerable empirical variation characterizes union responses to job loss. In some countries, organized labor typically tolerates high levels of job loss without industrial action – the United States is a well-known example –

whereas in others unions lead strikes over workforce reductions with relative frequency. This section presents some data comparing the extent of industrial action over job loss in four countries. On the basis of the propositions presented in the preceding section, I propose that the main factor distinguishing countries with relatively high (low) rates of conflict over workforce reductions is the absence (presence) of institutions protecting union activists from dismissal during the course of personnel reductions.

This is a coarse-grained argument. It captures the essence of the four propositions I have advanced, all of which suppose that disputes over job loss occur only when trade union activists are targeted (although not always then). Appropriate comparative data do not exist allowing us to assess cross-nationally subtler hypotheses regarding the impact of informational imperfections or exogenous subsidies. As far as activists are concerned, however, existing data permit some general assessments, because some countries have institutions protecting union representatives during job loss whereas others do not, and information on such institutions can be collected, albeit with some difficulty.

The four countries chosen for analysis here are those used in the case studies that follow. Not coincidentally, they offer maximum variation on both strike rates over job loss and the institutional protections afforded union activists on the shopfloor.

The comparative importance of strikes over workforce reductions is illustrated by the data presented in Figure 1.1, showing the proportion of industrial disputes waged over job loss in Japan, the United States, Great Britain, and Italy for as much of the postwar period as data permit. The figure graphs the number of strikes over workforce reductions as a proportion of the total number of industrial actions in the four economies for every year between 1942 and 1990, depending on data availability.[21] Some idea of the extent of industrial action in the four countries can be gleaned from the following absolute numbers. In 1970 (a year for which data are available for all four countries) there were 5,716 industrial disputes in the United States, of which only 170 were classed as having to do with dismissals. In Italy in the same year there were 4,162 disputes of which 321 involved dismissals. In the United Kingdom, of a total of 3,906 disputes, 123 involved dismissals. And in Japan, finally, there were 4,441 disputes, only 100 of which had to do with dismissals. In absolute as well as relative terms, then, disputes over workforce reductions were frequent in Italy in 1970, whereas the other three countries all had far fewer such industrial actions.

Examining the data over time, the figure shows that the proportion of strikes over workforce reductions was greatest in Japan in the 1940s and 1950s, although not uniquely so. The Japanese peak of 1949 is unmatched

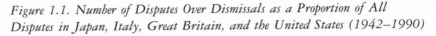

Figure 1.1. Number of Disputes Over Dismissals as a Proportion of All Disputes in Japan, Italy, Great Britain, and the United States (1942–1990)

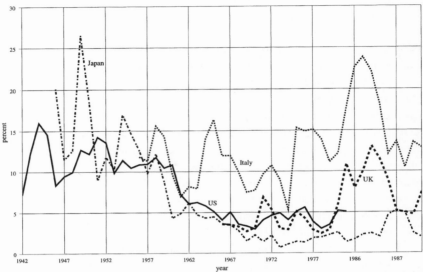

Sources: For Japan, Ministry of Labour, *Year Book of Labour Statistics* (Tokyo: Ministry of Labour, various years). For Italy, Istituto Nazionale di Statistica, *Annuario di statistiche del lavoro* and *Annuario statististo italiano* (Rome: ISTAT, various years). For Great Britain, Department of Employment, *Employment Gazette* (London: HMSO, various issues). For the United States, Bureau of Labor Statistics, *Bulletin* (Washington, D.C.: U.S. Government Printing Office, various issues).

by any of the other three countries, but Italian proportions after the mid-1970s are also quite high. There, the proportion of industrial disputes caused by issues involving job loss rose immediately after the first oil shock of 1974 to more than 15 percent, and has stayed above 10 percent for every year since 1975. Even in the 1950s and 1960s, however, Italian unions exhibited a relatively high propensity to strike over job loss, as the proportion of disputes classed this way was often more than 10 percent.[22] In the United States, by contrast, rates were relatively low even in the 1940s and 1950s, and have never gone above 10 percent since 1961.[23] Britain, finally, exhibits very low rates of disputes over workforce reductions throughout the 1960s and 1970s,[24] while in the 1980s such conflicts have become relatively more frequent, sometimes exceeding 10 percent of the total.

    This comparison shows that Japanese unions in the early postwar period exhibited the highest propensity to strike over large-scale dismissals, much higher than American unions, considerably higher than British unions, and even somewhat higher than Italian unions. The theory I have advanced proposes that institutional variations in the protections accorded shopfloor union activists should correspond to these variations in dispute rates across countries. Strike frequency over job loss should vary according to the extent to which shopfloor union activists are protected during large-scale personnel reductions. The following sections offer brief country-by-country discussions of this hypothesis.

JAPAN

Japan is an especially interesting case because strikes over workforce reductions were common in the 1940s and 1950s but became quite rare afterward. After World War II and through the 1950s, disputes over workforce reductions were frequent, comprising more than a quarter of all strikes at their peak in 1949, for instance. In 1960, however, the number of such conflicts tumbled to under 10 percent – indeed, in most of the following years, to less than 5 percent – where it has consistently remained until the present. This drop mirrors the general pattern of industrial conflict in Japan. Strike propensity generally was high in the 1950s (higher than in most other advanced capitalist nations), and remained so until the mid-1960s, after which it declined so that by the late 1970s Japanese strike rates were lower than major Western European countries, with the exception of Germany (Hanami 1984: 206; Korpi and Shalev 1980).

The theory presented here predicts that the decline in the frequency of strikes over workforce reductions in Japan parallels the development of institutions protecting union activists. And this is largely the case. In the 1940s and 1950s, Japanese firms exercised complete discretion in selecting those to be expelled during workforce reductions. Even after the end of the Red Purge in 1949–50, which constituted a direct attack on labor's right to organize, enterprises continued to single out union activists throughout the 1950s, systematically attempting to weaken unions affiliated with what had become Japan's major confederation, Sōhyō, and promoting "second" unions to compete with those affiliated with Sōhyō. The typical pattern of a dispute over workforce reductions in the 1950s thus went as follows: the company dismisses a certain number of employees, who nonetheless continue to report to work; a lockout ensues; numbers of workers – possibly a coalition of those who knew they would not be fired and those hoping that by strike breaking they could convince the firm to retain them – secede from the original union, forming a second union; the company and the new union reach an agreement and the latter orders its members to report to work; in attempting to reenter the factory, violence occurs at the factory gates; eventually, the original union is reduced to minority status and forced to settle on disadvantageous terms (Fujita 1974: 323 and 347; see also Koike 1988: 171). One analyst has argued that these union schisms constitute a "conspicuous feature" of postwar Japanese labor relations, one that had led to multiple enterprise unionism with unexpected frequency (Kawanishi 1992: 33). Corroborating this, another argues that "most of the major strikes in postwar Japan have been solved [sic] by this method" (Nakayama 1964: 1).

In these disputes over workforce reductions, at least through the first half of the 1950s, "union activists were *always* the target of discharge" (Fujita 1974: 354; emphasis added). As Kazuo Koike writes:

> Prior to the mid-1950s when layoffs were more common, if the number of volunteers [for layoffs] did not meet the quota, managements [sic] would make the additional selections, usually choosing older workers (45 years of age or older), those with poor attendance records, and those who were "less efficient." The last item, in particular, tended to be used to lay off active union members such as shop stewards. (Koike 1983a: 49)

Even in the 1980s, another scholar writes that "There is no established rule or agreement on dismissal like the 'seniority' principle in the U.S.A. Therefore, management also uses these dismissal methods in its attempts to weed union activists from its work force" (Shigeyoshi 1984: 5).

Workforce reductions still occur in Japan, and in large numbers. But after the 1950s, unionized workers were largely protected from them with the development of what is called "lifetime employment" (described in detail in Chapter 5). Indeed, Koike (1983a: 49) has argued that after the long and costly strikes of the 1950s, firms "have since become very cautious in their selection of the workers to be laid off." Taishiro Shirai (1968: 33o) too notes that, because disputes over workforce reductions in Japan have been especially costly, firms have learned not to trigger such strikes. In the 1970s, for instance, when recession resulted in noticeable numbers of layoffs, "Management was careful not to resort to the nomination of candidates for redundancies, but maintained instead a system of advertising for volunteers" (Koike 1987: 91). The same had been true when workforce reductions were required even in the years of labor shortage in the 1960s (Ujihara 1974: 160). As a result, trade unions have tended to cooperate in workforce reductions affecting their members since 1960. Firms have stopped targeting union activists – indeed, union members altogether – in workforce reductions. This has allowed unions to gain stability on the shopfloor. No longer threatened when workforce reductions take place, unions no longer mobilize their members to oppose such reductions. Industrial disputes over job loss largely ceased in Japan once firms no longer targeted union activists in the course of large-scale personnel reductions.

UNITED STATES

In the United States, union militants enjoy almost complete protection from expulsion from the firm thanks to seniority arrangements (Abraham and Medoff 1984: 90). Seniority orders job loss according to when one was hired, with the most recently hired the first to be let go. In this context, disputes over job loss are rare because (as Chapter 4 demonstrates in greater detail) union representatives tend to enjoy more seniority than the average worker. Moreover, as the theory presented here would lead us to expect, as seniority arrangements have become virtually universal in the years since World War II, the incidence of disputes over workforce reductions has fallen even further. This is true despite the fact that American firms resort to layoffs with considerably greater frequency than firms do in Europe or in Japan (Moy and Sorrentino 1981). The American data verify that the frequency of layoffs does not by itself necessarily engender frequent industrial conflict.

ITALY

Italian unions also enjoy seniority provisions when redundancies occur. A 1965 agreement between the country's three union confederations and management bodies stipulates three criteria to use in the event of permanent workforce reductions (*licenziamenti*): the technical-productive requirements of the firm, seniority, and the family responsibilities of the employee (Ventura 1990: sec. 6.4). Temporary layoffs, however, are entirely unregulated because the courts have ruled that the provisions regarding redundancies are not applicable (Scognamiglio 1990: 447; Ventura 1990: sec. 6.8). Moreover, Italian firms have used temporary layoffs to the almost complete exclusion of permanent workforce dismissals since legislation was adopted in the 1970s allowing public funds to be used to subsidize the costs of temporary layoffs to the firm (Padoa-Schioppa 1988). As the hypothesis I have presented would lead us to expect, the incidence of industrial action over workforce reductions has grown in Italy with the increasing number of institutionally unregulated layoffs that have taken place since the first oil shock.

UNITED KINGDOM

In Britain, finally, there is considerable variation in the institutional protections afforded union representatives during the course of workforce reductions. Seniority – there called "last in/first out" (LIFO) – although the single most important ordering device for workforce reductions, is applied considerably less frequently than in the United States. While it may be true that it constitutes "the most widely used method for choosing who in a slump will be made compulsorily redundant" (Oswald and Turnball 1985: 82), results of a 1984 survey of enterprises found that LIFO constituted the basis of selection in fewer than half the cases involved (Millward and Stevens 1986: 221). Corroborating this, the results of a 1985 mail survey of the 31 largest unions affiliated with the Trades Union Congress (TUC) found that only 28 percent of the 25 unions responding reported that LIFO proved of principal importance in the selection of the redundant (Booth 1987: 405–6). Seniority, the author concludes, "does not appear to be of primary importance in the management of redundancies in Britain, . . . an interesting contrast to the U.S. experience" (Booth 1987: 409). When seniority does not obtain, management exercises discretion in the selection of those to be dismissed. Given this, it is not surprising that British rates of conflict over discharges have fluctuated considerably in the years for which data are available, comprising more than 10 percent of the total number of strikes in the latter part of the 1980s (when job loss in Britain rose).

CONCLUSIONS

This preliminary four-country analysis corroborates that industrial action over job loss occurs most often not where job loss itself is most frequent – by all accounts, the United States – but instead where institutional protections for union representatives on the shopfloor are weakest. This constitutes *prima facie* evidence in favor of the realism of the assumption that firms prefer to target union activists during the course of large-scale workforce reductions, provided that statutory or other restrictions preventing them from doing so do not exist. As later chapters demonstrate in detail, these protections are most secure where seniority provisions regulate layoffs or where union members are virtually immune to job loss altogether.

This aggregate analysis necessarily offers only a first test of the arguments developed here. The case studies constituting the bulk of this study are the heart of the empirical evidence corroborating my interpretation of interactions between firms and unions during the course of large-scale personnel reductions.

THE RANK AND FILE

Thus far, I have said nothing about ordinary workers. The reason is that, as I have already argued, ordinary workers do not lead strikes, trade unions do. Thus, the preferences of the union organization are critical to understanding industrial actions, and these preferences do not directly reflect the preferences of ordinary workers. Indeed, I argue later in this book that in situations of mass workforce reductions, the preferences of ordinary workers are typically so divided as to allow unions almost complete latitude in choosing the appropriate course of action.

Assuming that ordinary workers maximize some combination of income (consumption) and leisure, we may imagine that they respond to the threat of downsizing as follows. First, individual employees will evaluate their chances of being let go depending on the information the firm has communicated to them (the criteria for selecting those to be expelled may or may not be clearly delineated and communicated). They will then consider their estimation of this probability in conjunction with their own preference for income versus leisure, the probabilities they judge exist for obtaining new employment, the probable rate of pay for such employment, and the replacement income they can expect to receive while unemployed. Most of the time, most workers prefer to remain employed with the firm rather than being forcibly expelled. The most obvious division to appear among the rank and file during the course of workforce reductions is thus based on the distinction between those likely to be laid off and those likely to be retained. Those likely to be laid off are much more likely to support industrial action, despite its costs to them in terms of lost pay and other inconveniences. Where workers have certain knowledge regarding their probabilities for expulsion – where, in other words, the firm has made the lists public – we can expect the most serious conflicts of interest among employees to arise.

Although the interests of workers act as one constraint on the union, precisely because they are inevitably so divided in their reactions to large-scale job loss, the interests of ordinary workers cannot *determine* the reaction of the union. Moreover, if unions did represent the preferences of the average employee in these situations, strikes over workforce reductions would almost never occur, since the average employee is usually not threatened. Hence, it is analytically infeasible to explain industrial action in the course of workforce reductions exclusively on the basis of employee preferences. As the earlier discussion of organizational maintenance suggested, the union has its own organizational interests, and these are not necessarily identical to the interests of workers. Many workers may be let go without jeopardizing the union's organizational interest, and while the union may prefer that workforce reductions not occur, the costs to the union are low. The extent of the threat of personnel reductions to workers is not equivalent to the extent of the threat to the union. The empirical studies that follow substantiate that where interests diverge, the behavior of the union is better predicted on the basis of its own organizational interests than as a function of the interests of the employees who are its members.

2

GAMES ANALYZING JOB LOSS

In Chapter 1, I presented the assumptions that underlie the game-theoretic analysis of job loss as well as the major results derived from that analysis. The goal was to acquaint the reader with the substantive logic of the games. The current chapter presents the games themselves. A second section discusses the rationale for case selection.

THE SIMPLE JOB LOSS GAME

The simplest possible interaction over workforce reductions is represented in Figure 2.1. The firm announces that job loss is required and has to decide whether to target union activists or not. Since the firm moves first, it is known as Player 1. If the firm targets activists, the union has to decide whether to strike or not. Since it moves second, the union is Player 2. The payoffs for each player are listed in order (Player 1, Player 2) at the three terminal nodes of the game.

The three assumptions presented in Chapter 1 allow us to order the payoffs for each player. There we said that the firm's most preferred outcome is to target activists and not face a strike (b_1). The reason, as the reader will recall, is that we assumed that firms wanted to exploit mass workforce reductions to target trade union representatives, thereby undermining union organization. However, firms were not prepared to pay the costs of a strike if one ensued. The firm's second most preferred outcome is simply not to target activists at all (c_1). Finally, it least prefers to target activists and have a strike ensue (a_1). The union for its part prefers that the firm not target

Figure 2.1. The Simple Job Loss Game

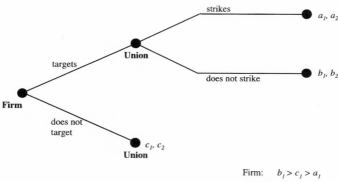

Firm: $b_1 > c_1 > a_1$
Union: $c_2 > b_2 > a_2$

activists in the first place (c_2). After that, it prefers that the firm target but that industrial action not follow (b_2). Its third preference is that the firm target activists and that a strike ensue (a_2). The order of the preferences is listed for each player below the game tree.

This game is simply solved using a technique known as backwards induction (for descriptions, see Gibbons 1992: 58–61; Ordeshook 1992: 63–73). We begin at the last move of the game – in this case, the union's choice between striking and not striking. We know, by assumption, that the union prefers not to strike if the firm targets its activists. We therefore can discard ("prune") the branch of the tree that is labeled "strikes," since by assumption this move will not occur. Moreover, since this is a game of complete information, the firm too knows that if it targets union activists, the union will not strike. That is, the firm can anticipate the other player's move, because it knows that the union is rational and will do whatever is most to its own advantage. The decision the firm faces, then, is really between not targeting (which results in a payoff of c_1) and targeting/no strike (with a payoff of b_1). We know, by assumption, that the firm prefers b_1 to c_1; this ordering is clearly indicated below the game tree in the firm's preference ordering, which is in turn simply formal notation for the three assumptions presented in Chapter 1. Thus, the only possible equilibrium outcome for this game is that, in the course of large-scale personnel reductions, the firm target activists and the union acquiesce.

The reader may object that I have ordered the payoffs improperly, and that the union would strike if it knew that the threat of targeting activists would be withdrawn. That is, the game does not allow for the possibility that the union can "win" a strike against the targeting of its activists in the course of workforce reductions. Figure 2.2 shows, however, that this can never be the case.

The Simple Job Loss Game, Extended Version, is identical to the previous game, with the addition of the decision by the firm, should a strike occur, either to go ahead and fire activists or to concede and not fire. The order of payoffs for each player is again indicated below the game tree. As in the earlier game, we assume that the firm prefers to target union activists and not face a strike (c_1) and secondarily not to target at all rather than face a strike (d_1). Should a strike occur, however, we assume that the firm prefers to go ahead and fire the union activists it has targeted rather than conceding ($a_1 > b_1$). The union's preference ordering is similar to that of the previous game. It most prefers that, if job loss is to occur, the firm not include union organizers among those to be let go (d_2), but if the firm does target, the union prefers not to engage in a costly dispute (c_2). If, however, the firm targets activists and the union strikes, the union would obviously prefer that the firm withdraw the threat to fire activists rather than going ahead ($b_2 > a_2$).

The game is solved using the same technique of backwards induction already used for the Simple Job Loss Game depicted in Figure 2.1. We begin at the final move of the game, the firm's decision whether to fire union representatives. Given the firm's preference structure, if the union strikes, the firm will not concede but will instead make good on its threat to fire activists. Knowing this, the union refrains from striking in the first place. And knowing this, in turn, the firm goes ahead and targets union activists. As in the first game, the unique equilibrium outcome of the game is for the firm to target union organizers and for the union to acquiesce.[1]

Figure 2.2. The Simple Job Loss Game, Extended Version

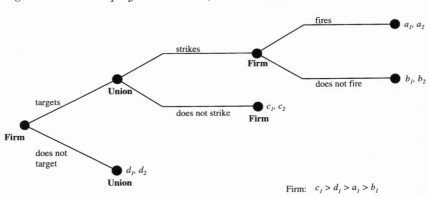

Firm: $c_1 > d_1 > a_1 > b_1$

Union: $d_2 > c_2 > b_2 > a_2$

The Simple Job Loss Game, both in its original and extended versions, thus presents us with a paradox. If both the firm and the union are fully informed and fully rational, industrial action will never occur when personnel reductions take place. Yet simple empirical observation reveals that industrial action can well occur in such situations. Apparently, we need to complicate the Job Loss Game to construct a model that comes closer to reality.

THE JOB LOSS GAME WITH A STRIKE-PRONE UNION

One possibility is that industrial action in response to the threat to effect personnel reductions may occur if the costs to the union are unusually low – that is, if the union has good reason to believe it can actually "win" the strike by holding out longer than the firm can bear. One way this can occur is for the union to receive a subsidy for the costs of a strike from an outside player. This outside player may be a national organization of trade unions, with access to financial resources far greater than those wielded by the organization encompassing any single group of employees, or it may be a political party that is favorable to the claims of the labor movement, or it may even be the government.[2] But if the union receives a subsidy in the event of industrial action, the order of its preferences changes, and with it the equilibrium outcome. I will label such a union "strike-prone" to indicate that, thanks to external support, it can tolerate the costs of industrial action more than an ordinary union. The strike-prone union prefers industrial action over nonengagement in the event that its shopfloor activists are targeted for dismissal.

Figure 2.3 depicts the interaction between the firm and a strike-prone union. The order of preferences for the firm is the same as it was in the Simple Job Loss Game. The union, however, receives a subsidy if a strike occurs (represented in a payoff of $a_2 + y_2$, where y_2 is some subsidy that more than offsets the difference in the payoffs between not striking and striking). Because of this, the order of the union's preferences is different than in the Simple Job Loss Game. The strike-prone union most prefers that the firm not target activists at all, but if the firm does do so, then it prefers to strike over not doing so ($c_2 > a_2 + y_2 > b_2$).

Using the method of backwards induction, we first prune the branch where the union does not strike since, faced with the choice between striking and not striking, the union prefers to strike (because $a_2 + y_2 > b_2$). Given, however, that the union will definitely strike, the firm – which finds industrial

Figure 2.3. The Job Loss Game with a Strike-Prone Union

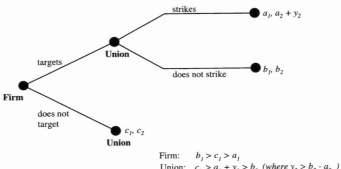

Firm: $b_1 > c_1 > a_1$
Union: $c_2 > a_2 + y_2 > b_2$ *(where $y_2 > b_2 - a_2$)*

action costly – refrains from targeting union activists during the course of
personnel reductions (because $c_1 > a_1$). Thus, the only equilibrium outcome
of the Job Loss Game with a Strike-Prone Union is for the firm not to
target activists, and for no strike to ensue. In other words, if the union,
thanks to the support of some external player, can credibly threaten industrial
action, the firm will refrain from targeting its activists in the first place.

Such an outcome is obviously one that any trade union would prefer
to the outcome that occurs in the Simple Job Loss Game, where the firm
targets union activists and the union is forced to acquiesce. As a result, all
unions will strive to develop reputations for toughness or to cultivate the
impression that they can credibly threaten industrial action if the firm targets
their activists. All unions have an incentive to appear to be strike-prone.

But such a reputation is likely to be difficult to acquire. By assumption,
the ordinary trade union cannot afford to be strike-prone, since it lacks
the resources to undertake industrial action. Circumscribing the union
organization to employees of the firm, it is empirically plausible to class
most unions as "ordinary" rather than "subsidized." Whatever the costs of
industrial action, they are likely to exceed the amount a single organization
of employees can amass into a strike fund. The historical development of
organizations linking unions in different firms to each other – and eventually
into national union confederations – was in part a consequence of precisely
the inability of single unions to bear the costs of industrial action, and the
need of all unions for labor movement solidarity. But since even national
union confederations can subsidize only some of their affiliates' strikes, no
matter how well organized the labor movement, a reputation for toughness
remains difficult to achieve and then maintain.[3]

Two implications of this analysis are worth highlighting. First, even
with a strike-prone union, a strike in the course of workforce reductions

never occurs. It is the credible *threat* of industrial action that prevents it. Second, ordinary unions have strong incentives to try to confuse management about whether they are strike-prone or not. Ordinary unions will do what they can to get the firm to believe they might actually enjoy the externally supplied resources allowing them to prefer industrial action to acquiescence in the event that the firm targets union activists. The union, in short, will strategically withhold information from the firm regarding what is called its "type," or its preference ordering. This leads to consideration of the third game in the sequence, the Job Loss Game with One-Sided Incomplete Information.

THE JOB LOSS GAME WITH ONE-SIDED INCOMPLETE INFORMATION

I have argued that trade unions have strong incentives to try to convince the firms they deal with that they are strike-prone, and that they have sufficient external resources to risk industrial action in the event that the firm targets union activists during personnel reductions. This kind of situation is referred to as one of incomplete information; that is, at least one player is uncertain about another's preference ordering. In the case at hand, the firm is uncertain how much the trade union values industrial peace or, conversely, whether it has adequate (external) resources to risk a strike. Figure 2.4 depicts the interactions that ensue in such a situation.

Figure 2.4. The Job Loss Game with One-Sided Incomplete Information

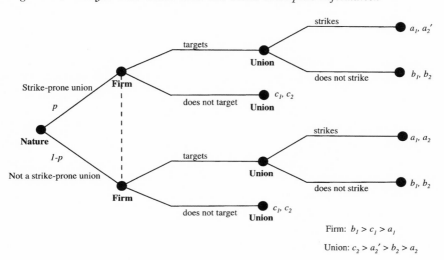

Firm: $b_1 > c_1 > a_1$

Union: $c_2 > a_2' > b_2 > a_2$

The first move is made by a player commonly referred to as "Nature," meaning simply that some initial feature of the situation is given by a probability distribution. In this case, nature determines with probability p that the union is strike-prone (that is, that it has adequate external resources to risk industrial conflict) and with probability $1 - p$ that the union is an ordinary, non-strike-prone one (and hence values industrial peace more highly than responding to the firm's threat).

The firm, which seeks large-scale personnel reductions, moves next. However, as the dashed line connecting the firm that faces a strike-prone union and the firm that faces an ordinary union indicates, the firm does not know which type of union it confronts. (The dashed line indicates incomplete information; in this case, that the firm does not know where on the game tree its own location lies.) Thus, the firm moves without certain knowledge of the union's preference ordering.

The third and final move in the game is the union's, which decides whether to strike or not. Unlike the firm, the union knows its opponent's preferences; that is, it knows its own exact location on the game tree.

Solving a game with incomplete information is more complex than solving a game with complete information. The method of backwards induction is technically inappropriate. Instead, we must put ourselves in the position of the firm, and imagine what it could expect to gain if it targeted activists and the union turned out to be strike-prone (or not) versus what the firm could expect to gain if it did not target and the union turned out to be strike-prone (or not). The two equations representing these possibilities are

$$EU_t = (a_1 \cdot p) + (b_1 \cdot (1 - p)) \tag{1}$$
$$EU_{nt} = (c_1 \cdot p) + (c_1 \cdot (1 - p)) \tag{2}$$

where EU_t represents the expected utility to the firm if it targets union activists during the course of personnel reductions and EU_{nt} represents the expected utility if it does not target them.

A strike can occur only if $EU_t > EU_{nt}$ – that is, if the expected utility of targeting is greater than the expected utility of not targeting (since strikes occur only in the case that the firm actually targets union activists, which it does only if the expected utility of doing so is greater than that of not). Solving both Eq. (1) and Eq. (2) in terms of p finds that the firm targets if

$$p < \frac{b_1 - c_1}{b_1 - a_1} \tag{3}$$

and that if the firm targets, a strike results with probability p. Put more simply, the firm targets if it thinks that the probability that the union is strike-prone is low, and refrains from targeting if it thinks that the probability is high that the union is strike-prone. If, believing that the union is unlikely to be strike-prone, the firm targets a union that is actually strike-prone, a strike will ensue.

This result is critical for present purposes. It demonstrates that, *even if both parties are fully rational, strikes may occur if one of the parties lacks complete information*. Whereas the first three games examined earlier all ended without industrial action, once incomplete information is introduced, strikes may occur.

For the empirical applications that follow, the language of the model may be recast to make it useful for a wider range of cases. In some situations it may be useful to think of the union as strike-prone or not, as we have done thus far — that is, whether the union receives additional resources from an external player such as a national labor federation, confederation, or labor-affiliated political party. Often, however, it will be useful instead to distinguish unions with low tolerances for the targeting of activists from those with higher tolerances. Varying degrees of tolerance make some unions unable to bear the dismissal of even a few activists and others able to withstand the expulsion of substantial numbers before reacting. I shall argue at greater length in Chapter 4 that the main determinant of the degree of tolerance, or threshold, experienced by a particular union is its ability to replace the activists lost to workforce reductions. This, in turn, is usually largely a function of the extent of recent union membership in the enterprise. (In Chapter 6, I also examine other institutional determinants for variations in the union threshold, determinants particularly relevant to the Japanese system of industrial relations.) Strikes over workforce reductions are most likely when unionization rates have been unstable in the preceding period, since it is in such a situation that the firm is most likely to suffer from imperfect (i.e. obsolete) information regarding the union's threshold. This terminology generates a model identical to that depicted in Figure 2.4, with the difference that instead of not knowing if it faces a strike-prone or an ordinary union, the firm does not know if it faces a low-tolerance or a high-tolerance union.

SOME ADDITIONAL IMPLICATIONS

The mathematical solution to the Job Loss Game with One-Sided Incomplete Information is not in itself very meaningful empirically, but there are some additional insights that can be derived from the model that do have potential empirical relevance. Strikes occur only if $EU_t > EU_{nt}$; the following two equations represent this inequality:

$$p(a_1 - b_1) + b_1 > c_1 \tag{4}$$
$$b_1 - p(b_1 - a_1) > c_1 \tag{5}$$

On the basis of these inequalities, we know that strikes become more likely as b_1 increases, as c_1 decreases, as p decreases, and as a_1 increases. Interpreting generates the following conclusions:

- As the costs of a strike to the firm decline, strikes become more likely (since a risk-neutral firm will be more likely to target activists as the costs of industrial action fall);
- As the benefits from targeting without engendering industrial conflict increase to the firm, strikes become more likely (since the firm will have a greater incentive to target, thereby risking industrial conflict more often);
- As the payoff from not targeting falls, strikes become more likely (because the firm is more likely to target union activists, thereby risking conflict more often);
- As the probability of encountering a strike-prone (or low-threshold) union falls, strikes become more likely (since the firm undertakes targeting more often).

These results are difficult to test empirically, since they all involve changes in payoffs over time. Most of the variables are difficult to operationalize and measure, especially over time. It is difficult to know what data to collect that could appropriately and systematically assess falling payoffs to the firm from not targeting, or changes in the probability of encountering a strike-prone union. So in this study, I restrict investigation in two ways. First, as I shall elaborate, I use a series of carefully arrayed case studies rather than systematic data sets. Second, I test a small number of simpler hypotheses – already presented in Chapter 1 – hypotheses that do not require information about changes over time.

THE JOB LOSS GAME WITH A STRIKE-PRONE UNION AND TRIGGER-HAPPY FIRM

Thus far, we have found that industrial action over workforce reductions occurs only in situations characterized by incomplete information. Indeed, I showed that if one player – namely, the union – valued defending its

activists even if this called for industrial action over acquiescence to targeting, a dispute would not result. Instead, the firm would refrain from
targeting. (Conversely, if the firm's preference ordering is that of the
trigger-happy firm depicted in Figure 2.5, but the union is an ordinary
[not strike-prone] union, the equilibrium solution is that the firm always
targets, and the union always acquiesces.) The same is not the case, however,
where *both* parties enjoy externally supplied resources such that the costs
of conflict are lower than those of acquiescence. In this case, too, strikes
may occur. Figure 2.5 represents the interaction when both players have a
preference for industrial action over nonengagement.

Because this is a game of complete information, the technique of backwards induction described previously can be used to solve it. Examining
the game shows that the equilibrium solution is that the firm targets
and a strike ensues. Thus, *if both parties strictly prefer industrial action over
nonengagement, strikes may occur*, even if both are rational and fully informed.
If we continue to adhere to the three assumptions initially laid out, these
preferences appear only thanks to the intrusion of other actors, whose
resources change the payoffs of our two original antagonists. In what follows,
empirical applications of this model will also be explored.

CONCLUSIONS

The major results of these games were already presented in Chapter 1 in
the form of four hypotheses. The hypotheses were derived deductively from
the game-theoretic models, and will be used to guide the empirical research
presented in subsequent chapters.

*Figure 2.5. The Job Loss Game with a Strike-Prone Union and a Trigger-
Happy Firm*

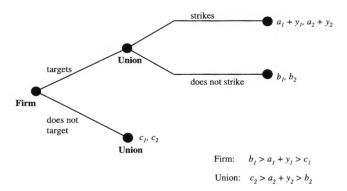

Firm: $b_1 > a_1 + y_1 > c_1$

Union: $c_2 > a_2 + y_2 > b_2$

RESEARCH DESIGN AND CASE SELECTION

The basic research design of this study is what Adam Przeworski and Henry Teune (1970) call the "most different systems" design. This design matches selected cases along subnational processes and relationships identified as theoretically important while maximizing the national settings from which cases are drawn. Such a design allows the analyst to identify patterns of causal relationships that obtain regardless of the national system in which they are located. As a result, system-level variables can themselves be excluded as causally important. That is, specific characteristics of national histories and national cultures cannot be invoked in the explanation of sub-system-level relationships that prevail across different national histories and cultures.

The most different systems design, although originally endorsed by Przeworski and Teune, was little used in comparative studies until scholars began cannibalizing economic theory for applied political analysis (for examples, see Levi 1988; Olson 1982; Rogowski 1989). Since economic theory assumes that actors are fundamentally similar regardless of the national and cultural context in which they find themselves – that is, that they are all rational, maximizing agents – it lends itself especially well to the most different systems design.

For present purposes, a case is defined as a set of events (which may or may not result in industrial action) surrounding mass job loss. Case selection was guided by the attempt to maximize the variation in the settings selected for analysis. All had to be settings in which modern labor organizations existed and were operational, thus precluding the inclusion of nondemocratic regimes (when labor unions are not fully functional) or societies in which modern industry had not already gained considerable ground. This effectively limited the pool of countries to the advanced industrial democratic nations affiliated with the OECD. I wanted enough cases to convince skeptical readers that the economic analysis I have advanced is more compelling than the alternative that cultural and historical approaches might provide, but not so many cases that each could not be explored in some detail. This consideration urged me to select cases where interactions over workforce reductions had already been well studied or where considerable amounts of relevant information were readily available.

The cases investigated in the most detail are drawn from three countries – Italy, Britain, and Japan – with additional materials taken from a fourth – the United States. Cases concern two industries – engineering (especially the automobile sector) and coal mining. The specific disputes investigated span nearly the full postwar period, ranging from reductions in force in the Japanese coal industry in 1953 to the British miner's strike of 1984–85. The cases are arrayed as paired comparisons. In the paired comparisons, I use what Przeworski and Teune (1970) call the "most similar systems" design. I first examine large-scale workforce reductions in major British and Italian automobile firms in the period around 1980. Despite their numerous similarities, the two cases exhibit different outcomes. At the Fiat works in Italy, organized labor battled layoffs with industrial action. Like its counterpart at Fiat, management at British Leyland (BL) sought to reduce the size of its workforce quite substantially and to regain managerial prerogatives on the shopfloor. Unlike its Italian counterpart, however, management at BL successfully accomplished these goals without provoking major industrial action.

The second set of comparisons I investigate concern workforce reductions in the British and Japanese coal industries. Here, too, divergent outcomes occur, but across time, not national boundaries. In Britain, the National Union of Mineworkers undertook industrial action against pit closures in the mid-1980s, although the same union had repeatedly acquiesced in large-scale closures through the 1950s and 1960s. In Japan, the union organizing miners at the Mitsui company's Miike mine struck over redundancies in 1953 and won. Six years later, however, in an even longer and more bitter dispute, it lost to the same company.

The American materials, by contrast with those on Japan, Britain, and Italy, are not industry-specific, nor do they detail particular disputes. They are instead broadly historical, spanning most of the twentieth century, and are used to explore the reasons for the development of rules that prevent targeting activists during large-scale workforce reductions. They are presented in the concluding chapter of this study, offering additional indirect verification for some of the hypotheses presented in Chapter 1.

The case studies are used to illustrate the four central propositions I have presented. Taken as a group, they show that it is analytically compelling to consider interactions over workforce reductions at the microlevel, without reference to national history or culture. In addition, they show that the same deductively derived set of theoretical propositions can be used for cases as diverse as Japanese mining in the 1950s, Italian autoworkers in the 1980s, and American steelworkers over three decades. The next four chapters present detailed empirical materials. Chapters are ordered as paired comparisons. I first analyze events surrounding workforce reductions in the Italian and British auto industries and then turn to events in the British and Japanese coal industries. The first of each set of chapters is descriptive, the second analytical. A final chapter presents some extensions and implications of the analysis.

3

JOB LOSS IN THE ITALIAN AND BRITISH AUTOMOBILE INDUSTRIES

Major reductions in force took place almost simultaneously at British Leyland and at Fiat, following on the heels of the second oil shock. Conditions at BL and Fiat were at that time strikingly similar. In both firms, newly appointed and aggressively antilabor managing directors or chairmen announced massive job reductions as part of more general plans for firm restructuring and reorganization. Both firms had been suffering from poor productivity and losing market shares to foreign competitors. In both cases, too, poor productivity was viewed by management as a result of an unnecessarily large workforce, seen in turn as a function of poor industrial relations. Union organizations at BL and at Fiat enjoyed reputations as highly militant and strike-prone, with strongly entrenched stop steward organizations in whose leadership organs Communist Party members figured prominently.

Given these similar conditions, management's decision to tackle the bloated workforce became invested with similar significance. One study has summarized the major issue involved in both cases as the "re-establishment of managerial authority," including the very authority to effect workforce reductions. Comparing the outcomes at British Leyland and Fiat, Wolfgang Streeck (1985: 21) notes, "The more or less complete recovery of the two companies by the mid-1980s is accounted for mainly by the fact that management prevailed on this crucial, and cruel subject. . . ." Both firms were intransigently committed to effecting massive workforce reductions.

Nonetheless, at Fiat organized labor responded with industrial action, whereas at British Leyland, the unions ultimately acquiesced in job loss. This analytic puzzle is explained in the next two chapters. The current chapter provides descriptive information about the two firms, their union organizations, and the manpower policies characteristic of each context. I then detail the events that occurred around manpower reductions in the period after 1979. The following chapter uses the propositions generated by the game-theoretic analysis presented in Chapters 1 and 2 to analyze why the outcomes of two such similar cases differed.

INDUSTRIAL REORGANIZATION AT FIAT AND BRITISH LEYLAND

The 35-day Fiat strike in the fall of 1980 was Italy's single most important industrial dispute of the 1980s and arguably of the last 30 years. Intense and dramatic, the final weeks of the strike witnessed a complete blockade of Fiat's plants, open threats of a factory occupation, and a polarization of public (and working-class) opinion that eventually resulted in a procession through the streets of Turin on the part of the self-proclaimed "silent majority" demanding an end to the dispute and the right to work.

The strike was precipitated by the firm's announcement that it was going to make large numbers of employees redundant as part of the restructuring called for by the changing nature of international competition in the automobile industry. Even when the threat of redundancies was withdrawn, however, and instead only temporary layoffs were at stake, the strike continued – indeed, at that point, it actually intensified.

Because the firm was known for a long history of poor industrial relations, an unusually high degree of shopfloor militancy, and a particularly ideological local union movement, the strike did not seem to Italian observers as though it were out of character for the actors involved. In the main, it was ascribed to an explosive combination of a management team absolutely determined to regain authority on the shopfloor and a small, highly ideological, and increasingly unrepresentative shop steward movement, one driven mainly by expressive and noninstrumental goals.

The outcome was generally considered disastrous for organized labor. Although ultimately the firm agreed not to fire any employees, the strike was nonetheless felt to be a defeat of major proportions for the Italian union movement. Standard contemporary histories use it to mark the final act of the era of labor strength that had begun with the wave of militancy in the late 1960s (after the events in 1969 usually referred to as the Hot Autumn) and as initiating a period of weakness for the Italian labor movement generally. The decade that followed was characterized by a decline in working-class real incomes, increasing unemployment rates, and widespread industrial restructuring.

Like its Italian counterpart, Britain's major automobile producer has long been the focus of public scrutiny and a symbol of the country's supposedly poor industrial relations. A powerful shop steward movement with recognized rights over jobs and manning, a complex and unwieldy bargaining system, a plethora of unions, and an excess of industrial disputes all characterized British Leyland in the decade preceding restructuring. Although Britain had been Europe's largest car manufacturer between 1932 and 1955 (Wood 1988: 56), by the 1970s the country's automobile industry was generally considered an internationally poor performer, with BL a major part of the problem.

Appointed in 1977 by the outgoing Labour government, BL's aggressive managing director, Michael Edwardes, was entrusted with the job of restoring BL's profitability and international competitiveness. Regaining managerial authority on the shopfloor was seen as crucial to these ends. As at Fiat, restructuring called for mass workforce reductions. Inside the company, top management considered its labor problems broadly similar to those found at Fiat in the same period (reported in Scarbrough 1982: II, 11). But unlike the events that transpired in its Italian competitor, BL's management effected personnel reductions and restructuring without engendering a major industrial dispute. Gaining the agreement of organized labor was not easy, but ultimately the firm successfully stripped stewards of much of their bargaining power, radically reduced the size of the workforce, and established new collective bargaining procedures without a major strike. Organized labor acquiesced, in short.

THE ACTORS

Four different actors came directly into play during events at the two firms: the firms themselves, the various trade unions, the shop stewards, and ordinary employees. The next four sections provide some basic information about each.

THE FIRMS

Founded in 1899, in the years after World War II Fiat became Italy's largest private enterprise and one of Europe's leading producers of automobiles. In 1979, just prior to the massive personnel reductions with which we are concerned, the firm employed some 141,000 persons in Italy who were engaged in automobile production, while an equal number were employed in other sectors, ranging from tractors to aviation (figures from Comito

1982: appendix, table 5). Despite its size, the firm was still run by its founding family, the Agnellis, and was still based primarily in Turin, where it was born nearly a century earlier.

The company dominated local employment in the province, accounting for one-third of all employees in industrial sectors and more than half of those in the metalworking industries (Golden 1988: 194, table 28). Among its numerous plants in Turin, Mirafiori was the largest; indeed, prior to the layoffs, Mirafiori was Europe's largest auto factory. In 1980, at the height of its employment, the plant alone employed more than 73,000 persons (Golden 1988: 240, table 30).

In the late 1970s the company reorganized its operations, establishing a new divisional structure. Each division was accountable for its own balance sheet. Automobiles comprised the largest division. Isolating the position of Fiat's automobile sector had the effect of bringing to light its disastrous financial state, and the poor financial position of the firm more generally (Locke 1992: 260). While large-scale workforce reductions were not the first option the company considered, it quickly began sounding out the trade unions on possible productivity improvements.

Like Fiat, British Leyland was also heavily concentrated geographically, in this case in the Coventry area (Thoms and Donnelly 1985). By the 1970s the firm was Britain's last remaining domestically owned car producer. Employing some 155,000 persons in the United Kingdom in 1979 (Wilks 1984: 206, table 8.2), by the late 1970s "on every conventional indicator BL performed extremely badly" (Wilks 1984: 206). Michael Edwardes was appointed Chairman and Chief Executive in 1977 in an attempt to reverse the company's declining fortunes. Like Fiat's management, Edwardes favored a divisional structure, in part as an effort to shake up the company and restore managerial competence and authority. As at Fiat, workforce reductions were not the first or the only aspect of reorganization enacted by the company's new management. But in both firms large-scale job loss quickly appeared inevitable following the 1979 oil shock and the precipitous decline in demand that ensued.

THE UNIONS

At both Fiat and BL organized labor is divided into competing unions. At Fiat, however, union structure is relatively simple, in that the three competitors are all organized as industrial unions, each affiliated with one of the country's ideologically distinct confederations, the Confederazione Generale Italiana del Lavoro (CGIL), the Confederazione Italiana Sindacati Lavoratori (CISL), and the Unione Italiana del Lavoro (UIL). At BL, by contrast, union structure is considerably more complex, involving myriad craft, industrial, and general unions.

The largest Italian industrial union, the Federazione Lavoratori Metalmeccanici (FLM), comprises three separate unions, each affiliated with one of Italy's competing confederations: the Federazione Italiana Metallurgici (FIM-CISL), the Federazione Impiegati Operai Metallurgici (FIOM-CGIL), and the Unione Italiana dei Lavoratori-Metallurgici (UILM-UIL). In 1982 with nearly 1 million members enrolled, the FLM organized fully one-third of all industrial unionists in the country. Over half of these belonged to the FIOM alone (527,000), with the FIM next in size (296,000), and the UILM the smallest (141,000) (reported in Golden 1988: 90).

Although nationally unionization in the metalworking sector was probably over 50 percent in 1980, the FLM's organizational strength in the Fiat works was far lower. In 1979, for instance, unionization in Turinese Fiat plants peaked at 34 percent, while unionization in other metalworking plants in the province was another full 15 percentage points higher (Golden 1988: 180, table 19). Historically, trade unions had never been especially strong at Fiat, however.

Despite this, the firm generally served as a focal point for the Italian labor movement as a whole. Events there inevitably received considerable public attention, and even national union officials often busied themselves with collective bargaining for the company. Although national federations in conjunction with Italy's business associations established wage minima, collective bargaining over wages and other so-called "normative" issues also occurred for individual firms. At Fiat, firm-level collective bargaining was considerably more complex than in most other companies. Three members of the FLM's national Secretariat were officially responsible for automobiles and thus greatly, although not exclusively, attentive to events at Fiat. Typically, wage bargaining for the company as a whole proceeded under their direction. At the same time, the FLM had established a Coordinamento, which brought together shop stewards and full-time union officials from Fiat plants across Italy. Finally, in Turin itself the firm tended to absorb most of the local union's resources and attention.

The provincial FLM of the time comprised 105 full-time officials (excluding secretarial and administrative staff). These men were young (their average age was 37), most of them having become union officials only in the years following Italy's strike wave centered around 1969 (Golden 1988: 174, table 14). For trade union purposes, the province was then divided into ten zones (*Leghe*), of which the fifth was solely responsible for Mirafiori. The sociological composition of union officials there differed somewhat from that of FLM officials generally in the province. Union personnel in the

Quinta Lega in 1980 were relatively better educated, and came from white-collar and technical backgrounds rather than out of the manual working class. Moreover, they had surprisingly little experience in collective bargaining (Carmignani 1984: 45).

Trade unionism in the British automobile industry was considerably more complex than in the Italian, itself already a relatively complex situation. At Longbridge, BL's largest facility, the 1970s found 11 unions affiliated with the Confederation of Shipbuilding and Engineering Unions (CSEU), of which the Transport and General Workers Union (TGWU) had been the largest since the 1960s. The Amalgamated Union of Engineering Workers (AUEW), formerly the Amalgamated Engineering Union (AEU), was the second largest union in BL. Together, the two probably organized more than 90 percent of manual workers in the automobile industry (Seglow and Wallace 1984: 31).

The AUEW and the TGWU differed in their internal distributions of power. The basic unit of each was the branch. In the AUEW, these were in turn grouped into districts, ruled by district committees, comprising both union stewards and elected representatives. District committees were quite powerful, since they determined whether strike benefits should be paid or not. Overall, the AUEW was a relatively decentralized union, in which districts and stewards exercised considerable autonomy, and in which full-time officials have historically been especially few (Marsh and Coker 1963: 181). It is generally considered a more internally democratic union than the TGWU, and since the 1930s has been more closely identified with the establishment and promotion of steward organization.

The TGWU's structure also comprised branches grouped into districts. However, in this union, full-time district officers were appointed not elected. Moreover, stewards had no constitutionally recognized position in the TGWU. Strike action could only be sanctioned centrally, not at district level, as was instead effectively the case in the AUEW. For these reasons, the TGWU is considered more centralized than the AUEW, although the previous two general secretaries of the TGWU, Frank Cousins and Jack Jones, had both been strong supporters of increasing steward power and influence.

Unionized only after World War II and with great difficulty (see Tolliday 1987), by the mid-1960s BL's unionization was nearly 100 percent among manual workers. Nonetheless, the collective bargaining structure in the industry in general (and in BL in particular) remained complex and fragmented. Employers could affiliate with the Engineering Employers' Federation (EEF), which in turn negotiated with the CSEU. Previously affiliated, BL withdrew from the EEF in 1980 as part of its restructuring effort. At the same time, 58 hourly paid bargaining units existed in the 34 plants of BL Cars in 1975 (when BL Cars was established). Settlement dates extended across nine months of the year, and wide variations existed in pay and conditions. There were, for instance, fully 25 different layoff arrangements (Scullion 1981: 17). Bargaining fragmentation was thus very marked at BL.

SHOP STEWARDS AND LAY OFFICIALS

In 1983, there were nearly 1,400 shop stewards in the Turinese Fiat plants, of whom nearly half (43 percent) were members of the FIOM and another one-quarter were unaffiliated with any of the three confederations (Golden 1988: 188, table 23). The FIM and the UILM were about equal in strength. Nearly half of Fiat's delegates (596 in 1983) were located in Mirafiori alone (Golden 1988: 235, table 29). Shop stewards (known then in Italy as *delegati*) combined into factory councils (*consigli di fabbrica*), the largest of which was known as the *Consiglione* at Mirafiori.

The shop stewards involved in the 1980 strike were newly elected but not inexperienced. Elections at the Turinese Fiat works had been held under FLM auspices in March of that year, and more than 2,000 union representatives elected. About 60 percent had already served as shop stewards (reported in *Flmese* 1980: 16). At that time Italian stewards were elected on blank ballots, by all employees in a shop or department.

As in Fiat, shop stewards at BL were usually elected at mass meetings through an open show of hands. The ratio of stewards to employees was better in BL than in Fiat. In the company's entire Car Division, for instance, there were about 4,000 stewards in 1976, or one for every 23 manual workers (Seglow and Wallace 1984: 44).

The internal structure of steward organizations in Britain and Italy was similar. In Britain, senior stewards, also known as "convenors," could be elected either by all stewards or directly by the union's membership. It was the senior stewards who constituted the core of the steward organization in the plant. In 1977, there were 11 senior stewards of 700 stewards at Longbridge (representing 16,700 union members). Of these 11, 4 were members of the TGWU, 2 of the AUEW, and 5 of other unions (Seglow and Wallace 1984: 45).

Whereas at Fiat the national FLM had established a Coordinamento that brought together stewards from Fiat plants across Italy, in Britain, by contrast, national unions had resisted establishing similar bodies linking stewards in different plants of the same companies. Combines, as they were called in the United Kingdom, were discouraged because they were seen as threats to regular channels of decision making and to the authority of national unions. Nor were they recognized by management in Britain.

Finally, and again similarly to the situation at Fiat, by the late 1970s steward organization at BL had become generationally distinct and isolated. At Longbridge the core organization in the postwar decades consisted of perhaps 20 Communists, a group that apparently failed during the 1970s to recruit a younger generation (Jefferys 1988: 82).

THE RANK AND FILE

In 1979 Fiat employed some 150,000 persons in Turin. The ordinary blue-collar Fiat worker in Turin in 1979 was male, in his thirties, southern Italian by birth, with no more than a high-school education, and had been hired sometime after the Hot Autumn (Accornero, Baldissera, and Scamuzzi 1980: 2–3). A small proportion of the workforce – about one-fifth – was younger, having been hired during the most recent wave of expansion in 1978–79, when approximately 15,000 new employees had been recruited (Belforte and Ciatti 1980: 19).

I have already noted that only 34 percent of Fiat's blue-collar employees in the province were union members (Golden 1988: 180, table 19). This percentage, however, understates the relationship between the rank and file and organized labor. Two-thirds of Fiat's blue-collar employees reported that they always or often participated in strikes having to do with collective bargaining issues, for instance (Accornero et al. 1980: 8). Despite this, survey evidence shows that ordinary workers exhibited relative moderation in their views of labor – management relations and were not highly conflict-prone, believing that collaboration between the parties was both possible and necessary.[1]

As in Fiat, British Leyland had begun to shed workers in 1975 and 1976, following the first oil crisis, but by the latter part of the decade was engaged in new hiring once again (Willman and Winch 1985: 33). This proved only temporary, however, as the second oil crisis provoked an even more serious crisis for the firm. Although prior to the 1970s the skilled workforce of the West Midlands automobile industry – the geographical heartland of BL – had enjoyed relatively high wages and protection from major structural dislocations, after 1980 the industrial basis there began to collapse (Taylor 1981: 65–69). Workforce reductions rippled across the area.

The reactions of employees in the automobile industry are difficult to gauge. There exist no surveys of rank-and-file attitudes of BL employees such as are available for Fiat. Nonetheless, under Edwardes's leadership, a whole series of issues had been put directly to the workforce for approval rather than waiting out the lengthy process of obtaining the agreement of BL's stewards prior to initiating internal reform. The ballot results give some information on rank-and-file sentiments.

Table 3.1 presents results from five separate BL ballots between 1977 and 1980 (the last of which was organized by the CSEU; the first four, by the firm). Employees at British Leyland approved the reform of collective bargaining proposed in 1977, a parity payments scheme in 1978, and the controversial recovery plan in 1979. The recovery plan in particular passed by an extremely wide margin. On the other hand, employees rejected the establishment of a company-wide incentive scheme in 1978. Likewise, when balloted by the CSEU, they rejected the "Blue Newspaper" in 1980 (detailed later in this chapter).

Although it is difficult to draw many conclusions from these data, one thing stands out. Most employees at British Leyland were clearly uninterested in confronting the firm through major industrial action over the recovery plan, despite the fact that it involved large-scale workforce reductions. Ballot results from 1979 reveal that nearly 90 percent of those who voted approved the plan, and with it the proposed layoffs. Earlier, too, employees had shown considerable willingness to allow Edwardes to institute

Table 3.1. *Ballot results at British Leyland, 1977–80*

Date of ballot	Issue	Yes	No	No. of voters	Eligible voters (turnout)
October 1977	Bargaining reform	59,029 (65%)	31,304 (35%)	90,333	103,605 (87%)
April 1978	Incentive scheme	21,759 (32%)	46,106 (68%)	67,940	97,000 (70%)
December 1978	Parity payments	48,702 (66%)	25,403 (34%)	74,105	95,000 (78%)
October 1979	Edwardes recovery plan	106,062 (87%)	15,541 (13%)	121,603	166,603 (73%)
February 1980[a]	Pay offer ("Blue Newspaper")	41,422 (59%)[b]	28,623 (41%)	70,045	85,115 (82%)

[a]Ballot organized by CSEU.
[b]A "yes" indicated voter favored rejection of offer.
Sources: TGWU, reported in Paul Willman and Graham Winch, *Innovation and Management Control: Labour Relations at BL Cars* (Cambridge: Cambridge University Press, 1985), 185, table 9.1.

a series of reforms that shop stewards in general opposed and that had the effect of diminishing steward autonomy. The ballot results give little support to the interpretation that stewards at BL represented a highly militant rank and file that sought a direct confrontation with management over rationalization and workforce reductions. In this regard, the situations at Fiat and at BL appear strikingly similar.

INDUSTRIAL RELATIONS IN THE FIRMS

Prior to 1980, Fiat was known for its poor industrial relations. Strikes were extremely frequent in the decade following the Hot Autumn of 1969 (Buran 1982). The shop stewards, although not officially recognized as such by the company, enjoyed extensive influence over the daily decisions affecting the deployment of the labor force on the shopfloor and affecting workloads. Management considered that it had lost authority on the shopfloor in the years since the Hot Autumn and the birth of the steward movement.

The company had long been known for its hostility to organized labor. In the 1950s, under U.S. prodding, management had gone after members of Partito Comunista Italiano (PCI) in the factory, wrecking the FIOM and reducing the PCI virtually to insignificance. Fiat had even tried to establish a company union, although its efforts failed.

Like its Italian counterpart, Britain's major automobile producer was known for its poor industrial relations. In the 1970s, industrial relations were identified as the main factor damaging the productivity of British automobile production compared with other European producers (Jones and Prais 1978; but cf. Marsden et al. 1985: 3–7). Observers focused on the impact of the job controls exercised by shop steward organizations, which were held to have engendered considerable excess labor as well as various other inefficiencies. Recognized in numerous written agreements, job controls fell under what was termed "mutuality," which officially required shop steward acquiescence in any changes in shopfloor work routines.

These problems had become sufficiently pressing as to engender a government study released in 1975, commonly known as the Ryder Report, after its principal author, Sir Don Ryder (see Ryder 1975). A Participation Scheme was established in 1975 on the basis of the Report, aimed at improving productivity by gaining shop steward cooperation. The scheme enjoyed strong support from stewards, including those Communists who later opposed workforce reductions (Scarbrough 1986: 102).

The Ryder Report also emphasized the inefficiencies generated by the fragmentation of bargaining units in BL, a fragmentation seen as partially responsible for the relatively high levels of industrial disputes in the firm. Negotiations to standardize pay and conditions across BL Cars began in 1976, but made slow progress. Symptomatic was a 1977 toolroom dispute, when skilled toolmakers across BL plants demanded separate bargaining rights in an effort to restore wage differentials (Scullion 1981). The danger of a further proliferation of bargaining units helped precipitate a reform of bargaining structures in the company, and in November of 1979 an agreement was reached that established uniform company bargaining (Willman 1984: 6–8).

In May of 1975, again thanks to the Ryder Report, the British Leyland Motor Company became simply British Leyland, a publicly owned corporation. The government's holdings were vested in the National Enterprise Board (NEB) in February 1976 (see Wilks 1984: ch. 5). In 1977, however, Lord Ryder resigned from the NEB, and the Labour government named Michael Edwardes to the position of company Chairman. At this point, the firm's handling of industrial relations altered. Known for his tough views and antiunion attitudes, Edwardes was widely considered ready to take on organized labor in an attempt to restore company profitability, replacing BL's earlier strategy of inclusion with a strategy of confrontation.

We have already seen that collective bargaining had been extremely fragmented in BL. The introduction of measured day-work (MDW) in place of piece rates in the early 1970s altered the tasks that stewards performed – it was they, after all, who had previously been responsible for bargaining and monitoring the piece rates – although, given the difficulties in negotiating and monitoring piece rates, stewards in Britain often favored the change (Flanders 1973: 376). Even with measured day-work, stewards at BL retained substantial influence on the shopfloor. Formal agreements guaranteeing stewards' mutuality were won in many BL plants; indeed, at Longbridge, mutuality was achieved in exchange for allowing the establishment of MDW to proceed (Scarbrough 1982: I, 154). Stewards at BL thus enjoyed greater levels of shopfloor influence than stewards in other automobile firms in Britain.

The Ryder Report recommended bargaining be consolidated into fewer bargaining units and renewal dates (Ryder 1975: 35–37). In 1976 negotiations began to standardize pay and conditions across the company's plants and agreement was reached by 1979 to establish company bargaining (Scullion 1981). Workers supported such a move, voting in favor by a margin of two to one in 1977 (see Table 3.1). Pay bargaining was thus shifted up to the plant, although mutuality meant that stewards still retained the right to bargain over work practices, job assignment, and labor mobility on the shopfloor.

MANPOWER PLANNING AND POLICY

In the early postwar period, Fiat had hired and fired at will, and was known for using politically sensitive criteria in making such decisions. Hiring, for instance, often occurred on the basis of recommendations by the parish priest. By the 1970s, this was no longer the case. National legislation and a union attentive to the dangers of political discrimination forced the company to hire from government unemployment lists. Legislation adopted in 1969 protected workers from the kinds of politically motivated individual dismissals that had been common in the 1950s, especially at the height of the Cold War.

Nonetheless, the memories of the 1950s remained strong. In the middle of that decade, the firm had used the shift from a primarily skilled to a semiskilled labor force to effect the expulsion of a whole generation of Communist union militants. The company threatened to fire workers who voted for the FIOM's representatives in the elections to the *commissioni interne* (internal commissions). As a result, unionization plummeted and the FIOM was virtually destroyed for more than a decade (Della Rocca 1977).

In the 1970s, individual dismissals for malfeasance were still legally possible, although Italy's Statuto dei Lavoratori offered shop stewards protection against unjustified dismissal. Workforce reductions for economic reasons also carried with them complex legal restrictions. Redundancies legally required prior notification, as well as selection that took into account ability, seniority, and need. Redundancies were by and large a thing of the past, however. A national layoff fund (the Cassa Integrazione Guadagni [CIG]) made temporary layoffs far more attractive to Italian employers, since a large part of the bill was picked up by the government. The provisions governing redundancies were held legally not to obtain in cases of temporary layoff. This effectively allowed firms complete discretion in the selection of those to be laid off. Since the CIG guaranteed about 90 percent of a worker's most recent wage, organized labor also had a strong incentive to favor its use rather than redundancies, despite the absence of legal stipulations regarding selection criteria for the former (Treu 1982). At Fiat, temporary layoffs had most recently occurred in 1974 as a result of the first oil shock. These had been negotiated with organized labor, and had not resulted in industrial action.

Manpower planning and policy, although largely left to the discretion of the firm in Britain, is more likely to be the subject of collective agreements than in Italy. The established procedures regulating job loss at BL protected shop stewards in the reorganization of the late 1970s. Indeed, they had been designed to do just that. The formative events occurred in 1956 and are worth detailing because, as we know from Chapters 1 and 2, the protection of stewards during downsizing is theoretically relevant.

Although 1955 had proved a record year for all the main vehicle-producing countries, in 1956 British auto manufacturers were subjected to a severe market crisis. A variety of factors was important, including a drop of 20 percent in new car registrations because of fear of petrol rationing due to the Suez crisis; indeed, rationing was imposed in December (Maxcy and Silberston 1959: 16). At this time, most British automakers practiced "hire and fire" policies in response to cyclical (as well as seasonal [Lewchuk 1986: 146]) fluctuations. At Ford, a "Continuity of Employment" clause guaranteed hours reductions rather than layoffs in response to cyclical fluctuations; but in Coventry, by contrast, federated employers (as those affiliated with the EEF are known) regularly used labor shedding instead (Salmon 1988: 191–92). For this reason, in the years following the Second World War – as had been the case in the interwar era as well (described in Salmon 1983: 172–73) – "the questions of managerial control over redundancy and the issue of steward victimization were among the most serious obstacles confronting workplace organisation" (Salmon 1988: 192; see also Jefferys 1988: 64). This was true even in the few firms in which union influence seemed strong and where management accorded recognition to organized labor. When it came to redundancies, the lack of established selection criteria and procedures led to severe industrial conflicts. At the Standard Motor Company, for instance, which after World War II had virtually abolished the direct supervision of employees, instituting in its stead higher wages and a gang system of production, a conciliatory and highly cooperative system of collective bargaining collapsed between 1954 and 1956 as a result of a strike over redundancies (Melman 1958). Even at Standard, with its progressive management, discrimination was practiced against shopfloor activists; in the redundancies of 1956, nearly one-half of the firm's stewards were included (Salmon 1988: 208).

Between 1947 and 1956, there were 44 strikes against redundancies in the British motor industry, involving 97,000 workers and accounting for 549,000 days lost. Of these, 18 were directed against the inclusion of shop stewards on redundancy lists. Although these strikes accounted for less than 17 percent of the total workers involved, they constituted 58 percent of the working days lost (Salmon 1988: 192). In other words, relatively small groups of workers (usually affiliated with only one union) undertook relatively lengthy strikes in defense of trade union organization in this period, mainly because management "had a policy of selecting those it wished to be rid of when selecting for redundancy" (company sources,

Austin Rover, letter to the author, 1989). One detailed analysis of strike data from the period has concluded that "workplaces did not generally aspire to oppose redundancies as such, but more the method or manner with which redundancies were carried out." In particular, they attempted to prevent firms using mass redundancies to pick off workplace leaders, thereby undermining shopfloor worker and union organization (Salmon 1983: 339).

Typically single-union affairs, it was not surprising that most of these strikes failed. At the same time, the various unions involved failed to agree in principle on how redundancies ought to be confronted, with the main issue of contention whether stewards ought to play any real role in helping select those to be let go (Salmon 1983: 415). But in 1951 a strike at Jaguar managed to gain the reinstatement of stewards made redundant. More important, a pathbreaking agreement was signed protecting stewards from discriminatory selection with the establishment of seniority rules for redundancies (Salmon 1988: 198–99). At the same time, strikes in other car manufacturers did not fare as well. In 1951 mass workforce reductions at Austin included Sidney Pegg, an AEU steward and Secretary of the Longbridge Communist Party, and his colleague Bills (first name unknown), and for this reason the dispute became known as the "Pegg and Bills strike." A strike involving more than 10,000 workers in their defense collapsed after only a few days, and although eventually all 760 made redundant were rehired, Pegg and Bills were not (Jefferys 1988: 66–67; Salmon 1988: 198). In 1952, another 800 redundancies included seven stewards, among whom John McHugh, a leading National Union of Vehicle Builders (NUVB) steward. Six hundred of these men were eventually rehired, but not McHugh, despite winning a legal battle for the right to be reinstated. An 11-week strike by the NUVB in 1953 in McHugh's defense was defeated when workers affiliated with other unions crossed picket lines. By the end of the strike, management had successfully dismissed one-sixth of Longbridge's stewards. Union density in 1953 fell to 60 percent as a result (Jefferys 1988: 68–71).

The British Motor Corporation (BMC; later British Leyland) declared 6,000 redundant as a result of the collapse of auto sales in 1956. An uneven strike, led by national union officials of the major unions but without the support of a majority of the workforce, ensued. Unlike the strike earlier in the decade, it was the first official multiunion, company-wide strike in the firm's history (Jefferys 1988: 72). Even so, most employees continued to report to work. At Longbridge, where 3,000 men had been made redundant, only 20 percent of the workforce struck. Nonetheless, union solidarity paid off. The strike ended with "an agreed method . . . for the handling of future redundancies" (Salmon 1988: 206). The method employed is referred to in Britain as "last in/first out," or what we know as seniority (British Motor Corporation [BMC] 1956). Mirroring the 1951 Jaguar agreement, BMC agreed that in the future senior stewards would be involved in the administration of redundancy and that selection of the redundant would thereby use the workplace knowledge of shop stewards. This was the first time the company offered any recognized role to shop stewards. Eighteen months after the strike, the leading steward at Longbridge could claim nearly total unionization at the plant (Salmon 1988: 206–7). Fear of victimization, which had so hindered the development of shopfloor union organization in the company, became a thing of the past. And with the boom of 1959, the workers dismissed in 1956 were all finally rehired (Jefferys 1988: 73).

Prompted by the events of 1956, in 1961 the EEF agreed to give advance warning in cases of mass redundancies (Marsh, Hackmann, and Miller 1981: 150). And in 1965 Parliament enacted the Redundancy Payments Act (Jefferys 1988: 75–76). The Act deliberately avoided imposing seniority or other criteria on firms – indeed, it fails to specify any particular method of selection – and instead was designed to free management to use efficiency criteria at a time when LIFO was viewed as fostering inefficiency on the firm (Fryer 1973: 5). The Act's main goal, however, was the prevention of industrial disputes over redundancy, especially through the provision of severance payments. By the 1970s, both statutory and extrastatutory redundancy payments were widespread in the United Kingdom. Statutory redundancy payments are made by the firm, rising with seniority (Booth 1987: 402–3). Some extrastatutory payments predate the original 1965 legislation. In the late 1970s these were typically used by large companies to encourage certain categories of employees, especially older workers, to volunteer to take redundancy (Booth 1987: 404).

Other legislation affects workforce reductions as well. The 1975 Employment Protection Act requires employers to give the Department of Employment as well as trade unions advance notice of collective redundancies, notice ranging from one to three months (White 1983: 33–35). The Act also requires that companies communicate the numbers of projected redundancies, the reason for them, the method of selection to be used, and the procedures to be observed (Marsh et al. 1981: 150). These two pieces of legislation have helped substantially reduce disputes over redundancies, the proportion of which one study estimates as under 5 percent in engineering in the early 1970s (Marsh et al. 1981: 151). By the 1980s research found that in the relatively few cases where compulsory redundancies were used to manage workforce reductions in Britain, LIFO was used as the selection criterion in about half (Millward and Stevens 1986: 221; see also

Oswald and Turnbull 1985: 89). Union activists were thereby largely (but not entirely) protected from dismissal during downturns.

By the 1970s BL stewards enjoyed even greater protection than that established by law. A 1976 agreement signed at plant level between CSEU signatory unions and the firm reestablished the Engineering Disputes Procedure. Section 6 of this outlined a procedure to avoid redundancies. The agreement strongly established mutuality (Willman and Winch 1985: 113–14). In the event of workforce reductions, stewards could realistically expect total job protection.

THE 1980 FIAT STRIKE

In the fall of 1979 Fiat dismissed 61 individual employees, among them some union activists, on grounds of malfeasance. The move was highly public, as the company insisted that it was attempting to regain authority on the shopfloor. Organized labor largely failed to respond to what was perceived as a deliberate provocation. While a strike was called in defense of the 61, it failed to attract much support and instead, a lengthy debate within the labor movement ensued in which it was argued (even if not agreed) that the firm may have had legitimate grounds for the firings (see Amendola 1979). Indeed, in a variety of ways organized labor reluctantly acquiesced in the dismissals. National confederal officials in particular privately signaled the firm that they were looking for an excuse so they would not be forced to defend the dismissed employees (Romiti 1988: 97), although ultimately legal action (which the union lost) was pursued.

Based on its initial meetings with national confederal officials regarding the dismissals, management interpreted union reaction as indicating tacit acknowledgment that they lacked adequate control over local union officials and shopfloor activists (Romiti 1988: 101). As Fiat's Managing Director Cesare Romiti explained:

> The behavior of the union after the [events surrounding the] 61 opened our eyes. It was still an immense body, a huge and apparently healthy but contradictory body. At Rome they decided on one policy and in Turin they followed another. The whole thing gave the impression, which we had not had earlier, of impotent weakness. We at Fiat were the first to understand that the union had put itself on a course that was extremely dangerous for itself. And we understood before others the reasons for this weakness. How could a union not be weak when it was made up above all of leaders without authority over factory employees, of bureaucrats who represented only themselves, of professional shop stewards who no longer responded to anyone else, of factory councils which did not dare

expose themselves to the electoral scrutiny of the workers, of decision making bodies which behaved in contradictory ways and which never wanted to expose themselves to referenda by the rank and file, of membership cards automatically renewed and this thanks to the firm which deducted the dues? . . . This was the kind of union we had before our eyes in Turin at the end of 1979. (Romiti 1988: 101)

In the months following the 61 dismissals, the company also dismissed hundreds of employees for chronic absenteeism (Romiti 1988: 100). Presumably as a result of this, absenteeism fell substantially.

Next in the sequence of events preceding the strike, the company's growing profitability and productivity problems were subjected to public scrutiny. In March, although the company then denied any particular economic difficulties, the PCI held a national conference to investigate Fiat's position in the context of the second oil crisis and concluded that the company was likely to be in for hard times. Among other things, the party proposed that the government intervene with a Piano Auto (Auto Plan), or some kind of national planning initiative for the automobile sector, an initiative that organized labor, too, repeatedly called for during the events that followed.

A month later secret meetings were held between management and national officials of the FLM in which the company raised issues of productivity and flexibility in the use of labor. The FLM's officials rejected continuing negotiations on these issues on the grounds that, after an informal sounding, the most important of Fiat's shop stewards had vetoed the proposal (Bonazzi 1984: 35; Carmignani 1984).

In May Fiat confirmed the economic difficulties it had earlier denied with the announcement that 78,000 of its 137,000 auto workers in Italy (total figures from Comito 1982: appendix, table 5) were being put on short work through the CIG. By June, however, under pressure from its bankers, the company was threatening mass redundancies instead, arguing that temporary layoffs were proving inadequate to resolve its financial and productivity difficulties (Agnelli 1980). In itself, the threat of large-scale workforce reductions was motivated primarily by external economic pressures. The 1979 oil shock hit Fiat hard, undermining its competitive position in Europe. At the same time, the firm's bankers began to exert considerable pressure on the company to get its house in order.

The response of organized labor was to insist that workforce reductions occur on the basis of worksharing (which in this context meant rotating employees temporarily in and out of the CIG), natural wastage, and early retirements. Indeed, organized labor repeatedly insisted it would acquiesce in workforce reductions if they were carried out using such measures.

This was precisely what the firm refused to do. One argument the company made was that rotating layoffs among employees was not equivalent to a permanent reduction in the size of the labor force; indeed, the company claimed that rotation would effectively avoid any permanent reduction in the number of its employees. Organized labor responded that the firm's need to reduce the number of its employees could be handled through attrition and natural wastage, the rates of which could be expected to increase were worksharing used as a bridge mechanism. Such a response left considerable uncertainty about whether organized labor genuinely accepted the need for mass workforce reductions or not.

These differences led to a breakdown in negotiations in early July. At the end of that month, Fiat replaced its Managing Director with Cesare Romiti, a man notorious for his hawkish views on industrial relations. On September 10 the company formally announced that it intended to fire 14,000 employees, almost all from its automobile division (Federazione CGIL-CISL-UIL Piemonte 1980: x–xi; Federazione Lavoratori Metalmeccanici Torino [FLM Torino] n.d.: 1–2).

This announcement followed a secret evening meeting between national officials from the three metalworkers' unions and Fiat's management. Because of the political situation – the Italian government had recently resigned – the firm was on the point of converting the threat of redundancies into layoffs. At this meeting, both sides expressed considerable unease at the prospect of a strike, apparently sharing a genuine willingness to try to prevent the situation from getting out of control. Union officials promised they would dampen industrial action, moving to more "articulated" tactics (short, rotating or revolving strikes) if management agreed to discuss selection criteria for precisely whom would be laid off and how the processes of expulsion and reentry would be managed.

The union leaders left the meeting believing that they had achieved an understanding along these lines. Monday morning, they were awakened with the information that the company had just sent out letters laying off 23,000 workers. Upon seeing the lists of those laid off, union leaders maintained that shop stewards, especially the more militant and active among them, were disproportionately included (Dina 1981: 16–17) and that a preliminary analysis of the data revealed the use of "politically discriminatory and antiunion" criteria ([FLM Torino] n.d.: 11). One verbatim report of a local leader's public response reads:

> The criteria used can be schematically summarized as follows: there are lots of women, there are lots of sick people, above all there are lots of shop stewards and combative workers, the so-called avant-garde. Comrades, there are squads without a steward any more; or there are squads in which the steward is surrounded by emptiness. This is, in essence, the objective that Fiat wanted to attain with the 14,000 redundancies; the form has been changed but the substance remains.

> And it is because of this, comrades, that we propose . . . the blockade
> of the gates of all Fiat plants. . . . (Marco Giatti, quoted in Perotti
> and Revelli 1986: 56)

Echoing this, the FLM's posters lining the factory gates stressed the use of
unilateral and discriminatory selection criteria (see the photo in Perotti and
Revelli 1986: 57).

At this point, organized labor committed itself irrevocably to an intransigent stance. In a meeting with shop stewards that morning, union officials
made the decision to blockade the Fiat works with 24-hour picket lines.
Even then, however, research among participants has found that if from
the beginning, "20 percent foresaw defeat, to which one must add another
10 percent who had generally negative outlooks . . . [another] 22 percent
understood that things were going badly once Fiat mailed the lay-off letters
(30 Sept.) . . ." (Bonazzi 1984: 36).[2] In other words, according to extensive
interviews undertaken by Giuseppe Bonazzi and Fabrizio Carmignani,[3] by
the time that organized labor committed irrevocably to an intransigent
stance, a majority of union officials and shop stewards appeared to know
that they were committing to their own defeat. This commitment to an
apparently self-defeating course of action is theoretically deeply puzzling.

The factory blockade lasted another 15 days, an extraordinary accom-
plishment in a country in which unions are without strike funds.[4] Pickets
were set up at Fiat's gates and the company effectively shut down, at least
in Turin. But if this kept employees out, it did not necessarily convince
them of the merits of the union's action. By the end of the strike, for
instance, pickets were being bussed in from Lombardy, so few Turinese
Fiat workers remained willing to stand outside company gates.

The strike captured national attention, remaining headline news for its
duration and exciting public opinion. The PCI officially supported the
strike, and Enrico Berlinguer, the party's General Secretary, spoke to striking
workers in front of Mirafiori's gates, offering them the party's complete
solidarity. When asked, he committed the party to accompany the rank
and file into the enterprise were an occupation of the factory to occur.
Privately, however, the party's local leadership remained in contact with
the firm and was attempting to mediate the conflict.

To the surprise of all concerned, on October 14 some 40,000 Fiat
employees took to the streets of Turin in a silent procession demanding
"the right to work" (see Baldissera 1984). Although the firm had helped
organize the demonstration, its success caught the company by surprise.
Mainly involving better paid technical employees, white-collar staff, and
foremen, the "march of the forty thousand," as it came to be known,
effectively signaled the end of the strike. An agreement (available in Federazi-

one CGIL-CISL-UIL Piemonte 1980: xxv–xxvii, along with most other relevant documents) was signed in Rome early on the morning of July 15.

With this agreement, the threat of redundancies was formally withdrawn. Instead, it provided incentives encouraging voluntary quits and early retirement, arrangements for transfers of workers among different Fiat plants within the Piedmont area, and extensive use of the Cassa Integrazione Straordinaria, which was to be used to lay off 23,000 workers as of October 6 for up to three years. Organized labor's initial reaction was cautious optimism. The agreement was officially called a "partial victory," mainly on the grounds that no redundancies were actually to take place. Union militants, however, experienced the end of the strike as a defeat, and within a few years organized labor as a whole conceded that the conflict had ended in defeat.

WORKFORCE REDUCTIONS IN BRITISH LEYLAND, 1979–80

British Leyland began cutting jobs in February 1978, with the closure of one plant and the loss of 3,000 jobs. Restructuring really only got underway the following year, however. In June 1979, Edwardes announced a Recovery Plan involving personnel reductions of some 25,000 and 13 plant closures. Immediately establishing a BL Emergency Committee, shop stewards voted to oppose the Plan. In September the TGWU also formally rejected the Plan. The Confederation of Shipbuilding and Engineering Unions took a more moderate position, however, and eventually the organization's executive supported the Recovery Plan and recommended to employees that they accept it. The executive's initial suspicion of the Plan had apparently been further moderated after their meeting with government representatives in October which convinced union officials that public funds to avoid workforce reductions would not be available (Wilks 1984: 214).

The company balloted the workforce on the Recovery Plan in October (see the results reported in Table 3.1). Employees turned out to vote by a rate of four to one; voters approved the Plan by 87 percent. Edwardes then produced a 92-page "Draft Agreement" detailing the changes in working practices sought by the company. The document, extending an earlier reorganization of the company's complex collective bargaining structure, proposed an end to mutuality, or the myriad agreements that gave shop stewards rights to negotiate virtually all matters of work effort, job performance, and demarcations.

In November, despite the rank and file's evident support for the Recovery Plan, the senior shop steward at the company's major Longbridge facility, a Communist and skilled toolroom worker – a man referred to by the popular press as "the most powerful shop steward in British industry" (Fryer 1979: 63) – took on the Recovery Plan by coauthoring a pamphlet exhorting workers to resist Edwardes's reorganization and in particular to mobilize against plant closures and job loss even with "work-ins and occupations" if necessary (Leyland Combine Trade Union Committee n.d.: 13). The company responded by sacking the senior steward, Derek Robinson, and issuing warnings to his three coauthors.

The TGWU called for industrial action to protest the sacking, and some 40,000 BL employees struck or were laid off as the result of the strike. But Robinson's own union, the AUEW, proved reluctant to support his case. Although the AUEW formally supported its steward and launched an inquiry into his dismissal (Wilks 1984: 211), local AUEW officials supported the company's Draft Agreement and the diminution in steward power it entailed (reported in Scarbrough 1982: II, 82; also Jefferys 1988: 79–80).[5]

With the two major unions at Longbridge divided, strike action protesting Robinson's dismissal fizzled. Lacking the AUEW's support, the TGWU was forced to reconsider its position. Eventually, the inquiry sponsored by the AUEW's executive found that Robinson had been improperly dismissed and sanctioned official industrial action in support of his reinstatement. At the same time, however, the AUEW decided that the actual decision to strike be put directly to the Longbridge workforce, thereby guaranteeing that no strike would occur. Not surprisingly, Robinson's fellow employees refused to undertake industrial action in support of his reinstatement and rejected a strike call at a mass meeting held in February. It was at this point that union acquiescence to workforce reductions was assured. As a result, "there has been little or no overt struggle against the plant closures" (Marsden et al. 1985: 10) that took place at British Leyland in the 1980s.

In January 1980, the unions decided to ballot the workforce on the November 1979 package. The February ballot attracted about half of BL's workforce, of which 59 percent voted to reject the company's offer (see Table 3.1). In March, having failed to gain employee agreement to the 92-page document on new pay and working practices, the company issued what was commonly called the "Blue Newspaper," a shortened "Final Draft of Proposed Agreement on Bargaining, Pay, Employee Benefits and Productivity" (British Leyland Cars 1980) aimed at the manual workforce. Management then announced that anyone reporting to work on April 8 would be considered to have accepted the changes. The TGWU called for industrial action whereas the AUEW recommended that members report to work on April 8. On April 12, the TGWU made the dispute official. The union backed down two days later, however, when management threatened to fire anyone on strike. The end of mutuality was thereby unilaterally imposed and new working practices speedily implemented (Willman 1984: 9).

SUBSEQUENT OUTCOMES

Evaluating the impact of restructuring and workforce reductions at BL and Fiat is fraught with difficulty. The issues are politically sensitive, and any interpretation likely to be controversial. Moreover, as in any situation where labor is on the defensive, knowing just how badly labor has suffered calls for assessing a multitude of indicators, not all of which point in the same direction.

Despite such qualifications, I argue that overall the evidence supports the interpretation that trade unionism at BL emerged less damaged than that at Fiat, although even in the latter case management was surprisingly restrained. (For more detailed interpretations, see Chapter 7.) At Fiat, union density, low before the strike, plummeted afterward. In the company's Turinese plants, unionization fell 10 percentage points between 1979 and 1983, from 34 to 24 percent (Golden 1988: 180, table 19). Strikes virtually ceased. The shop steward organizations, although still nominally intact, were effectively stripped of bargaining power. The number of stewards in Mirafiori fell by 25 percent, from about 800 just before the conflict to about 600 three years later (Golden 1988: 235, table 29). During this same period Mirafiori's workforce dropped from around 70,000 to 52,000, that is, also by 25 percent (Golden 1988: 240, table 30). The loss of stewards was thus exactly proportional to the loss of jobs and the firm did not expel activists in disproportionate numbers. Nonetheless, a striking symptom of the situation was the FLM's inability to hold new elections for shop stewards on the required triennial basis. Instead, elections were delayed for a decade.

The firm's health subsequently recovered. Productivity improved and absenteeism fell. Union sources report that on the assembly line at the Rivalta plant absenteeism had been 18 percent in 1979 but was down to only 8 percent in 1981 (Federazione Lavoratori Metalmeccanici [FLM] Fiat Rivalta 1982). Fiat's market position improved so much that by the mid-1980s the firm was one of Europe's strongest competitors in the automobile industry.

The company's workforce in the automobile sector was substantially reduced. Between January of 1980 and 1982 the company lost nearly one-third of its employees in the automobile division in Turin, where employment dropped from 102,000 to 70,000. More than half of this reduction (18,000) can be attributed to layoffs; another 4,000 persons took voluntary redundancy; 3,000 took early retirement, and more than 3,000 were fired, mainly for excessive absenteeism (data reported in Istituto per lo Sviluppo della Formazione Professionale dei Lavoratori [ISFOL] Regione Piemonte 1983: 33).

Studies show that layoffs have not proven as disastrous for most former employees as might have been feared (see Bonazzi et al. 1987). Layoffs have had a large impact on the local economy, however, since so much of it involves Fiat. In 1984, for instance, fully one-quarter of all layoffs in Italy were concentrated in the province of Turin (reported in Bagnasco 1986: 58).

Exactly whom did the firm lay off in the end? Despite the agreement ending the strike, organized labor remained without any voice in the firm's selection criteria. The available data appear to show that although the firm refrained from laying off shop stewards in disproportionate numbers, it did expel union members in substantially larger numbers than their proportions would have warranted. Table 3.2 shows that in the body works at Mirafiori, for instance, unionization in 1981 was only 27 percent, whereas just over half of those employees from the body works who were at that time in the Cassa Integrazione Guadagni were union members.[6] Similar disproportions affect all the various shops for which data are available (see also Baroncini 1985: 156–58).

Shop stewards, however, enjoyed protection proportional to their numbers. Among the 23,000 workers included in the first round of layoffs – those stipulated in October 1980 – were 300 stewards (Revelli 1989: 106), or about one steward for every 75 workers laid off.[7] The persons who were laid off disproportionately to their numbers overall were the less skilled, the youngest and most junior employees, female employees (who also figured disproportionately among the young and most junior, making causal effects difficult to disentangle), and – although on this there are little real data – the physically impaired, chronically ill, and so forth (see ISFOL–Regione Piemonte 1983: ch. 2). This tends to corroborate that the firm did target union members in the layoffs, since the most recently hired did not intersect substantially with the most unionized. One estimate has it that in the stamping and body works at Mirafiori fewer than 20 percent of the young workers hired in 1978 were union members, a figure notably lower than that overall (which was 34 percent in 1977 for Mirafiori generally) (Belforte and Ciatti 1980: 99).

British Leyland's workforce in the United Kingdom was halved between 1978 and 1982, declining from 164,000 to 80,000 (Centre for Policy Studies 1983: 31, table 12; cf. Willman and Winch 1985: 20, table 2.2).

Table 3.2. *Overall unionization compared with rates of layoff for union members in various Fiat plants and sections, 1981*

Plant/department	Unionization rate (%)	No. of laid off workers[a]	No. of laid off union members	Percent of unionized workers on layoff
Mirafiori				
Carrozzeria	27	3,800	1,948	51
Meccanica	26	1,400	1,045	75
Presse	29	850	624	73
Rivalta				
Carrozzeria	29	2,300	1,354	59
Meccanica	21	250	151	60
Presse	31	200	144	72
Lingotto				
Carrozzeria	n.a.	1,060	555	52
Presse	n.a.	160	77	48
Lancia Chivasso	n.a.	1,250	1,069	86
Total	n.a.	11,270	6,967	62

[a]Does not include 6,300 employees laid off in October 1980 who had taken voluntary redundancy by the end of 1981.
Sources: FLM Turin, reported in Mario Bessone et al., "Dossier Fiat Auto: il prezzo dei profitti," *Azimut*, 2, no. 5 (May-June 1983), 117, table B, and Ada Becchi Collidà and Serafino Negrelli, *La transizione nell'industria e nelle relazioni industiali: l'auto e il caso Fiat* (Milan: Franco Angeli, 1986), 166–67, tables 3 and 4.

Ten BL facilities were closed between 1979 and 1986 (company sources). In Coventry, where most of the firm's production was based, BL's workforce declined from 27,000 in 1975 to 8,000 seven years later (Thoms and Donnelly 1985; see also Walker 1987). The company's workforce fell across Britain from 192,000 in 1978 – before restructuring began – to 103,000 in 1983 (Willman and Winch 1985: 20, table 2.2). Only a third of this decline can be attributed to plant shutdowns (Jones 1983: 17; cf. Law 1985: 11); thus, large numbers of employees were expelled even in plants still operating, attesting to a reduction in what was presumably a previously bloated workforce. But there were virtually no forced dismissals. With a handful of exceptions involving white-collar staff (and excluding situations

of plant closure), voluntary redundancies, natural wastage, and early retirements were used instead (company sources; Marsden et al. 1985: 64). One
indicator of the effectiveness of these measures in getting the oldest part
of the workforce out of the firm is provided by census data, which show
that the median age of laborers in the automobile industry fell from 49 to
46 years between 1971 and 1981 (reported in Marsden et al. 1985: 72).

Job loss on this scale has naturally been quite disruptive of trade union
shopfloor power. But union structures in BL plants appear to have survived
largely intact. Between 1980 and 1982, for instance, the number of stewards
at the company's Longbridge plant fell from 800 to 400, "principally because
of a high rate of resignations after the Robinson dismissal and the new
working practices" (Willman and Winch 1985: 159). Over the same period,
however, employment in the plant fell by 30 percent (reported in Willman
and Winch 1985: 204 n12); thus, the relative decline not due to job loss
in the number of stewards was 20 percent. The influence of the stewards
in shopfloor bargaining and job controls was initially reduced, mainly as a
result of the imposition of the Blue Newspaper and the end of mutuality
agreements. Facilities for full-time stewards were withdrawn and the number
of Longbridge stewards on full-time release fell from 11 in 1977 (Seglow
and Wallace 1984: 45) to 8 in 1981 and then to 2 (Willman and Winch
1985: 159). But interviews with the stewards themselves found that "it
would be exaggeration to say that the shop-steward organisation at Longbridge was 'broken' . . ." (Willman and Winch 1985: 160, see also 180;
also reported in Marsden et al. 1985: 110). In 1982 a new procedural
agreement was signed, reconstituting steward organization, providing for
the automatic deduction of union dues from members' pay, defining the
role of stewards, securing facilities for them, and recognizing the possibility
that senior stewards could enjoy full-time release (Willman and Winch
1985: 175). While steward organization in BL never regained mutuality
and stewards are therefore no longer involved in effort bargaining, the
shopfloor organization that emerged otherwise survived the job loss. One
study has summed up the impact by arguing that "stewards at Longbridge
(as well as other BL plants) felt that their organisation has survived the
events of 1980 and was in some ways 'fitter' despite reduced facilities"
(Willman and Winch 1985: 180).

By the end of 1984 BL's management claimed that its Longbridge
facility was Europe's most efficient automobile plant (Marsden et al. 1985:
1–2). Substantial improvements in productivity took place, as output rose
from 5.59 vehicles per worker-year in 1980 to 14.2 by 1983, according to the
company (reported in Willman 1984: 10). After 1980 substantial declines in
industrial disputes also occurred (see Willman 1984).

CONCLUSIONS

This chapter has given readers information about union responses to job loss in the Italian and British automobile industries in the period immediately following the second oil shock. Despite the similarities in the industrial relations characterizing Fiat and British Leyland in the 1970s, industrial action in response to the threat of large-scale workforce reductions took place only at Fiat. The next chapter uses insights derived from the games presented in Chapter 2 to understand these different outcomes.

4

TRIGGERS OF INDUSTRIAL ACTION

When the managers at Fiat and BL launched similar attacks on organized labor at the end of the 1970s, they sought to eliminate surplus labor and to strip shop stewards of the job controls they exercised on the shopfloor. These changes were meant to restore productivity in a context of heightened international competitiveness. Both companies were successful in these aims. Some plants were closed and employees let go; in plants kept open, personnel reductions, often substantial, were achieved using natural wastage, early retirement provisions, voluntary redundancies, and/or temporary layoffs. Between the late 1970s and the early- to mid-1980s both firms reduced their domestic employment levels by one-third to one-half. In neither case were many actually fired.

But the responses of their union movements differed. At Fiat organized labor – from the lowest shop steward to the highest confederal officer – resisted job loss with a long and bitter strike. At BL, conversely, attempts to muster resistance by shop stewards faltered in the face of the determined opposition of national union officials, who ensured labor's acquiescence to job loss and restructuring. Large-scale job loss at British Leyland and at Fiat thus engendered distinctly different responses by organized labor.

The game-theoretic analysis developed in Chapters 1 and 2 suggests explanations for these diverse outcomes. As the four propositions advanced in Chapter 1 assert, there are two possible reasons why the union movement at Fiat could have engaged in industrial conflict in 1980:

- either the firm targeted union activists in greater numbers than the union could tolerate (or the firm failed to understand that the union could afford to strike if activists were targeted);

- or both the union and the firm preferred a conflict because the costs were usually low to each; that is, each could expect to receive a subsidy from an outside actor.

Conversely, there are two possible reasons why the union movement at BL should have failed to undertake industrial action in 1980:

- either institutions existed that prevented the firm from targeting union representatives during the course of workforce reductions;
- or the union enjoyed a sufficient reputation for toughness that the firm refrained from targeting union representatives altogether.

The present chapter demonstrates that the first of each set of hypotheses is applicable to the relevant case. At Fiat, labor struck because the firm inadvertently targeted too many activists for the union to tolerate. At BL, labor refrained from industrial action because existing collective agreements enforced seniority provisions, which in turn prevented the targeting of activists during the course of workforce reductions.

The present chapter falls into two sections. In the first I explain how we operationalize the concept of union thresholds for empirical work, as well as why the presence or absence of seniority-based layoffs should have such a dramatic effect on the outcome of interactions between unions and firms over workforce reductions. In the second section I illustrate the propositions stated with reference to the two cases described in Chapter 3.

UNION THRESHOLDS AND SENIORITY-BASED LAYOFFS

In this chapter I seek to show that industrial action at Fiat occurred when too many union activists were inadvertently targeted during the course of layoffs, whereas industrial action at BL was forestalled in similar circumstances because seniority provisions were in place protecting activists from dismissal. The two major concepts involved in these arguments are union thresholds and seniority.

WHERE UNION THRESHOLDS LIE

In Chapter 1, I proposed that one reason why unions respond to job loss with industrial action is that the firm during the course of workforce reductions inadvertently targets "too many" union activists for dismissal for the union to tolerate.

Where should this threshold lie? Put another way, what distinguishes a low-threshold union, unable to tolerate the dismissal of more than a few activists, from its high-threshold counterpart, able to allow the expulsion of relatively many activists without reaction?

The discussion in Chapter 1 concerning organizational maintenance suggests an answer. The most important consideration will be the ease with which the organization can replace those shopfloor representatives who are lost. As a general rule, as I already noted in Chapter 1, unions experience considerable difficulty in securing member participation and recruiting activists. These difficulties are nonetheless more or less severe depending on particular features of the situation. Above all, where unions organize relatively few members out of the pool of potential members – where union density is low, in other words – they will, all else equal, experience greater difficulty in recruiting militants than where they organize relatively many members. Historically, it has been common for firms to target activists precisely in efforts to frustrate unionization drives – that is, during times when unionization rates were still relatively low – as the case materials in the last chapter describing unionization efforts in the British automobile industry in the 1950s illustrate. Targeting in such circumstances is likely to elicit a strike since, where the union is relatively weak but devoting considerable resources to enrolling new members, it will be especially easy for the firm to misidentify the union threshold, thereby provoking industrial action. In such a context, the union has an incentive to generate deliberately confusing information about its own ability to recruit and replace activists, thereby easily but inadvertently misleading the firm into targeting over threshold.[1]

Empirically, the degree of unionization in the firm is one determinant of the union's tolerance for the dismissal of activists. Union density, however, cannot offer a complete explanation. The cause of industrial conflict is *not* that the union will collapse if it loses more than a few activists, but rather that the firm does not *know* how many the union can tolerate losing. An operational determinant of strikes over imperfect information is the rate at which union density has been changing in the period preceding workforce reductions. If unionization has been changing rapidly, the firm is less likely to have an accurate and up-to-date understanding of how many activists the union can afford to lose. Moreover, if unionization has been increasing, there may exist a discrepancy between the unionization rate and the activist replacement rate: it may actually be more difficult to replace activists than the unionization rate suggests because many union members are still relatively new and their loyalty not fully secured. The interpretation of events at the Fiat works in 1980 that will be offered in the next section corroborates this argument. At Fiat unionization has historically been low and the recruitment of activists extremely problematic. Nonetheless, unionization had risen considerably in the decade before 1980. In part for this reason, the union's trigger point was lower than the firm had expected.

SENIORITY AS AN INSTITUTION
PREVENTING TARGETING

Modeling union preferences, as we have seen in Chapter 1, remains an unsettled matter, in part because selecting an appropriate maximand is problematic (Farber 1986: 1047). Among the various models currently used in the field of labor economics is one focused on seniority. Proponents contend that the seniority model bridges the classic bilateral monopoly model (see Dunlop 1944), in which unions maximize wages within the constraints given by the labor demand curve set by the firm, and the efficient bargaining model (McDonald and Solow 1981), in which labor and management bargain over both wages and employment. The seniority model acknowledges the apparent disinterest unions typically exhibit in Anglo-American and some continental countries in bargaining over employment levels while claiming that bargaining outcomes nonetheless may prove efficient (Oswald 1993). This last point is not a claim we need to evaluate here. Instead, I focus on the empirical utility of the model.

Arguing that "With lay-offs by seniority . . . the union is indifferent about employment" (Oswald 1986a: 79), the model explains this indifference with the observation that under seniority-based layoffs, in all but the most extreme of cases, "senior workers are insulated . . . from the threat of redundancy" (Oswald 1986a: 84), and that senior workers, in turn, comprise the majority of union members.

> Because even moderately large slumps therefore do not threaten the jobs of the bulk of employees (they know that it will be the young workers whose jobs will be cut), in any trade union with majority voting it is unlikely – so the model argues – that much emphasis will be given to the goal of [fighting] high unemployment. (Oswald 1986b: 183)

Extending the model for comparative application, it predicts that where workforce reductions are ordered by inverse seniority, democratically organized trade unions will acquiesce in job loss.

The seniority model exhibits two limitations that are relevant here. First, while proponents claim that "lay-offs and redundancies are normally made by inverse seniority within the firm" (Oswald 1986a: 77), in fact firms in OECD-member countries exhibit considerable variation in their use of seniority-based workforce reductions. In some countries firms generally do *not* employ seniority for ordering layoffs and redundancies. We shall see that Italy is one of these countries. The model fails to specify union preferences where layoffs do not take place according to organizational age, thereby restricting its empirical range.

Second, the seniority model typically employs a median-voter model of trade unionism, according to which the union maximizes the preferences of its median-aged member. This is empirically unsatisfactory because it ignores the internal structure of union organization, neglecting the possibility that leaders may have interests distinct from those of their members (Farber 1986; cf. Pizzorno 1978). The difference between leaders' and members' interests is demonstrated by the observation – among others – that unions may on occasion resist workforce reductions with industrial action even when the median-aged member is *not* threatened with job loss. In answer to this, I have proposed in Chapter 1 that we view the union as an organization with its *own* interests – organizational maintenance prime among them – which may well be distinct from the interests of its (median-aged) member.

For these two reasons, the seniority model is inadequate as a complete model for analyzing union behavior. Despite these limitations, its central insight – that unions are relatively indifferent to job loss where seniority-based layoffs obtain – is compatible with the models developed in Chapter 1 and may usefully guide empirical inquiry.

Let us now introduce some institutional variation. Jon Elster (1992: ch. 3) provides a useful categorization of the principles by which workforce reductions (as well as other allocative decisions) may proceed. These are

- egalitarian principles (e.g. worksharing);
- time-related principles (e.g. seniority);
- status-based principles (e.g. gender);
- welfare-based principles (e.g. need);
- efficiency-based principles (e.g. productivity);
- power-based principles (e.g. managerial discretion)[2]

All of these have at various times been used (or are still used) in deciding whom to let go when workforce reductions occur. Seniority is only one possible mechanism for ordering expulsions from the workplace. Although it is certainly the most important in the United States, it is less common elsewhere and is hardly used at all in some countries.[3]

Of all the possible selection criteria firms use for workforce reductions, seniority carries with it some unique side-effects. Where seniority is used, union activists will generally be protected in situations of mass employment reductions, since activists are rarely found among the more junior employees. One review of studies of shopfloor union activists found that in most respects they were indistinguishable from ordinary members except that "they were older . . . [and] had been with the company and in the union longer" (Klandermans 1986: 195). (For additional evidence, see Anderson 1979; Huszczo 1983; Perline and Lorenz 1970.) Because of this, only in catastrophic cases will expulsions include so many activists as to cripple the union for the future. Where managerial discretion obtains, by contrast, firms may include as many activists among those to be laid off as they choose.

Thus, when seniority orders layoffs, the organizational integrity of the union is not threatened. Thanks to seniority, the firm is unlikely *ever* to exceed the union's threshold of tolerance for expelling activists. In such settings, industrial conflict over job loss will therefore almost never ensue.

INTERPRETING THE EVIDENCE

I now show that the events surrounding workforce reductions at Fiat and British Leyland can be interpreted using the conceptual materials just presented. In the first case, the firm targeted too many activists for the union to bear – and the union's threshold was lower than expected, given a history of chronically low unionization combined with recent substantial improvements in recruitment. In the second case, that of BL, seniority rules effectively prevented activists from being selected at all during the course of workforce reductions. After forwarding these interpretations, I proceed to consider a number of alternative hypotheses.

As the descriptive materials presented in Chapter 3 showed, the events that occurred around 1980 at British Leyland and at Fiat were similar; so too were the positions and goals of the firms. Both cases took place almost simultaneously, following on the heels of the second oil shock. Conditions at BL and Fiat were at that time quite alike. In both firms, newly appointed and aggressively antilabor managing directors or chairmen announced massive job reductions as part of more general plans for firm restructuring and reorganization.

The place of both firms in their national industrial relations landscapes was also alike. Industrial relations at British Leyland are often taken as indicative of British manufacturing more generally (Willman and Winch 1985: 188). Historically Fiat has been viewed in the same light. Indeed, these two firms are virtually synonymous with their national automobile industries, making company and sectoral analysis almost indistinguishable here. And given the sheer size of the automobile industry as well as the national and even international publicity that events in these firms receive, outcomes here carry an importance far exceeding that usually characterizing single firms.

The union organizations in the two firms were also similar. At BL and at Fiat, trade union organizations were militant and strike-prone with very visible and powerful shop steward organizations.

Finally, the situations facing employees were similar in both firms. Fiat and BL are centered in monoindustrial regions whose occupational structures are dominated by the automobile industry. Job loss was thus especially threatening to employees, since work in other local industries was unlikely to be easily found. Mass workforce reductions in autos were also likely to carry with them considerable secondary unemployment, as the effects rippled through the local economies. In both cases, however, the threat to autoworkers was more of temporary layoff or voluntary severance than of forced redundancy, and workforce reductions were achieved with the nearly total protection of employees' incomes.

Despite these impressive similarities, the outcomes of the two cases differed, as the detailed descriptions in the last chapter showed. I now show why. I begin by examining the extent to which seniority rules are used to order workforce reductions in Italy and Britain.

SENIORITY-BASED LAYOFFS IN ITALY AND THE UNITED KINGDOM

In neither Italy nor Britain are seniority-based workforce reductions universal. Nonetheless, they are considerably more common in the latter than the former. In Italy, seniority provisions for layoffs are effectively absent, as was already noted in Chapter 1. The situation is complicated by a clear discrepancy between the legal and actual conditions. A 1965 agreement between the country's three union confederations and management bodies stipulates three criteria to use in the event of permanent workforce reductions involving firings of workers. These are the technical-productive requirements of the firm, seniority, and the family responsibilities of the employee. However, no standard system for weighting these various factors exists, nor do collective agreements commonly specify such matters (Ventura 1990: sec. 6.4 and 6.7).

Even if seniority should play some role in allocating permanent job loss, firms effectively evade such a requirement by avoiding permanent workforce reductions altogether. The CIG – Italy's state-sponsored layoff fund – makes it highly advantageous for firms to undertake technically temporary layoffs (during which period employees formally retain their employment relationship to the firm) rather than actually firing them. Legislation adopted in the 1970s extended the CIG to a virtually indefinite duration, and since then recourse to permanent workforce reductions has all but vanished in Italy (see Padoa-Schioppa 1988). Instead, firms use the nominally temporary CIG even for workforce reductions that are effectively permanent. In fact, cases exist of groups of workers "temporarily suspended" from work for up to 15 years. And in ordering the selection of persons for temporary layoff, Italian labor courts have ruled that the provisions of the agreement regulating permanent workforce reductions do not apply (Scognamiglio 1990: 447; Ventura 1990: sec. 6.8). This has left the selection of persons for temporary layoff without statutory regulation. In effect, firms may use their own discretion, bound only by local collective agreements and Italy's global labor legislation – the Statuto dei Lavoratori – the country's equivalent of the Wagner Act, with its unjust dismissal protection.

Empirical evidence on the selection criteria for individuals to be put into the CIG is hard to come by, but it appears that rotation is the most commonly employed device. One study of collective agreements regarding temporary layoffs in the textile industry found that just over 40 percent of cases involved layoffs of selected groups of employees (CIG a zero ore). Of this 40 percent, 38 percent of the agreements rotated layoffs among employees. Another 47 percent of the sample of agreements examined involved part-time layoffs with rotation (i.e. rotated worksharing). In all, nearly two-thirds (63 percent) of the collective agreements sampled involved rotating employees who were to be laid off or subjected to reduced working hours (reported in Padoa-Schioppa 1988: 105).

In Italy, in sum, two principles for the allocation of job loss are currently commonly employed. These are, on the one hand, managerial discretion and, on the other, the egalitarian solutions of rotating layoffs among employees in conjunction with worksharing.

Like Italy, British firms also use a variety of devices for the selection of those to be expelled from the firm. Seniority is the single most important ordering device for workforce reductions but is still far from universal as the empirical evidence already presented in Chapter 1 showed. The vulnerability of older British employees to job loss was heightened by legislation enacted in 1965 that scales redundancy payments according to length of service, a feature that was apparently intended to encourage management to shed older employees, thereby rejuvenating their workforces (Fryer 1973; Mukherjee 1973: 99–113). At the same time, various temporary provisions in the 1970s and 1980s compensated firms that used worksharing or other measures rather than redundancies (Metcalf 1986). Indeed, casual observation suggests that worksharing may be more common in Britain than in the United States but less common than in Italy, although it is difficult to be sure given the apparent absence of systematic cross-national data. In the British automobile industry, for instance, worksharing apparently remained relatively common in the era after World War II, even as it was disappearing in the United States. For many years Ford U.K. guaranteed hours reductions rather than layoffs in the event of a cyclical downturn. Elsewhere in the industry where layoffs were frequent, some of the unions organizing autoworkers refused to adopt policies regarding the allocation of job loss and in particular refused to participate in sanctioning norms for the selection of those to be made redundant (Salmon 1988: 191 and 194). Like their Italian counterparts, British unions have exhibited considerable hesitation, and even overt resistance, to endorsing seniority.

These observations suggest that industrial conflict over workforce reductions may occur in both Italy and Britain, but will likely be more frequent in the latter (as the data presented in Figure 1.1 confirm). In individual cases, we would expect that industrial conflict would occur in Britain only in firms not using seniority-based layoffs; in both cases as well, the union's threshold of tolerance for the dismissal of activists would have to be surpassed for conflict to occur.

ANALYZING THE TWO CASES

In the Fiat case, evidence shows that management had reason to believe that the union would acquiesce in some degree of job loss, even if this involved expelling union activists. The announcement of forced redundancies – which would obviously have provoked considerable controversy and public outcry in a situation where redundancies had become virtually unknown for large industry – was not necessarily meant to provoke industrial action in response. Instead, on the basis of information gained during the fall of 1979, the firm appears to have come to believe that the union's threshold for the expulsion of activists had moved up. With the firing of the 61 employees for malfeasance, Fiat's management appeared to believe that national union leaders had tacitly agreed that things were out of control on the shopfloor and that expelling some especially troublesome activists would be in everyone's best interest. Indeed, we may interpret the events surrounding the 61 dismissals as an early attempt on the part of the company's management to gain information about the union's trigger point in the defense of its activists. The failure of the subsequent strike to protest the dismissals management put down to a lack of will on the part of organized labor, since management by and large believes that "strikes succeed when the union wants them to succeed" (Romiti 1988: 66). As we have seen, in a variety of ways organized labor reluctantly acquiesced in the dismissals (Romiti 1988: 97). The firm interpreted this as tacit acknowledgment by national union officials that they exercised incomplete control over local union officials and shopfloor activists (Romiti 1988: 101); arguably, management began to believe that national officials considered this enough of a problem that they had raised their threshold for the protection of activists, despite a history of weak unionization at Fiat. The firm considered that it shared a problem with national union leaders, a problem that targeting shopfloor activists could help solve.

Instead, however, organized labor opposed managerial discretion in the selection of those to be let go. The unions insisted that workforce reductions occur on the basis of worksharing through the rotation of layoffs, natural wastage, and early retirements. Worksharing would have had the effect of largely protecting shopfloor activists; like everyone else, they would have been rotated in and out of the factory, but – according to what we can infer from the evidence – in numbers below the union's trigger point. Indeed, organized labor repeatedly insisted it would acquiesce in workforce reductions on the condition that they be carried out using worksharing.

This was precisely what the firm refused to do. On the basis of the information gathered during the events surrounding the dismissal of the 61, we may infer the firm believed it could expel activists and shop stewards in higher numbers than would be achieved with worksharing without hitting the union's trigger point. This interpretation explains the most curious feature of the strike: the intensification of strike action *after* the firm converted the threat to fire into only temporary layoffs. It was only then that Fiat plants were blockaded, as union officials repeatedly and publicly argued that the firm was discriminating in its selection of those to be laid off. When the lists of persons laid off were made public, the union maintained that shop stewards, especially the most militant and active among them, were disproportionately affected (Dina 1981: 16–17) and that the firm was using antiunion criteria for selection. As one of the union's leading negotiators explained, "No union, not in Italy, not in Germany or the United States, would have been in a position to make acceptable proposals once the problem was defined this way. It was not simply a matter of reducing personnel (though this was serious and extensive) but of a reduction *that would occur in the ways and on terms decided by Fiat*" (Dealessandri, in Dealessandri and Magnabosco 1987: 93; emphasis added). Thus, the issue that engendered such bitter conflict at Fiat was not job loss per se but rather management's insistence on exercising discretionary selection criteria.

Evidence thus shows that the union was relatively indifferent to the numbers involved and to whether these were forced redundancies or temporary layoffs. Instead, its principal concern lay with the selection of individuals for layoff, and it was only the company's decision to use unilateral selection procedures – indicated by the public announcement of the lists of those selected to be laid off – that caused labor to harden its tactics and to block-ade the factory. Even in the last hours of negotiations, following the march of the 40,000, as the unions were literally desperate to settle, the very final points under discussion concerned how to measure whether shop stewards were protected from layoffs in disproportionate numbers and what criteria to establish for the reentry of laid-off employees so as to protect the organiza-tion on the shopfloor as much as possible (personal observation by the author).

Thus, in inadvertently targeting more activists for layoff than the union was prepared to tolerate, Fiat's management provoked a serious labor dispute. The dispute could have been avoided if the firm had singled out fewer activists for expulsion. In part because of the multiplicity of actors involved, in part because the union appeared organizationally stronger in 1980 than was actually the case, the company misread the genuine desire of national union officials for greater control over their shopfloor representatives as a commitment to raise the threshold for the expulsion of activists. This, however, was something that national officials neither wanted nor would have been able to do. Although unionization in Turinese Fiat plants was 34 percent in 1979, a historic high, I have provided evidence (see Chapter 3, page 46) that the March 1980 elections showed that the union's ability to recruit new shop stewards was still extremely problematic.

The case of British Leyland is easily interpreted in light of the theory of seniority already proposed. The procedures regulating job loss at BL protected shop stewards. Indeed, as we have seen in Chapter 3, they had been designed in the 1950s to do just that. When it came to management's threats to undertake extensive workforce reductions in the late 1970s, organized labor could justifiably imagine that if redundancies were used, they would occur according to seniority (company sources). Not only had custom and practice long established the use of seniority, but numerous written agreements dating back nearly 25 years guaranteed it. In sharp contrast to the situation at Fiat, precedent too established that workforce reductions would occur at BL while protecting union organization on the shopfloor.

This allows us to reconsider the attack on selected shop stewards at BL. It is true that management targeted Longbridge's senior steward, Derek Robinson, and it was at this point that a response, had one been forthcoming, could have been expected. Indeed, we have seen that the TGWU called for industrial action to protest the Robinson sacking, but that Robinson's own union, the AUEW, equivocated. The theory proposed here interprets this as a difference in the trigger points of the TGWU and the AUEW. That is, we would expect the TGWU to be the union potentially facing greater difficulty in attracting shop stewards and for whom, therefore, any threat to steward organizational integrity would be taken more seriously.[4]

In some respects, this is indirectly confirmed by the little available evidence. Although the TGWU is the larger of the two unions in terms of national membership, its shop steward organization is less developed. Stewards occupy no official place in the TGWU's hierarchy, and have less autonomy than stewards in the AUEW. For instance, strike action is sanctioned at the district level in the AUEW but centrally in the TGWU. Despite this, from the 1960s on, presidents of the TGWU have striven to encourage steward power and influence. One result of this hierarchical imbalance – encouraging the growth and activity of actors without according them secure constitutional status – has been greater obvious strains between shop stewards and full-time officials in the TGWU than in the AUEW (Seglow and Wallace 1984: 28). It is therefore plausible that the TGWU generally experienced greater difficulty in recruiting stewards than did the AUEW, since activism would be a more problematic and difficult role in the TGWU.[5]

ALTERNATIVE HYPOTHESES

Comparative consideration of events at BL and Fiat can be used to reject a series of arguments meant to explain one or the other of the two cases. The criteria employed is that, given the notable similarities exhibited between these two cases, any explanation of one outcome must also explain the other. The same independent variables must work for both cases. Thus, rival hypotheses can be evaluated according to whether the independent variables proposed exhibit variation appropriate to the observed outcomes.

The Ideology of Shop Stewards and Union Officials

The most systematic study of the Fiat strike (Bonazzi 1984; Carmignani 1984) argues that it was the company's highly ideological steward organization that engendered militant resistance to job loss – a steward organization that vetoed less radical proposals from above (Bonazzi 1984), despite a relatively moderate rank and file that tended to acknowledge that the firm's labor force was too large (Bonazzi 1988: 5). The incentive for stewards to engage in radical ideological position-taking came, according to this view, as an attempt to compensate for their cooptation into shopfloor decision making and their roles as agents of social control vis-à-vis the rest of the workforce (Bonazzi 1987).

As we have seen, however, thanks to the Ryder Plan, shop stewards at BL had also become involved in shopfloor social control (see Scarbrough 1986: 109–10; Willman and Winch 1985: 83), and they too engaged in ideological position-taking of a kind more or less identical to that of their Italian colleagues. Both groups of stewards reacted similarly to the threat of workforce reductions, expressing preferences for militant resistance to job loss, resistance extending even to threats of factory occupations. But in one case national union offices ultimately repudiated the stewards, whereas in the other they supported their claims. An explanation focused on shop stewards alone is inadequate for understanding why different outcomes resulted.

A variant on this argument focuses more generally on the relative importance of ideology in the Italian and British labor movements. The Italian labor movement is often depicted as highly ideological while the British union movement, which was historically invested in job control unionism, is not. For the cases at hand, the available empirical evidence fails to corroborate such a distinction. Consider, for instance, an official Amalgamated Union of Engineering Workers – Technical, Administrative and Supervisory Section (AUEW–TASS) pamphlet probably dating from 1978, with a forward by the General Secretary, analyzing Edwardes's proposal for layoffs and the closure of the BL plant, Speke No. 2. "The Edwardes plan must be rejected," wrote the General Secretary:

> while BL should be expanded not contracted, and it should be expanded largely with government help. Indeed, the entire British automobile industry (including its foreign-owned components) should be nationalized into a single firm which should in turn receive vast public financing. This new nationalized firm should be managed through a single management board, one that included workers and trade union representatives. (Ken Gill, in AUEW-TASS n.d: 9)

The call to reject workforce reductions by nationalizing the industry is even more extreme than the Italian union's call for government subsidies to the automobile industry in the form of a Piano Auto, or Auto Plan. At the national level, in other words, there is no evidence that British union officials were less ideological than their Italian counterparts.

The Influence of Shop Stewards

If the preferences of stewards at Fiat and BL were indistinguishable, perhaps stewards in Italy enjoyed greater autonomy and influence than stewards in Britain; that is, perhaps in cases of disagreement between national officials and stewards, stewards in Italy are either capable of independent action or able to force national officials to act according to the preferences of the stewards. If this is the case, Italian shopfloor representatives may somehow have prevailed in their views over responses to job loss, whereas British stewards were unable to convince national union leaders to resist.

If anything, however, the empirical evidence suggests that it is British, not Italian, stewards, who enjoy greater autonomy and discretion (for Britain, I draw on Batstone, Boraston, and Frenkel 1977 and Clegg 1979: ch. 2 and 213–21; for Italy, on Golden 1988: 103–10). Relations between stewards and union officials have historically been tenser in Britain than in Italy and the British steward system often developed in opposition to national unionism. In collective bargaining, British stewards generally enjoy greater freedom from union supervision and control, even though in some instances their loyalty to national organization may be high (Edwards and Scullion 1982).

Perhaps the stewards were less important to national officials in Britain than in Italy; perhaps British union elites did not care if the company attacked the stewards. This, however, seems unlikely. In both cases, stewards would have been relatively difficult to replace *en masse*. Of the situation at British Leyland, for instance, two analysts write: "The apathy of the average member and his consequent abstention from the affairs of the Branch, the grassroots decision-making body of the union, makes it possible for minorities of 'extremists' to gain a voice in the government of the union out of all proportion to their actual numbers" (Seglow and Wallace 1984: 22). Since the branch structure was especially strong in the AUEW, where district committees are quite powerful and control such resources as the decision to pay strike benefits or not, the AUEW should have been even more sensitive to the need to protect its stewards than the TGWU. Yet we have seen that the opposite was the case.

Differences in steward autonomy and influence are not, therefore, enough to explain the different outcomes. In Italy as much as in Britain, national unions chose whether to endorse or repudiate steward action. Their decisions did not necessarily coincide with the preferences of shop stewards or with the apparent degree of steward autonomy and influence. While it is true that stewards supplied the crucial impulse behind the Fiat strike, they did so *only because national officials allowed them*. Nothing in the constitution of Italian unionism prevented national officials from repudiating their stewards, thereby suffocating strike action as their British counterparts did. In the British case union officials (especially in the AUEW) refused to back a strike, although it was supported by an ostensibly more powerful steward movement, whereas in the Italian case national union leaders supported industrial action. This suggests that they viewed it in their own interests to do so.

The Structure of Trade Unions

Perhaps if authority relations within the two union movements were fundamentally similar, outcomes would have been different had the structures of organized labor differed. This view has been advanced by those who argue that at BL, "the plant-based and sectionalized union structure was too decentralized to provide a cohesive defense of their members' interests in the crises of the late 1970s" (Marsden et al. 1985: 140), suggesting that resistance would have occurred had organized labor only been less fragmented and more centralized. Events at Fiat reveal that this attention to structure is misplaced. At Fiat a union movement, in many ways as fragmented and decentralized as that at BL, nonetheless mustered a "cohesive defense." It did so because, despite the handicaps of structure, national union officials backed shop stewards in their determination to resist layoffs.

The Credibility of the Threat

Perhaps BL's management successfully convinced British national union officials that it was not bluffing in its threats to close the firm entirely if labor tried to repudiate the Recovery Plan with a long strike, whereas Fiat's failed to convince Italian union officials that a last-minute rescue operation (funded by the government) would not be forthcoming rather than allow the firm to declare bankruptcy. Evidence for this comes from BL's own management, which subsequently stressed the importance it placed on convincing national union officials (as well as the rank and file) that the government was no longer prepared to bail out the company with funds except under conditions of severe enterprise contraction and restructuring (Edwardes 1983). But Fiat's management, too, repeatedly and explicitly strove to insure the credibility of its threat, even appointing a new managing director known for his hard line on labor issues. And while shop stewards and some local union officials never found the company's commitment to redundancies credible, continuing rather to believe that a last-minute government rescue operation could be engineered (Bonazzi 1984; Carmignani 1984), this misperception fails to distinguish the two cases, since management at both firms report that shop stewards failed to grasp the extent of the danger to the company, endorsing militant strategies despite the more moderate views of both national union officials and the rank and file.

The Preferences of Employees

Finally, perhaps the reactions of union officials in the two countries differed because employees exhibited different preferences. Employees at Fiat may have opposed workforce reductions more strenuously than did those at BL, for instance, and union leaders may have merely been representing the different preferences or strategies of the majority of their members. But here, too, evidence fails to support the hypothesis.

Even before events unfolded, FLM officials had information indicating that substantial numbers of Fiat employees were likely to view militant opposition to workforce reductions with disfavor. The highly publicized results of the PCI's survey conducted earlier in the year indicated that the company's manual employees were largely moderate in their orientations to industrial relations, favoring cooperation rather than antagonism between labor and management (Accornero, Carmignani, and Magna 1985: 35). Indeed, if the union had not suspected that it would encounter trouble with the rank and file, it would not have turned to the highly atypical tactics used during the strike, tactics that suggested the union knew it lacked majority support from the rank and file. The controversial decision to blockade the factory was symptomatic of a deeply divided rank and file: why surround a factory with 24-hour picket lines if not to keep some employees from reporting to work? And in fact, toward the end of the strike, groups of workers did try to enter the factory gates.

All five of the hypotheses presented can be ruled out because they fail to show variation on the proposed independent variables that corresponds to the variations in observed outcomes for the two cases. At both Fiat and BL, the rank and file appeared relatively moderate and largely unprepared to resist job loss. Moreover, employee views were well known to union officials. In both cases, national union officials appear to have found management's threat fully credible and to have recognized that substantial job loss was inevitable. In both cases, militant and ideological shop stewards nonetheless endorsed active resistance to job loss, even threatening factory occupations.

The preferences of the average worker and the modal steward are thus indistinguishable across the two cases. But in one, national officials selected resistance to job loss. In the other they chose not to undertake major industrial action. The reason, I have argued, stems from the different degrees of organizational threat characteristic of the two cases. At Fiat more union activists were targeted for expulsion than at BL, and at Fiat the number was more than the Federazione Lavoratori Metalmeccanici could tolerate. At BL, by contrast, with the exception of the dismissal of Derek Robinson (carried out as an individual dismissal, on grounds not dissimilar to those used for the 61 at Fiat), seniority procedures largely protected shop stewards from forced layoff.

CONCLUSIONS

This chapter has made two major claims. First, I have argued that firms may trigger disputes over job loss if, thanks to incomplete information, they target more union activists than the union can bear to see expelled from the firm. This argument was illustrated with the case of the Fiat strike in 1980. Second, I noted that firms were exceedingly unlikely to target too many activists where seniority systems were in place, since seniority has the effect of protecting union activists during workforce reductions. The case of workforce reductions at British Leyland in 1979 and 1980 illustrates the latter argument.

The second case shows the special importance of workplace institutions for the likelihood of industrial conflict. Strikes can be prevented where workplace institutions, such as seniority, guarantee the organizational integrity of the trade union. Strikes may occur, conversely, where such protections are absent and where the firm's own absence of complete information causes it inadvertently to select a strategy too confrontational for organized labor to acquiesce. Incomplete information is not the only source of industrial conflict over workforce reductions, however. We now turn to two more cases of large-scale workforce reductions to illustrate the importance that other actors may have on the payoffs of the firm and the union.

5

PIT CLOSURES IN THE JAPANESE AND BRITISH MINING INDUSTRIES

Perhaps more than any other industry, coal mining in the twentieth century has confronted massive job loss. To some extent, this has been an inevitable product of geology; as the coal seam becomes exhausted at a site, the pit must be closed, thereby throwing miners out of work or at least forcing them to relocate to pits still in operation. Other job loss occurred with the increasing mechanization of the industry, especially in the period since World War II, when coal was increasingly mined with less labor. But the major part of global job loss has come from the changing position of coal in world energy markets. Coal quite literally fueled the Industrial Revolution, thereafter serving as the world's principal source of energy for nearly 200 years. But sometime after the Second World War oil began to displace coal. Global employment in coal fell drastically as a result.

Because coal is traditionally mined in relatively isolated locations, the closure of pits has not infrequently confronted entire villages with the loss of their major source of male employment. The social consequences of pit closures have thus proved devastating in many instances. Rank-and-file protests, which have often been community-based, have not been unusual in a geographically isolated industry that has been in decline everywhere for nearly a half-century. These protests have often elicited widespread public sympathy; the figure of the miner, undertaking dirty and dangerous work that most people are relieved that they do not do, tends to evoke admiration and compassion. Nonetheless, full-blown, union-sanctioned strikes against pit closures (as opposed to short-lived wildcat action) have been rare.

The few occasions when union-sponsored industrial action has occurred have been instances of high international drama. This chapter examines three trade union strikes against pit closures: a four-month dispute in Japan in 1953; a strike lasting more than a year, again in Japan, in 1959–60; and the year-long dispute of Britain's miners in 1984–85. The 1959–60 Japanese strike was the world's major conflict in coal after an international downturn hit the industry in 1957. The miners' strike of 1984–85 was Britain's largest industrial conflict since the General Strike of 1926 and the OECD's greatest major conflict against job loss in the 1980s. Both were, in other words, exceptionally important disputes.

Coal is often cited as one of the most conflict-prone industries (Kerr and Siegal 1964). Accordingly, the massive disputes that surrounded job loss in the mines in Britain and Japan seem at first glance unsurprising. But even coal is not uniformly conflict-prone; cross-national data for its strike rates in various European countries and the United States during the twentieth century vary considerably (Rimlinger 1959). The variation, however, has never been fully or adequately explained.[1]

The specific comparison presented here is analytically especially challenging. Although British industrial relations are well known as highly conflictual – and the British miners' strike characteristic in that regard – contemporary Japanese labor relations are not. Indeed, the stereotype of Japanese labor relations is that they are especially peaceable and harmonious. Yet even in Japan, large-scale job loss in the mining industry has met massive and violent industrial conflict. So while the two cases reflect the two extremes of national labor relations – peaceable and harmonious, on the one hand; bitter and conflict-prone, on the other – unions in the mining industry have reacted similarly to the threat of pit closures. That union organizations in such different national industrial relations systems should react in the same fashion presents something of a puzzle.

At the same time, reverting to an industry-based explanation is clearly inadequate, as British history in particular illustrates. For the British mining union has sometimes fought pit closures and at other times quietly acquiesced. The National Union of Mineworkers battled closures in the 1980s, but had repeatedly acquiesced despite the loss of two-thirds of the industry's pits and one-quarter million men between 1957 and 1968. The claim that coal mining unions are generally conflict-prone or even that the British union is especially so is thus obviously false.

The next chapter will unravel these puzzles. For both Britain and Japan my analysis turns largely on the importance of third parties in altering the payoffs for the firm and for organized labor. The current chapter provides descriptive materials on the coal industries in Japan and Britain, on trade unionism and manpower policy in the industries, and on the three strikes. The organization of the presentation parallels that used for the presentation of descriptive materials on the British and Italian automobile industries in Chapter 3.

PIT CLOSURES IN JAPAN AND BRITAIN

Employment in the Japanese mining industry experienced fluctuations during the 1950s, falling from 620,000 in 1953 to 460,000 just three years later due to an international crisis in the industry, but thereafter it rebounded. At the end of the decade, however, the permanent shift of the Japanese economy from coal to petroleum-based energy sources caused mining jobs to plummet from a new peak of 610,000 in 1959 to 540,000 in 1960 and then to 460,000 the year after that (Ministry of Labor, Japan, various years).

Both periods of job loss – the middle and the end of the decade – produced major industrial disputes over the terms of workforce reductions. Among the most important were those at the Miike mines, owned by one of Japan's most important mining companies, Mitsui. The mid-decade employment slump and the employment decline at the end of the decade resulted in different outcomes for organized labor at Mitsui, however. After a 113-day strike in 1953, Japanese miners employed at the Miike mines obtained a 1955 agreement giving their union the right to help select persons for layoff when necessary. Only five years later, however, labor lost these rights after a 262-day conflict, "the longest and largest strike in the history of Japanese labor relations" (Samuels 1987: 114; see also Roberts 1989: 447). Although it was a strike that focused the nation on the plight of Japanese miners, the union leading it was broken by defeat. Both strikes, as we shall see, were triggered when Mitsui targeted large numbers of union activists for dismissal.

British coal mines, too, lost considerable employment after 1957. But no organized industrial action over job loss occurred. Only in 1972 did the NUM officially adopt a policy opposed to pit closures (Allen 1981: 301), although by then, ironically, closures had temporarily ceased and the industry faced labor shortages (Ashworth 1986: 306). Industrial action against job loss took place only in 1984. The strike that occurred that year lasted more than a year, attracting international publicity. Like their Japanese counterparts some 25 years earlier, however, British miners in the mid-1980s were defeated in their efforts to halt pit closures, and the union leading them was at least partially displaced by a newly formed rival organization.

THE ACTORS

The organizational characteristics of the postwar mining industries in Japan and Britain differ considerably. British labor and capital are both formally more concentrated and centralized than their Japanese counterparts. (As detailed subsequently, Japanese actors are more cohesive informally than their official structures indicate but are still less so than the British.) This cross-national variation in the structure of labor market actors does not seem relevant to understanding different outcomes during pit closures, however.

Nationalized immediately after the Second World War with the Coal Industry (Nationalisation) Act of 1946, the British coal industry since then has been under a single employer, whereas the Japanese remains in numerous private hands. British labor too has been more cohesive than the Japanese. Although the British coal union contained powerful regional unions, area autonomy in the National Union of Mineworkers was radically reduced after 1945 and the national union correspondingly strengthened (Baldwin 1953). In Japan, by contrast, employer fragmentation has been matched by union fragmentation. Each colliery has an independent trade union, although these may federate into enterprise-wide organizations and then with a national mining union, known as Tanrō. Finally, related to these organizational differences, nationalization in the British industry ushered in more than two decades of industrial peace at the national level, decades when the National Coal Board (NCB) and the NUM enjoyed extremely friendly relations. Until the national strike of 1972 postwar industrial conflict in the British mining industry was purely local. In Japan mining remained one of the country's more conflict-prone industries for the period considered.

THE OWNERS

Ownership in the Japanese coal industry is extremely fragmented. The largest single coal owner was the Mitsui company, one of Japan's largest and most important industrial concerns (see Roberts 1989). In the 1950s the Mitsui Mining Company owned six of Japan's largest mines, employing on the order of 35,000 men (Cook 1967: 106; Martin 1961: 26) and producing 13 percent of Japan's coal (Japan Coal Miners' Union 1961: 1). Mitsui thus ranked as Japan's major producer in an extremely fragmented industry. The Miike mine, in turn, was Japan's largest, most modern colliery at the time, thus guaranteeing that events there would receive national attention.

Despite the fragmentation of ownership in the Japanese coal industry, business in Japan is well organized in a national association, Nikkeiren (Nihon Keieisha Dantai Renmei). Established in 1948, Nikkeiren allowed Japanese employers to coordinate their activities, especially as regards the shaping of the industrial relations system (Crawcour 1978: 238). For instance, Nikkeiren actively coordinated the wave of workforce reductions and plant closures that occurred after 1949 (Okamoto 1974: 174–75). During the 1950s Nikkeiren was especially aggressive in coordinating its members in the pursuit of an industrial relations system favorable to business. Its success in achieving a high level of business coordination is one of the features that makes contemporary Japanese wage bargaining considerably more cohesive than nominally appears to be the case, given that agreements are signed exclusively at the enterprise level (Levine 1984; Soskice 1990).

The British National Coal Board was formed in 1947 upon nationalization of the industry, and its chairman and members continued to be appointed by the government thereafter. Although nationalization was undertaken by the new Labour government, it was not opposed by the Conservatives; and even when Labour lost power in 1951, there was no significant shift in government policy toward the industry. Organized labor greeted nationalization with euphoria and, as we shall see in greater detail subsequently, national industrial relations in coal remained peaceable for decades afterward.

To some extent this pattern was broken at the end of the 1960s when a wave of unofficial strikes swept the coalfields, suggesting that rank-and-file militancy was growing. These protests were followed in 1972 by coal's first national strike since 1926 and then, two years later, by a second national dispute. Both of these concerned wages, and the second led the Conservative government of Edward Heath to call new elections and subsequently to resign after a Labour Party electoral victory ensued. But even though public opinion largely favored the miners' case for higher wages in the disputes of the 1970s, these disputes also helped set the stage for the rise of Margaret Thatcher in the Conservative Party and the Tories' eventual electoral victory in 1979. Thatcherism marked a radical change in government policy toward industrial relations and toward the coal industry in particular. Britain's public industries (including, as we have already seen, British Leyland) were well known for their high rates of disputes, excess labor, poor productivity, and lax management. Thatcher wanted these industries reformed, in part in order to prepare to sell off chunks of them into private hands. Coal, moreover, represented a special problem since an earlier Conservative government had been driven from office by a coal strike.

Determined that there would be no repetition of such a humiliating political disaster, Thatcher had already secretly prepared for a possible coal strike. The Ridley Report, named after its author, Nicholas Ridley, was leaked to the press in 1978 (*The Economist* 1978). It dealt with Conservative plans for the nationalized industries generally, but also included an appendix with specific suggestions for how to deal with the "political threat" that might arise from "the enemies of the next Tory government," among which coal figured prominently. The report outlined the following plans for the coal industry, which the report indicated the most likely battleground between a Thatcherite government and organized labor in the national- ized industries:

- Stockpiling of coal to prevent blackouts in the event of a strike;
- Contingency plans for the import of coal in the event of a dispute;
- Encouraging the recruitment of nonunion drivers to move coal by truck where necessary;
- Shifting power stations from coal to dual coal – oil firing as quickly as possible to reduce their vulnerability in the event of a dispute;
- The preparation of a large, mobile police squad to handle picketing (*The Economist* 1978: 22).

As early as 1978 the new Tory leadership showed itself prepared to subsidize the costs of a major industrial dispute in the coal industry.

In 1983 Thatcher appointed Ian MacGregor Chairman of the NCB. MacGregor had just finished a term as chairman of the British Steel Corpora- tion and had also been a member of the board of British Leyland. His goal for the coal industry, as was clearly articulated both by himself and by the government, was to help prepare the industry for privatization. As we have seen was also the case at Fiat and at BL, management's shift to a newly aggressive posture and its commitment to workforce reductions was also signaled by the appointment of a new chairman.

THE UNIONS

The Japanese labor movement is formally the OECD's most decentralized and fragmented, making even the relatively fragmented British seem cohe- sive by comparison. Unions in Japan are enterprise-based and collective agreements are all signed at the enterprise level (for comparative data, see Golden and Wallerstein 1996). Formal organizational fragmentation of the Japanese union movement was less in the 1950s than it subsequently became; indeed, as we shall see, the extent of organizational cohesion was one of the issues at stake in the great Miike strike of 1959–60. In the mining industry in particular, the labor movement boasted a relatively centralized national structure.

At the end of that decade, the Miike Coal Miners' Union enrolled 14,000 members, making it the largest affiliate of both Sankōren, Mitsui's enterprise union federation, and of Tanrō, the national industrial union of coal miners, whose membership then stood at about 200,000 (*Oriental Economist* 1959a: 654). In addition to its considerable size, the Miike union exercised evident influence over working conditions. For instance, although the quality of ore at Miike was high, productivity at the mine was relatively low, due in part to the strong pit-level powers the union had acquired in the aftermath of its 1953 strike (*Oriental Economist* 1960a: 38). The Miike union thus ranked as Japan's most powerful local union at the time (Martin 1961: 27).

The National Union of Mineworkers was established in 1945 when the Mineworkers' Federation of Great Britain (MFGB), originally organized in 1888, reestablished a more centralized organization out of the existing 22 autonomous area unions (Baldwin 1953). Even in the 1980s the areas retained considerable autonomy in the NUM. At that time the NUM comprised 14 semiautonomous geographic areas and five occupational divisions. Each area had its own rule book, offices, finances, staff, and elected officials. Areas, in turn, subdivided into branches – called lodges in the industry – also with elected officials. In most cases, the branch was equivalent to a pit, although occasionally very small pits were grouped into a single branch.

The national organization was composed of three elected officials – President, Vice-President, and Secretary – and a National Executive Council (NEC). The NEC included the three elected national officials as well as at least one representative of each area, regardless of how small. One additional representative was given to areas with more than 22,500 members, and a second for those with more than 55,000. In the mid-1980s the NEC had a total of 26 persons on it, weighted disproportionately toward small (and often rightwing) areas.

Like many British unions, the NUM has historically been divided between left and right. Until the election of Arthur Scargill as NUM President in 1981, the union was – to oversimplify somewhat – controlled by the right, and most of its areas were dominated by rightwing officials. However, the wave of unofficial mobilization that overtook especially the relatively prosperous parts of the coalfield in the late 1960s had brought with it a new generation of leaders, men much more likely to identify themselves with the left. In the 1960s and 1970s the left gradually gained prominence in the NUM's largest area, Yorkshire, where it successfully

wrested control from the right with the election of Scargill as Area President
in 1973 (Taylor 1984b: 173–75). As coal prospered after the oil crisis
following Scargill's election, and layoffs in the industry fell, the left gained
additional strength nationally. Finally, battling a divided right – which
put up three candidates to the single figure of Scargill on the left – the
left gained the NUM's national presidency in 1981 with an unprecedented
70 percent of the vote (Campbell and Warner 1985a: 3).[2]

Although the NUM is not the only union in the coal industry, at least
until its 1984 defeat it acted as an effective, if unofficial, closed shop for
manual labor. Nonmanual labor was organized into two other unions.
Supervisory personnel were organized as members of the National Association of Colliery Overman Deputies and Shotfirers (NACODS). NACODS
had some 16,000 members in the mid-1980s, most of whom acted as
foremen and who were responsible for the safety of the operation of the
pits (Adeney and Lloyd 1986: 196). A third union in the industry is
the British Association of Colliery Management (BACM), which organizes
managerial staff.

SHOP STEWARDS AND LAY OFFICIALS

Japanese collective bargaining agreements usually prohibit all but employees
of the individual firm from enjoying recognition to bargain. That is, contractual arrangements typically require Japanese union officials to be employed
by the enterprise for which they bargain; if they are not, the enterprise is
not obliged to recognize them for bargaining purposes (Kawada 1974: 246).
If an employee quits or loses his job, he is therefore no longer able to serve
as a union official for the organization negotiating for the firm's employees.
This is as true for coal as for the rest of the Japanese economy.

This feature of Japanese industrial relations renders unions especially
sensitive to the dismissal of union activists. In no other advanced capitalist
country is the figure of the shopfloor activist identical to that of the full-
time official. In Japan firing an activist is virtually tantamount to firing a
union official. The dismissal of even a few shopfloor activists may threaten
the viability of the whole union organization. It is this feature, I argue at
greater length in the following chapter, that lowers the threshold of Japanese
unions, making them more likely than unions elsewhere to respond to the
dismissal of even a small number of union representatives.

British local organization is by contrast more typical of advanced industrial societies generally: a national union with full-time officials of its own
bargains with, in this case, a single employer on behalf of all miners.
After the National Power Loading Agreement (NPLA) was adopted and

implemented between 1966 and 1971, thus abolishing piecework in the industry, national bargaining gained importance and wages were negotiated at the national rather than the local level. Nonetheless, local bargaining, especially over redundancies (see below) remained important and local organization strong. The latter was reflected in the strong role areas continued to play in the national NUM.

Rank-and-file representation in the coal mines is organized somewhat differently than in other industries in Britain. In mining the official branch organization usually includes a President, a Secretary, and a Treasurer – thereby mirroring the NUM's structure at the national level – a delegate responsible for maintaining contact with the union at the area level and up to 25 ordinary members (Edwards and Heery 1989: 12). Representatives are elected annually, and as at the national level, elections tend to be contested. Each branch sends delegates to the executive committee of its respective area (Edwards and Heery 1989: 115). All this makes the branch organization well developed in British coal mining; in 1981 for instance, one study found that between 60 and 70 percent of pits had a full-time branch representative (Edwards and Heery 1989: 116). In Yorkshire an additional and unique tier of rank-and-file representation called the panel exists, which comprises representatives from pits in each NCB administrative area (Edwards and Heery 1989: 97; Taylor 1984b: 169). The panels allow lay officials to coordinate their activities across the Yorkshire Area.

As in most other industries, in coal mining union activities were usually limited to only a select few. In the years prior to the strike, "Even in the mining industry, . . . lodge work fell increasingly to an activist minority" (Fryer 1985: 76). Although turnout in national and branch elections is high, attendance at branch meetings is typically low (Edwards and Heery 1989: 120). In their study of local unionism in the NUM, which used national surveys from both 1976–77 and 1980–81, Christine Edwards and Edmund Heery (1989: 121) found that "at the vast majority of pits less than five percent of the membership was actively involved in formal branch life." This, we have already seen, is a level that is typically the case for enterprise trade unionism in Britain.

THE RANK AND FILE

Although British miners had exhibited considerable industrial militancy in the national strikes of 1972 and 1974, during the 1980s they displayed less support for national conflict. Table 5.1 shows the results of every vote of the membership in British coal mining since 1970. Whereas workers had in large measure supported strike action in the 1970s, in the 1980s

Table 5.1. *NUM ballots, 1970–82*

Year	Issue	NEC recommendation	Ballot result		Agree with NEC?
1970	Strike ballot	Pro-strike	Yes	17.6%	Yes
			No	44.5%	
1971	Strike ballot	Pro-strike	Yes	58.8%	Yes
			No	41.2%	
1972	Strike ballot	Pro-strike	Yes	210,038 (97%)	Yes
			No	7,581	
1973	Strike ballot	Pro-strike	Yes	82,631 (33%)	No
			No	143,006	
1974	Strike ballot	Pro-strike	Yes	188,383 (81%)	Yes
			No	44,222	
1975	NCB agreement	Accept	Yes	171,755 (88%)	Yes
			No	23,686	
1979 (March)	NCB agreement	Accept	Yes	131,316 (85%)	Yes
			No	23,686	
1979 (Dec.)	Strike ballot	Pro-strike	Yes	107,656 (49%)	No
			No	113,160	
1980	NCB agreement	Accept	Yes	117,196 (56%)	Yes
			No	91,498	
1982	Strike ballot	Pro-strike	Yes	91,477 (45%)	No
			No	113,144	

Source: Adapted from Adrian Campbell and Malcolm Warner, "Leadership in the Miners' Union: Arthur Scargill's Rise to Power," *Journal of General Management*, 10, no. 3 (Spring 1985): 15, table 2.

the National Executive Committee's recommendations for industrial action went down to defeat three times. The first occurred in January of 1982 over pay claims; the second, in November of the same year, also over pay claims, though this time the pay issue was linked to that of pit closures; and the third occurred in March 1983, explicitly over pit closures. In this last instance, 61 percent of the NUM's membership across Britain voted against taking strike action to support South Wales miners in their efforts to resist closures (Beynon 1985: 11; Crick 1985: 93–96). Despite the radicalization of the NUM's national leadership, the evidence reveals that the union's membership remained cautious and moderate in its orientation. With British unemployment at nearly 14 percent in March 1983 (OECD 1983: 81), this reluctance to undertake industrial action was hardly surprising.

INDUSTRIAL RELATIONS IN
THE TWO INDUSTRIES

The patterns of postwar industrial relations in the mining industries in Japan and Britain were markedly different once the early years after World War II were over. Initially, industrial relations in both countries reflected the need to rebuild national economies. In Britain this involved nationalization; in Japan a spirit of collaboration. As the 1950s progressed, however, industrial relations in the Japanese mining industry became increasingly conflictual and eventually proved a battleground for the country's national business association to impose its vision of appropriate bargaining structures. Thereafter as employment in the industry fell substantially, industrial relations were marked by a quiescence reflected in Japanese industry more generally. In Britain, by contrast, industrial relations following nationalization remained peaceable nationally for decades, though there was considerable local conflict in mining. Only in the 1970s did industrial relations in coal become conflictual nationally, and they remained so until after the strike of 1984–85.

Japan emerged from World War II with its economy devastated. Under the direction of U.S. occupation authorities, priority was set on reestablishing production, breaking up the old industrial cartels, and establishing free trade unions. Enacted in 1945, the Trade Union Law protected the right to organize, the right to bargain, and the right to strike, while strictly prohibiting discrimination against union members (Levine 1958: 24; for a copy of the law in English, see Ayusawa 1962b: 156–70). In an extraordinary spurt of mass enthusiasm, union density rose from virtually nothing to more than 50 percent of the nonagricultural workforce within a few short years, the fastest growth of union membership in world history (Levine 1958: 26)

But as the Cold War set in, occupation policy shifted. Under the Dodge Line, initiated in 1949, priority moved to reducing inflation, effecting mass layoffs, and breaking up the Communist-dominated unions. Labor legislation, including the Trade Union Law, was overhauled, making organization more difficult (Garon 1987: 240). Waves of layoffs occurred in 1949 and 1950 in a "consolidation drive" designed to shed excess manpower and gain higher productivity with capital investments; over 100,000 employees were fired in railways alone (Gordon 1985: 389). In an operation known as the "Red Purge," management – with help from U.S. counterintelligence (Halberstam 1986: 123) – used the layoffs to single out union activists, many of whom were members of the recently legalized Communist Party (Levine 1958: 28). Organized labor lost every attempt to protect itself between 1949 and 1950, and whole unions collapsed as a result of the purges. In the electric power industry, for instance, 2,183 activists were dismissed in 1950, with the result that the union simply disintegrated on the shopfloor (Kawanishi 1992: 108). The country's largest labor federation, the Sanbetsu, fell into insignificance as its leaders were singled out for dismissal. In its place, Sōhyō, a breakaway federation established in 1950, quickly became the country's largest labor organization. Thanks to these attacks on union organization, membership fell from 7 million to 5 million.

It did not weaken without conflict, however. Even after the Red Purges and continuing throughout the 1950s, a series of major industrial conflicts marked management's attempts to regain managerial prerogatives after the wave of rank-and-file militancy that had occurred immediately after the war when labor had gained considerable shopfloor powers (Ichiyo 1984). Both of the mining strikes examined in detail in this chapter were part of this wave of defensive industrial actions.

The coal industry witnessed especially dramatic industrial disputes, disputes that centered on issues of workforce reductions and job security. One reason for the conspicuous disputes in coal lay with the unusual structure of trade union organization in the industry. At the end of the Second World War, collective bargaining in coal was industry-wide, although even then most bargaining in Japan was at the enterprise level. Coal had been deemed a priority sector by the government following the war, because production there was critical to postwar economic reconstruction. This meant that the organization of the industry was essentially under government control for some years (see Samuels 1987: ch. 3). The national employers' association in coal dissolved in 1953 and national bargaining ended. It was replaced by what is called "diagonal" enterprise bargaining: namely, collective bargaining at the level of the enterprise but in which national union officials from Tanrō, the national coal miners' union, participated (see Cook 1966: 72–75). This structure concentrated labor resources, facilitated rank-and-file mobilization and permitted intense and lengthy disputes. The involvement of national union officials in enterprise bargaining lent Tanrō the authority of an industrial union despite bargaining agreements at the enterprise level. In 1958, for instance, in a 14-day strike over summer bonuses, Tanrō "singled out Sumitomo Mining and staged an intensive strike at the mine while works were carried out as usual in other mines" (*Oriental Economist* 1958: 493). Tanrō was almost the only union in Japan with the capacity to coordinate national conflict in this fashion. In addition, the Red Purge had come relatively late to the coal industry, allowing Tanrō time to devise a counterstrategy. As a result, the union lost only 0.5 percent of its membership in the purge, compared to other unions, which had lost as much as 1.5 percent (reported in Hein 1990: 235–36). This meant that the miners' organization was more intact when it entered the 1950s than most other unions and that its links to the rank and file had not been as badly disrupted by the purges. As a result of these various factors, throughout the 1950s Tanrō was one of Japan's strongest unions and often served as "lead batter" in the coordinated annual spring wage rounds that began under Sōhyō's auspices in 1955 (Cook 1967: 105).

British industrial relations in coal were, as we have seen, considerably calmer. Between 1926 and 1972 British miners undertook no national strike action. In the first period this was largely the result of the defeat suffered in 1926. After World War II with the nationalization of the industry, labor and management developed amiable industrial relations; and during this period coal represented a classic instance of "corporatist" industrial relations (see Panitch 1976). In 1972 and again in 1974, however, the miners engaged in national industrial action over wages. Both were major strikes; indeed, the second forced the Conservative government of Edmund Heath to call new elections that resulted in a Labour victory.

Although national industrial relations in coal were cooperative and peaceable for many decades, the industry was often highly strike-prone locally. Indeed, in the 1950s and 1960s "mining still managed to have the worst disputes record of any industry" (Crick 1985: 17; see also Winterton 1981) even in the absence of any national strikes. This was part of a longer term pattern: one study found that "industrial unrest in the coal mining industry has dominated total strike activity in the United Kingdom" for much of the twentieth century (Pencavel 1970: 243). Strikes were usually local, often unofficial, and especially concentrated in the Yorkshire Area (e.g. Slaughter 1958). With only 20 percent of the country's miners, Yorkshire contributed 46 percent of days lost to strikes in the mining industry between 1950 and 1964 (McCormick 1969: 171; see also Crick 1985: 18). Overall, coal accounted for 13 percent of all industrial stoppages but only 2 percent of the country's labor force between 1947 and 1976, and between 1958 and 1968, it accounted for an astonishing 44 percent of all stoppages (McCormick 1979: 155).

Industrial relations in the British and Japanese mining industries have thus oscillated over time during the postwar era. Both have at different times been highly conflictual and antagonistic. These oscillations do not correspond to the structural features of their industrial relations systems.

MANPOWER PLANNING AND POLICY

Manpower planning has been as different in the Japanese and British coal industries as their union and employer organizations and their industrial relations systems. But here too the situation in Japan was different in the 1950s than is now the case and does not fit neatly with current stereotypes.

The feature of Japanese employment practices currently most frequently highlighted by observers is "lifetime employment," or the apparent commitment by the firm to the continued employment of the employees it hires as youths. However, extensive research by economists and industrial relations specialists has shown that this characterization constitutes an exaggerated stereotype of Japanese employment practices. Economists in particular have drawn attention to the extent to which Japanese labor markets resemble those in Western European countries. I discuss three qualifications that should be made to the concept of lifetime employment: its *limited scope,* its *similarity* to employment relations in other countries, and its relatively *recent development.*

LIFETIME EMPLOYMENT IN JAPAN

Lifetime employment affects only 20 to 30 percent of all Japanese employees (Boltho 1975: 35; Koike 1983b: 90; OECD 1977: 15; Tachibanaki 1987: 669; Taira 1962: 117). This form of implicit long-term contracting is used almost exclusively by large enterprises, and then only for their "regular" employees. In addition, large enterprises hire large numbers of so-called "temporary" employees who do not enjoy the same employment commitments as their permanent counterparts. Hired and fired quite regularly, temporary employees in large firms are used to buffer the firm from fluctuations in demand. As a result, in 1980 perhaps only 10 percent of Japanese men over 45 years of age had worked more than 20 years for the same firm (Tachibanaki 1984: 81), a figure not dissimilar to its U.S. equivalent (Hall 1982).

Recent research on labor adjustment in the 1970s (when pressures on firms to reduce employment were much higher than in the 1960s, a decade during which Japan faced labor shortages) has shown that "layoffs do occur and that their number in response to decreases in production is no less than in the West" (Koike 1983a: 48; see also Koike 1987).[3] Initially, labor adjustment after 1974 was carried out by shedding the traditionally more vulnerable employees: women, part-time, and "temporary" employees (Rohlen 1979: 238). The unionized enjoyed greater protection and it is this that allowed observers to conclude that "management will do all it can to avoid dismissing their *regular* labor force" (Shigeyoshi 1984: 2; emphasis added). By the latter part of the decade, however, large firms began expelling even permanent employees, although often by recruiting "volunteers" and offering voluntary early retirement. In about 20 percent of the cases in which large Japanese firms undertook forced redundancies in the 1970s, industrial action followed, thus substantiating a major claim advanced in this study (Koike 1988: 172–73).[4] Perhaps to mitigate such disruptions, in the 1970s the Japanese government passed legislation to buffer the effects of layoffs, including legislation granting firms subsidies to reduce layoffs (Kume 1988: 676; Pempel 1982: 105). One analyst estimates that the unemployment rate in Japan would have been more than double the 1.5 percent it actually attained in the mid-1970s in the absence of government subsidies allowing firms to furlough workers at government expense rather than firing (Rohlen 1979: 247).

Small- and medium-sized Japanese enterprises also typically fail to provide the protections associated with permanent employment. Wages are lower, jobs insecure, and working conditions generally worse (Koike 1983b: 89). Unions are uncommon in small firms. For instance, fewer than 10 percent of firms employing 30 to 99 persons have unions (Koike 1983b: 96). Wage differentials between large and small firms in Japan are unusually wide, arguably because of the effect of union wage bargaining in the former (Boltho 1975: 28–33; cf. Koike 1983b: 92).

Finally, even "permanent" employees are forced to retire at a comparatively young age (until recently, usually 55 years), but because pensions are not available until age 60, most "retired" workers immediately seek new employment (Pempel 1982: 142). In the late 1970s, for instance, the OECD reported that fully 80 percent of "retired" Japanese held jobs (OECD 1977: 36). Men who enjoy "permanent" employment are thereby forced into the parallel unstable labor market upon retirement, where they continue to work for years at lower wages and facing chronic employment insecurity.

As a result of the limited scope of permanent employment, overall mobility rates in Japan are not much different than in Western European countries (Cole 1971: 117).[5] A more noticeable difference characterizes mobility rates in the United States and Japan, but this is because employment elasticity in the United States is unusually high – higher, for instance, than in Western European countries (see Koike 1988: 69; Rohlen 1979: 254–55). Between 1950 and 1970 average monthly separation rates were between 2.0 and 2.5 percent in Japan but between 4.0 and 4.5 percent in the United States. However, even in Britain (where separation rates are on the higher end of the European spectrum), average monthly separation rates were very close to Japanese rates – 2.7 percent (Boltho 1975: 35). Koike presents data showing that in Japan, as elsewhere, the very young change jobs frequently, whereas men in their thirties and forties tend to remain with their firms. As a result, long-service workers are no more common in Japan than in member states of the European Community (Koike 1988: ch. 2; see also Hall 1982). Like firms in Western European countries, Japanese firms tend to use hours reductions and then worksharing arrangements when output declines rather than resorting early to reductions of employment as commonly occurs in the contemporary United States (Koike 1983a: 48; see also Moy and Sorrentino 1981).

Finally, to the extent that it exists, job security in Japan is a relatively new phenomenon, one that has developed chiefly in the last three decades.[6] "Lifetime employment" initially emerged in the 1920s but only in a select number of large enterprises (see Ōkōchi 1965 and Sumiya 1966). It became widespread in the 1950s although even then its scope remained highly uneven (Fruin 1975). Its development in the postwar era was part of the development of internal labor markets in Japan – also characteristic of other advanced capitalist nations – which in turn emerged with the need of employers to retain a highly skilled workforce (Cole 1972; Hanami 1972: 85; Kawanishi 1992: 29). For this reason, it is usually argued that the system of "lifetime employment" that emerged after World War II was substantially different than that of the pre- and interwar eras (e.g. Koshiro 1984). Corroborating the importance of internal labor markets, research has shown that, though Japanese employees exhibit strong commitments to their firms, this is largely the result of the incentives provided by the career expectations associated with strongly developed internal labor markets (Marsh and Mannari 1972). As one would expect of a system meant to tie employees to the firm, Japanese wages are usually characterized as "seniority" wages (that is, they rise steeply with seniority); and the large firm in Japan provides generous welfare benefits to its permanent employees, including health benefits, pensions, and housing (Dore 1973: ch. 12). Not surprisingly, Japanese firms successfully induce considerable loyalty among the permanent workforce (see Shalev 1990). Survey evidence shows that Japanese employees overwhelmingly prefer to remain with their current jobs (Tachibanaki 1984: 78–79).

For these three reasons – the limited scope of lifetime employment, its similarity to employment relations in other countries, and its relatively recent development – the current consensus is that Japanese labor markets and employment practices are not qualitatively different from those found in other advanced capitalist nations. In many regards, they resemble practices characteristic of the Western European nations. To the extent that they differ from those adopted by firms in the United States, the latter are also distinct from the practices generally found in Western Europe.

Although lifetime employment does not make Japanese labor markets as distinct as previously believed, this is not to say that they exhibit no special characteristics. Two specific institutional features of Japanese labor relations are the small *size* of unions and the common contractual provision *restricting bargaining recognition* to employees of the firm. In Japan almost all unions are enterprise unions; that is, they organize only employees of a particular firm. Moreover, only the enterprise union is entitled to sign collective agreements; and even when collective bargaining is nationally coordinated (as occurs with *shuntō*), the contracting parties on the union side remain the enterprise unions. This is enforced by the firm's refusal to recognize anyone other than its own employees as legitimate bargaining agents. In only a few industries – previously coal, as we have already seen – are union officials from outside the enterprise permitted to bargain on behalf of a firm's employees. The implications of these characteristics for how unions and firms interact over workforce reductions will be discussed in the following chapter.

THE DECLINE OF THE BRITISH COAL INDUSTRY, 1957–70

When the industry was nationalized in Britain immediately after World War II, mining was undergoing an expansion of capacity, but this lasted only until 1957. Thereafter, an era of managed decline set in, chiefly as a result of "the transformation of Europe's energy market from apparently chronic shortage to glut," as *The Economist* (1960b: 529) put it. Coal producers across Europe confronted excess capacity as usage shifted increasingly to oil-based and nuclear energy products. Excess capacity particularly affected Britain, Belgium, and Germany; but of the three countries, only Belgium, whose poor productivity made its coal especially uncompetitive, experienced acute industrial conflict in this period. Between 1958 and 1971 almost a half-million jobs, or two-thirds of the industry, were lost in British coal, without engendering national industrial action (for an overview, see Turner 1985). About half of this job loss was due to the introduction of mechanization in operating pits (certified with the National Power Loading Agreement of 1966); the other half resulted from closures, as pits were declared exhausted or too uneconomic to continue mining (Winterton 1985: 231).

Initially, job loss occurred without any redundancies or even, for the first two years, pit closures. Instead, Saturday work was abolished, recruitment restricted, and natural wastage allowed to play its part. Closures began only in 1959, but even then redundancies were initially infrequent (McCormick 1979: 104). Between 1959 and 1963, only 7,500 men took redundancy, despite a labor force reduction of 170,000. Marginal and exhausted pits were closed. Although this tended to concentrate job loss in those regions already suffering from relatively high unemployment (see *The Economist* 1959b: 863; Hudson and Sadler 1985), the process was handled to mitigate its social and political effects. Closures were gradual, with usually successful efforts made to redeploy the men involved. In 1959, for instance, facing an unexpectedly large decline in demand, the Coal Board announced the accelerated closure of 36 short-life collieries that would have been deemed exhausted in the following half-decade anyway; this entailed job loss for 13,000 miners, of whom only 9,000 could be easily redeployed in the industry. The National Coal Board chairman, Sir James Bowman, commented, "It is a bitter pill to swallow. But let us have it on the basis of planning. If it is to protect the great body of men employed in the industry we can only do it according to our lights and our convictions" (quoted in *The Economist* 1959c: 151). In 1960, *The Economist* (1960a: 223) would report that from the 90 pits closed between 1957 and 1959 and the 17,000 miners displaced, only 1,300 remained out of work.

Despite their growing scale, closures generated little pressure for national industrial conflict, for three reasons. First, until nearly the middle of the 1960s British policymakers misinterpreted the fall in demand for coal as temporary (Allen 1981: 40). The NUM therefore believed that were the Labour Party to be returned to power, changes in national policy could alter the industry's fortunes. After 1957 NUM leaders argued consistently that only the election of a Labour government would change the industry's closure policy (Allen 1981: 64). Second, as we have seen, the industry officially took care to "mitigate the social consequences" of closures (*The Economist* 1959a: 300). Finally, the government clearly indicated its intention to prevent as many closures as possible. After 1956, the British government granted no import contracts for coal until 1970. Protectionism too helped shelter the domestic coal industry from the growing effects of international competition.

The NUM was thus resigned to the need for pit closures and rather than opposing them, simply moderated wage demands in order to slow their pace (Ashworth 1986: 241). Indeed, Andrew Taylor (1984b) argues that it was this ongoing pattern of deliberate wage restraint that eventually helped spark a wave of unofficial strikes in the industry in 1968–72 and with them, the rise of a new generation of leftwing leadership in strong but traditionally moderate areas such as Yorkshire, a leadership that eventually organized the 1984–85 strike. At the same time, wage bargaining never entailed national industrial action. As *The Economist* put it:

One of the most significant features of postwar labour relations is that the miners, whose constant struggles with their employers lay at the bitter core of social and industrial strife in the 1920s, have in effect contracted out of the annual process of wage-bargaining-under-the-threat-of-official-strikes. They have agreed in advance always to submit their claims to arbitration. (*The Economist* 1960c: 439)

After Labour's electoral victory in 1964, however, the political disillusionment of the NUM gradually set in. Rather than reversing the policies toward coal undertaken by the Conservatives before them, Labour actually hastened the shrinkage of the industry (Allen 1981: 41–60). Beginning in 1965 when the NCB announced an accelerated pit closures program, the gradual tempo of closures intensified so that in 1967–68 redundancies comprised 3.3 percent of the national labor force in mining, compared to less than 1 percent annually in the five years before 1966–67 (Bulmer 1971: 5). By 1968 only 317 collieries remained open in Britain.

Despite their disappointment with the new Labour government, the NUM continued to accommodate closures and industrial relations in coal remained cordial. Small, localized disputes broke out but withered quickly thanks to an absence of NUM support nationally. One study of redundancy in the industry in the late 1960s found that the union response was one of "acquiescence" in which

the union did not see their [sic] role as either to enforce a "last in, first out" rule in relation to offers of alternative employment, or to seek to safeguard the jobs of members. . . . It was rather that the men should have the right to be made redundant if they wanted. (Bulmer 1971: 10–11)

Corroborating this interpretation, *The Economist* (1958: 1060) reported that, "There is little that the union can do but accept the closing of uneconomic pits that are becoming worked out, which has been going on for years. . . ." At the same time, miners wanted out of the industry, especially given the large lump-sum redundancy payments available. What conflict occurred concerned who would be made redundant, for "nothing in the redundancy situation made clear to the men why certain men were made redundant and why others were asked, repeatedly, to transfer to other pits. No clear criteria or principles of selection were apparent" (Bulmer 1971: 16). Men often expressed resentment at being forced to transfer rather than being allowed to take redundancy.

Massive labor migration followed the industry as miners from the Northeast and from Scotland were transferred to Yorkshire and the Midlands in the 1950s and 1960s (Rutledge 1977–78). This period of closures and transfers took place with the active cooperation of the NUM itself. For instance, a study carried out in the late 1970s found that redundancy

decisions were typically seen by both local management and union representatives in the mining industry as joint decisions – indeed, of all the various
decision areas negotiated locally, redundancy was the only one of which
this was true (Edwards 1983: 56). These findings were confirmed in a
parallel study in 1981 showing that, of 26 issues examined, redundancy
was consistently considered among the most important and branch officials
believed that they had "great" influence over redundancy selection (Edwards
and Heery 1989: 158–60). NUM branch officials reported that conflict over
the selection of those to be made redundant rarely or never occurred. Instead,
redundancy decisions largely meant selecting the "most deserving cases"
among those competing to be considered (Edwards 1983: 58).

During the 1960s as the scale of closures increased, the NCB and
the government were careful in their handling of the social and political
consequences. In his history of the industry, William Ashworth points out
(1986: 258) that, given the context of relatively full employment, the Coal
Board had a strong incentive to manage closures carefully in order to
maintain the morale of working miners since the most efficient production
of coal occurred in the regions with the strongest competition for labor.
So it is not surprising that these closures entailed very few actual redundancies. Of the 678,000 who had left mining jobs between 1957 and 1967,
less than 4.0 percent had been made redundant (Ashworth 1986: 261).

Moreover, there were greater attempts to cover the social costs as
the decade progressed. Especially under the Labour government, increased
financial help was given to those made redundant. Members of the Labour
cabinet apparently experienced considerable anguish over the closure policy
and were well aware that they needed to attend to the social impact of job
loss.[7] The already generous Redundancy Payments Act (1965), adopted soon
after Labour regained power, provides severance payments equivalent to
about six months' wages. This was supplemented by the Redundant Mineworkers (Payments Scheme) Order (RMPS) (1968), which provided that
miners made redundant at or above 55 years of age as of July 1967 would
receive for three years or until age 65 weekly benefits of 90 percent of their
previous net earnings (Bulmer 1971: 5). RMPS has been made increasingly
detailed and complicated with time in order to enhance its provisions (Rees
1985: 212); for example, as of March 1981, a redundant 55-year-old could
ultimately obtain a total theoretical maximum of more than 35,000 pounds
sterling in redundancy payments (Rees 1982: 181).

Decline of the coal industry in this period was by no means peculiar
to Britain. Parts of it were handled under European Community auspices
and, thanks to Community directives, mineworkers are entitled to a series
of supplementary financial benefits easing their involvement in a declining

industry. Coal mining is, of course, an unusual occupation for the physical toll it exacts and partly as a result, for the fact that men's skills decay with age. Mining is truly a young man's job; by the time they are in their fifties, most miners' productivity is in decline, and they are typically unable to perform all of the more skilled work of their past. Early retirement provisions are thus common to the industry across the advanced countries.

CONFLICT IN JAPAN: THE MIIKE STRIKES OF 1953 AND 1959–60

THE 1953 MIIKE STRIKE

With the end of the Korean War boom, demand for coal fell in Japan. In the mining industry 91,000 miners were let go between 1952 and 1954 in a major rationalization drive (Frantz 1984: 7). At the Mitsui company management sought to dismiss 5,738 men in late 1953. The company singled out those over 50 years of age, those with less than three years' seniority, those with poor attendance or poor productivity records, women, children, and those of "bad character." The latter proved a euphemism for union activists, who were deliberately included by the company as "uncooperative" (Hein 1990: 244). When Miike's enterprise union, an affiliate of Tanrō, opposed rationalization, Mitsui listed 1,815 men slotted for "voluntary" retirement instead.[8] A major dispute ensued, what has been called "one of the most serious disputes in postwar Japanese labor history" (Hanami 1979: 65).

As excerpts from the transcripts of the bargaining sessions between labor and management indicate, at issue were not workforce reductions as such but rather the attempt by the company to gain unilateral control over the selection of those for dismissal (see Hanami 1979: 65–67). On this critical issue, the company backed down and the strike ended in a victory for labor. Workforce reductions were carried out – at Miike, for instance, Mitsui cancelled only 1,815 of the 3,464 dismissals originally announced (Kume 1993: 166–67) – but the company relinquished the idea of "designated dismissals." In 1955 Mitsui signed an agreement with Sankōren in which it promised that it would not effect unilateral dismissals in the future (Japan Coal Miners' Union 1961: 5; Hein 1990: 244).[9] The strike cost the company more than four billion yen and labor's victory forced the company's president to resign (Roberts 1989: 448). The outcome was therefore not unlike that obtained by the unions at British Leyland in 1956; in both cases, although redundancies occurred, the firms agreed not to single out union activists in the future.[10] Such success made the Miike Coal Miners'

Union one of Japan's most powerful shopfloor organizations, and the Miike men emerged as Japan's best paid, best treated miners (Martin 1961: 27). As one observer put it, by the end of the decade, "The union's control of its members at the Miike Mine is literally fabulous" (*Oriental Economist* 1960a: 38).

THE MIIKE STRIKE OF 1959–60

By the end of the decade, however, Japan's coal industry, like its British counterpart, faced problems that were considerably more serious than those that had spurred the rationalization drive earlier in the decade. For one thing, despite rationalization in the early 1950s, Japanese coal companies had not invested adequately in their industry in the years after World War II; and even by the mid-1950s the failure to modernize was beginning to catch up with the industry (see Hein 1990: 216 and 232–33). By the late 1950s productivity in Japan was well below European levels at a time when even European producers were beginning to face excess capacity. In 1959 average monthly production per miner was 14.9 tons in Japan, compared to 29 tons in West Germany and 29.2 in Britain (reported in Kiyoshi 1962: 480). Second, the disadvantageous geography of Japanese coal meant that extraction was necessarily relatively expensive. This rendered coal increasingly uncompetitive as other sources of energy became more widely and more cheaply available. Finally, while coal had been heavily favored by the Korean War boom in the early 1950s, by the middle part of the decade the Japanese economy began turning to other sources of energy; and what eventually emerged as the secular and permanent decline of the Japanese coal industry set in. To make things worse, a sudden and severe worldwide depression of coal occurred in 1958, and world coal prices plummeted. This helped catalyze a major reorientation of policy on the part of both coal producers and the Japanese government, as both parties converged on the "energy revolution" and began working out programs to shift national resources from domestic coal to imported oil. In short, by the end of the 1950s the Japanese faced a permanently declining coal industry, one that "is experiencing in an acute form the same difficulties that are plaguing the coal business all over the world as a result of an energy revolution" (*Japan Quarterly* 1960: 6).

In 1959 a government report (the Arisawa Report) proposed that Japan confront the shift to imported oil by reducing the number of miners by one-third by 1963. The report projected job loss for 110,000 miners, largely from the larger unionized collieries (Martin 1961: 26). In a policy known as "scrap and build," resources were to go to the most efficient mines, while the less efficient were to be closed down. The goal was to cut personnel drastically and to raise productivity in the mines still operating, thereby making coal a more efficient competitor with imported oil (*Oriental Economist* 1959a: 654).

Following the Arisawa Report, Mitsui initiated its workforce reductions in standard Japanese fashion: in March of 1959 the company called for 6,000 volunteers to take early retirement. In five of its six mines adequate numbers of men came forward. But at the Miike mine, which had been asked to find 2,000 volunteers, the union produced a list of only 1,000 names and refused to nominate another 1,000 men. In response, in December 1959 the company itself designated another 1,277 Miike miners for dismissal, among whom figured 300 union activists, branded by management as "saboteurs" (Hein 1990: 323; Martin 1961: 28; *Oriental Economist* 1960a: 38). As the Japan Federation of Employers' Associations sternly reported:

> At Mitsui's Miike mine in Kyushu, management announced a reduction of 4,700 miners by naming for discharge those who had disrupted production as well as those who offered to retire voluntarily. . . . The management here has no intention of suppressing or breaking the union movement. Rather, it intends to discharge, from necessity, those who have habitually interrupted production over a long period. . . . (*JFEA News* 1960a: 2)

Even earlier Mitsui had clearly indicated that it believed special problems existed at the Miike mine, problems that would necessarily require purging 300 union activists from the ranks of the men there (*Oriental Economist* 1959b: 707). As one observer put it: "The company wanted not only to reduce the *quantity* of work force but to sift the *quality* of its personnel in the process of rationalization" (Ayusawa 1960: 30; emphasis in the original). In other words, management deliberately targeted union activists in selecting those to be let go. The secondary literature uniformly reports that the critical point triggering the dispute was management's attempt to pick off 300 activists, thereby effectively breaking organized labor's shopfloor power (Shinzō 1982: 449; Hirai 1991: 205).

Arguing that the dismissals represented an attempt to gain the "total destruction of the union," (Martin 1961: 28), Tanrō opposed the unilateral selection of those to be let go, "maintaining that, unless the management's proposal of laying the workers off by names is taken back, it will never cooperate with the management in the latter's effort to rationalize the industry" (*Oriental Economist* 1960a: 38). With Tanrō's backing, the Miike Coal Miners' Union therefore undertook to strike. Carefully planned to avoid provoking management, strike action was scheduled to occur only on Tuesdays and Fridays, "thus giving little excuse for a complete lockout"

(*Oriental Economist* 1960b: 131). Moreover, this kind of intermittent dispute would have allowed labor to continue virtually indefinitely since individual workers were losing little in pay.

Despite this, the Mitsui company proceeded to lock out the mines on January 25, 1960. Management had been divided between two wings, the more conciliatory of which wanted merely to reduce the number of mineworkers. The hawks, by contrast, sought to expel union activists as part of the mass dismissals. The company's top management in Tokyo was dominated by the former, whereas the hawks occupied managing positions at the Miike mine itself (Hirai 1991: 211–14). In December negotiations centered on the "quality" of proposed personnel reductions and a compromise seemed near. With the agreement of the Miike local, Sankōren and Tanrō prepared to concede workforce reductions on the condition that dismissals not be designated by management. Within the company the hawks were persuaded to relax their insistence on 300 designated dismissals and an agreement seemed likely (Hirai 1991: 230–31).

Management, however, suddenly hardened its stance, countering labor's offer with the additional requirements that the 300 previously designated activists take retirement, that another 10 activists be dismissed in disgrace, and that an additional 2,210 workers selected by management be dismissed as well (Hirai 1991: 226). The company specified exact names and notified 1,492 workers, including 670 activists and members of the Japan Socialist and Japan Communist parties, that they were scheduled for retirement as of December 2 (Shinzō 1982: 462–63; *Sōhyō News* 1960: 9). Apparently, the leading Japanese employers' association, Nikkeiren, along with the company's banks, had opposed concessions and successfully pressured the firm to readopt a hard-line position (Hirai 1991: 232).

At this point, collective bargaining broke down altogether and in January the lockout began. Organized labor countered with a strike. The strike and lockout ended only after 262 days of conflict, more than 1,000 arrests, over 1,500 injuries, the death of one miner on the picket lines, and the schism of the Miike Coal Miners' Union. During the strike, among the most violent of labor disputes in Japanese history, cumulatively more than 530,000 police were dispatched and 350,000 strike supporters were mobilized (Ayusawa 1966: 339; *JFEA News* 1960c: 3).

The company itself was well prepared for the dispute. In the earlier 1953 strike, Mitsui had found itself weakened as its competitors took advantage of events to encroach on its markets. During the 1959–60 strike, by contrast, cartelization of the mining industry successfully protected Mitsui. In a prestrike meeting with its competitors, 17 of Japan's biggest coal companies agreed to provide coal to Mitsui's clients during the strike but not to attempt to take over its markets (Frantz 1984: 15; Japan Coal Miners' Union 1961: 12; *Oriental Economist* 1960b: 131). Nikkeiren helped mobilize national support for the company among business circles, providing additional financial help (Martin 1961: 28; *Oriental Economist* 1960b: 131). In addition, thanks in part to the deep recession in coal in 1958, the company had stockpiled 12 million tons of coal prior to the dispute (reported in Ayusawa 1966: 337).

Five times during the course of the strike the union agreed to allow nonbinding arbitration by the Central Labor Relations Committee (CLRC), and five times the CLRC reconfirmed the dismissal of the 1,277 miners. The only concessions made to the union were to convert the dismissals back to "voluntary retirements" and to attach generous severance payments to the retirements. Notwithstanding the 1955 agreement between Mitsui and Sankōren, the commission repeatedly endorsed the company's unilateral selection of those to be let go, confirming management's insistence on purging "saboteurs" from the ranks of the employed.

As the strike and lockout progressed, the Miike Coal Miners' Union came under increasing pressure to capitulate. Two months after the lockout began, dissidents within the Miike union seceded and formed a second union, although "Nobody expected a union split at such an early date" (*Oriental Economist* 1960d: 263). Having gained the support of one-fifth of the union's Central Executive Committee (69 of 254 members) before breaking away in March 1960 (*JFEA News* 1960b: 4; Nakayama 1964: 2), the second union quickly enrolled more than 4,000 members, or one-third of Miike's miners, and with the company's help organized a back-to-work movement (Martin 1961: 28). This resulted in violence at the picket lines as groups of miners tried to enter the pits. The schism found Tanrō "surprised at its own organizational weakness. . ." (*JFEA News* 1960b: 4).

The schism had in part been triggered by conflicts among the various union organizations in play. The Miike Coal Miners' Union had received the support of the national coal union, Tanrō, which backed the strike action initiated at Miike. This was not the case for Sankōren, the Mitsui Coal Miners' Federation organizing all six of the Mitsui mines, of which Miike was but a part. Although initially opposed to the workforce reductions, Sankōren had agreed not to interfere with the company's attempt to enlist "volunteers" in obtaining workforce reductions. With a majority of its members employed at Mitsui's five other collieries, Sankōren eventually opposed the Miike strike, arguing that the colliery dispute was "hopeless" and that CLRC mediation ought to be accepted (*Oriental Economist* 1960c: 226). As a result of these differences with Sankōren, the Miike Coal Miners' Union seceded from its parent enterprise federation in April 1960 (Cook

1967: 106; Japan Coal Miners' Union 1961). Most other unions affiliated with Tanrō, however, continued to support industrial action on the grounds that "dismissal of specified workers . . . would dishearten union workers" (*Oriental Economist* 1960c: 226). Although Tanrō and Sōhyō both continued to support the Miike miners, the company was obviously helped by the fact that it could continue to work its five other mines, thereby reducing the financial impact of the Miike strike.

Nonetheless, the strike proved expensive for both sides. Badly in debt, the company was forced to seek "advances" on payments from clients, while Sōhyō orchestrated a major fund-raising drive and took out a large loan from the Workers' Bank, a loan on which it was paying 100,000 yen a day in interest alone (Ayusawa 1966: 338–39).

Finally, nine months after the company locked out its miners and facing certain defeat, the union accepted the CLRC plan despite great opposition by rank-and-file delegates from the Miike mines. The company thereby acquired the right to use designated dismissals (*Oriental Economist* 1960e: 509). Even so, the strike continued for another two months, in an effort by the Miike Coal Miners' Union to gain a nonrecrimination clause. In the end, nonrecrimination was agreed to but only for a period of five months.

THE BRITISH MINERS' STRIKE OF 1984–85

In 1974 the NCB, the Labour government, and the NUM agreed to a Plan for Coal that attempted to project future capacity, investment, and the employment needs of the industry. The Plan for Coal was written shortly after the first oil crisis of 1973, which effectively reversed 15 years of decline in the demand for coal. The second oil shock of 1979 was one factor rendering the Plan for Coal inoperative; a second was the election of the Conservative government the same year. Although the Tories' energy policy was never fully debated publicly, their handling of the mining industry seems to have differed from that of their Labour predecessors in three ways. First, the Tories were more committed to switching to nuclear energy than Labour had been. Second, they were determined in mining as in automobiles to force the nationalized industries to become profitable. And third, the Coal Board's strategy to achieve this appears to have consisted of a twofold endeavor: first, the closure of entire peripheral areas of the British coalfield and, second, large-scale investments in new large pit complexes enjoying high labor productivity (Burns, Newby, and Winterton 1985: 105). This latter effort involved considerable new automation as well as new systems for monitoring worker effort and productivity.

In line with these changed policies, in 1980 the government issued a Coal Industry Act requiring the NCB to balance its accounts by the 1983–84 fiscal year (Crick 1985: 86). Complete details were never publicly provided, but it seems that the Coal Board had in mind a workforce reduction of 20,000 (Crick 1985: 99) of some 181,000 colliery workers (Adeney and Lloyd 1986: 302; this is the figure as of March 1984; the total number of NCB employees then stood at 234,000) involving the closure of 20 pits in 1984–85 (Crick 1985: 99; Adeney and Lloyd 1986: 22). The Monopolies and Mergers Commission (MMC) report on the coal industry, released in 1983, outlined a long-term program for contraction of the industry by recommending the closure of uneconomic pits and the elimination of 3 to 4 million tons of capacity a year. One hundred forty-one of the 198 pits then in operation were declared unprofitable.

In 1981 the NCB officially announced a program involving 20 to 50 closures over the next five years. The NUM responded with a threat of a national strike and the Coal Board backed down. But the industry was clearly undergoing contraction. In 1982, for instance, 17 pits closed and 23,000 men left the industry (Adeney and Lloyd 1986: 22). Closures were occurring without industrial dispute, with the agreement of area unions, and in some cases even with the personal agreement of the NUM's President, Arthur Scargill (Goodman 1985: 35).

In late 1983 after rejecting a 5.2 percent pay offer, the NUM issued an overtime ban. The prospect of industrial conflict between the union and the Coal Board, backed by the Thatcher government, increased. But wages were not the issue that provoked outright conflict with the NCB. Instead, the issue of pit closures quickly rose to the fore.

The strike was precipitated by the announcement in early March of 1984 by the Yorkshire Area director of the NCB of the imminent closure of five pits, including one (Cortonwood) which had only a few months earlier seen miners transferred in to work it. Although in the year before the strike, 21 collieries had closed and 21,000 jobs had been lost (Rees 1985: 204), job loss had been effected according to national procedures specified in the industry. These typically involved as much as a half-year's notice to the area union (Rees 1985: 205ff). The Cortonwood announcement, by contrast, violated the Colliery Review Procedure. A few days later, the NCB informed organized labor that it projected closures of some 20 pits and job loss of 20,000 in 1984–85 alone.

In response to this threat of a mass workforce reduction, the Yorkshire Area of the NUM called a strike. It did so on the basis of a 1981 area ballot of Yorkshire's 66,000 members (a ballot that had received a 86 percent majority) mandating the Yorkshire NUM "to take various forms of industrial action (including strike action, if necessary) to stop the closure of any pit, unless on the grounds of exhaustion" (quoted in Crick 1985: 86).

Over the next few weeks, the national offices of the union in conjunction with the Yorkshire Area and a number of other regions tried to nationalize the strike. Flying pickets, as they were known, were sent into neighboring coalfields – notably Nottinghamshire – in an effort to "picket out" areas still working. At the same time, the Nottingham Area, the union's second largest after Yorkshire, also held a strike vote. Like miners in Cumberland, Derbyshire, Lancashire, and other areas, however, Notts miners failed to provide the 55 percent majority required for the strike to become official in their area; in fact, Nottingham miners came out 3 to 1 against strike action (Crick 1985: 102; Adeney and Lloyd 1986: 262). In South Wales, the third largest area in the NUM and one likely to be deeply affected by closures, 18 of 31 lodges voted against a strike (Adeney and Lloyd 1986: 96).[11] One month into the strike, a very substantial minority of NUM members continued to work or to try to work.

Coal miners thus responded in divided fashion to the threat of mass workforce reductions, as had also been the case in the Miike strike of 1959–60. Whereas their national union was fully united, compact in its decision to resist workforce reductions (Goodman 1985: 54), workers themselves were not. This division was so severe that it contributed to the subsequent establishment of a new rival trade union, the Union of Democratic Mineworkers (UDM), centered in those parts of the coalfield (mainly Nottinghamshire) where large numbers of miners had continued working during the strike. The sources of such internal divisiveness lay mainly with the differential impact of the threat of job loss on different segments of the workforce. From the perspective of the individual employee, redundancy, even if likely was not necessarily a bad prospect given the relatively generous financial compensation offered. This was particularly true for older miners, for whom redundancy effectively served as a form of early retirement. Moreover, the threat of redundancy was geographically distributed in a highly uneven fashion, with strike action most effective in those regions (such as Yorkshire and the peripheral coalfields in Scotland and Wales) in which the largest numbers of pits were likely to be shut and more miners working in areas (such as Nottinghamshire) least likely to be affected by closures (see Kahn 1988).

Perhaps the most contentious issue of the strike proved to be tactical, involving the decision by the NUM not to hold a national strike ballot. Although it appears that the union's leadership believed a national ballot would lose (Goodman 1985: 46–47), evidence on this point is far from conclusive. An opinion poll conducted after the first week of the strike found that 62 percent of British miners were prepared to strike over pit closures, whereas 33 percent were not (reported in Crick 1985: 103); in fact, "five separate opinion polls carried out between early March and early July showed that a 55 percent vote could easily have been achieved" (Crick 1985: 108). That some 60 percent of miners were on strike by April also suggests that a national strike ballot could have obtained its legal minimum.

No national strike vote was ever held, even though the union's rulebook required one for the strike to be an official national action. As a result, the strike technically remained a patchwork of geographically localized disputes. In September following legal action brought by two working miners against their union, the strike was legally declared "unofficial" and "unlawful" in the absence of a national ballot and the union's funds ordered sequestered (Goodman 1985: 122–23). Surreptitious ties between the miners suing the NUM and the Conservative Party were discovered, and there is some evidence that the Tories may have helped fund miners eager to bring legal action against their union.

The argument for the strike made by the NUM was that pits should be worked to "exhaustion," since it would be cheaper to keep miners working than to make them redundant in an era of high unemployment (see Glyn 1988b; more generally, see the collection in Cooper and Hopper 1988). On a number of separate occasions, the union's negotiating team effectively rejected possible agreements (Crick 1985: 156) and even at the end of the strike, the NUM's Executive continued unanimously to veto the NCB's final offer (Goodman 1985: 185). During the strike itself, there were six cycles of NCB – NUM negotiations, each of which failed to find a settlement to the dispute (Adeney and Lloyd 1986: 187). The most promising occurred in October, in conjunction with the resolution of a dispute between NACODS and the NCB. NACODS itself had voted overwhelmingly (83 percent) to strike but withdrew its threat after establishing a new review procedure for pit closures (Goodman 1985: 115). Had it struck, it could have effectively shut down the parts of the industry still working through the NUM strike. The NACODS agreement in many ways resolved the issues underlying the NUM strike; indeed, the Coal Board appeared to offer much to NACODS that the NUM had been demanding (Goodman 1985: 148–50).

Since coal stocks had been high before the strike began, winter failed to bring blackouts or other kinds of disruptions that would have directly affected the public. Despite the NUM's efforts to construct a "triple alliance" of coal, steel, and railway workers, even sympathetic industrial unions found themselves unable to guarantee supportive actions by their members. Dockworkers largely held out, refusing to unload foreign coal, but truck

drivers barely struck at all; electricians and power station engineers spoke
out openly against the strike; and steelworkers were visibly divided in their
responses. As one study of local mobilization during the strike observed,
"The NUM's appeal for support in a battle against voluntary redundancy
at £1,000 per year's service was being made to stewards who had often had
to swallow compulsory redundancies at 10 percent of that rate" (Mackney
1987: 93).

In the end, the miners found themselves virtually isolated in the labor
movement, reliant on collections often from middle-class sympathizers and
money from abroad. The NUM offered its participants no strike pay, but
the families of striking miners could collect supplementary benefits from
the government. Miners themselves were paid small sums for picketing,
although they were subject to often brutal political action. During the
course of the strike there were three deaths, 9,808 arrests in England and
Wales and another 1,483 in Scotland; and while figures on injuries are
unavailable, some indication is given by the number of police injuries,
which totaled 1,392 (Wallington 1985: 149–50). Miners were also faced
with stringent legal rulings cutting off part of government social security
payments during the strike and increasingly found themselves without
adequate food or, ironically, coal for heat. By all accounts striking miners
and their families held out with a fortitude that was genuinely heroic. This
lasted a full year, at which point they returned to work in defeat, without
even a written agreement to end the dispute. By the end of the strike
perhaps 60 percent of miners were working (Adeney and Lloyd 1986: 258).
As the theory proposed in this study would predict and as had also been
the case in the Miike dispute of 1959–60, the final issue that kept the
strike going from January through March 1985 was that of nonvictimization
of activists sacked during the course of the dispute (Winterton and Winterton 1989: 199). On this issue, as everything else, the union lost and
the NUM's Executive voted unanimously to reject the NCB's final offer
(Goodman 1985: 185).

SUBSEQUENT OUTCOMES

Despite the brief nonrecrimination clause won by the Miike union in 1960,
upon its expiration the company systematically targeted union organizers in
the pits. According to union sources, some 1,200 activists were subsequently
dismissed (Japan Coal Miners' Union 1961: 20). At the end of 1961, for
instance, the company dismissed 28 rank-and-file union members for strike
activity; and in late 1962 another 10 strike leaders were fired, including

the union's chairman (*Japan Labor Bulletin* 1963a: 2; *Sōhyō News* 1963: 1). By the end of 1962, "[m]ost leaders of the first union were discharged" (Cook 1966: 104 n20). In addition, the company announced that, "it had no intention of negotiating with the leaders who were no longer members of the Union. . . . A struggle led by discharged officials would be ineffective because they could not take full responsibility for the workers' advantage . . . " (quoted in *Sōhyō News* 1963: 1). This effectively ended the diagonal bargaining that had earlier characterized the industry, thereby marginalizing Tanrō. Finally, employees affiliated with the second union were given better transfers into higher paying jobs, the General Secretary of the original union charged (Shigeru 1960: 3).

All these actions further weakened the Miike Coal Miners' Union by encouraging workers to join the second union in its place. Not surprisingly, in the aftermath of the dispute the Miike Coal Miners' Union became the minority union at the Miike colliery. By 1961 the second union had 7,000 members at Miike, whereas the original union was left with only 4,000 (Cook 1966: 104 n20).

With few resources following such a lengthy and expensive dispute, Tanrō lent what remained to the Japan Socialist Party (JSP) in an ultimately successful effort to win better conditions for redundant mineworkers through national legislation, passed in 1963 (Cook 1967: 107; Hein 1990: 21 and 324–26). The very public campaign, undertaken by a "Struggle Congress" formed by the JSP, Tanrō, and Sōhyō, aimed to pressure the government on three fronts: "Tanrō will mobilise miners to come up to Tokyo to exert pressure on the Government through mass deputations, Sōhyō will organize general strikes by all the workers of the country, and the Socialist Party will develop a struggle within the Diet" (*Sōhyō News* 1962b: 3). The legislation that was adopted marked a turning point in the reluctant development of Japanese welfare state policies (see Pempel 1982: ch. 4); and the active labor market policy adopted for coal has been used for various industries, proving an important component in Japan's low unemployment rate (Kume 1991: 14).

Mines closed quickly after the defeat at Miike; indeed, more miners left the industry than projected (*Japan Labor Bulletin* 1963b: 3) and by 1964 voluntary quits were so high that labor shortages in coal were reported (*Japan Labor Bulletin* 1964a: 2, and 1964b: 2). Miners, at least those under 35, apparently had less difficulty finding new employment than had been expected (Cook 1967: 120), although it is doubtful that they enjoyed wages or working conditions comparable to those in the industry they had left.

In Britain, too, large-scale closures and job loss followed the NUM's defeat. Between the end of the strike and the summer of 1986, 27 pits had been shut and NCB employment had fallen from 234,000 in March 1984 to 175,000 (Adeney and Lloyd 1986: 302), a decline of some 25 percent. Productivity soared in the immediate aftermath of the dispute, in part, although not entirely as a result of the closure of the least efficient pits, so that within the first 18 months alone following the strike, average productivity increased some 17.5 percent (Glyn 1988a: 167).

The procedures used to conduct this mass workforce reduction did not extend to forced redundancies; indeed, from the beginning the Coal Board had promised that pit closures would not forcibly deprive any miner of employment in the industry (Goodman 1985: 15). Instead, a combination of early retirement and transfers was used. Men fifty years or older were offered voluntary early retirement, a practice often used in the frequent workforce reductions experienced by the industry in the 1960s and 1970s.

As in Japan, after the strike British coal miners sought voluntary redundancy in droves; typically, many more asked than places existed. The economic logic of their situation was transparent: severance payments in the coal mining industry, especially for men with many years' seniority, are among the most substantial for any group of manual workers in Britain.

Finally, where pits closed, men under fifty were offered transfers to other pits. The provisions of the 1965 Redundancy Payments Act make redundancy relevant to a particular place of work, such that employees offered alternate employment within daily traveling distance do not receive redundancy payments if they refuse a transfer (Bulmer 1971: 6).

As for the union, it faced severe competition from the UDM, which continued to be based largely in Nottinghamshire after breaking away from the NUM in 1985. By the end of 1986 the UDM probably organized 80 percent of Notts miners (Taylor 1988: 224). The Coal Board initially tried to pay UDM members higher wages than members of the NUM, but this was quickly ruled illegal. It then established a new conciliation procedure that allowed exclusive representation by whichever union had majority support in a pit (Taylor 1988: 224–26). At the same time, as two journalists observed, "Just how different things were to be emerged only after the strike was over. Miners returning to work in striking areas found whole networks of local agreements and pit deals about allowances and winding times unilaterally abrogated and the union branch excluded traditional consultations" (Adeney and Lloyd 1986: 187). Other studies report system-atic reductions in the influence of the NUM following the strike (Edwards and Heery 1989: ch. 10). As a result of these and other factors, one study reports that by March 1987 the industry had experienced approximately a 50 percent improvement in productivity over prestrike levels (Richardson and Wood 1989: 33). This was also a result of the introduction – against the NUM's objections – of a new payment system linking pay to output more closely.

The overall effects on the NUM were thus highly unfavorable. Various studies report that a disproportionate number of branch officials were sacked during the strike – in Scotland, for instance, apparently two-thirds of those sacked were NUM branch officials (Edwards and Heery 1989: 190 and 228). Peggy Kahn (1987: 77) concurs, reporting that over 700 miners were dismissed during the strike over alleged offenses. Peter Gibbon and Simon Bromley (1990: 76) report the number of those dismissed during and after the dispute as over 1,000. NUM membership fell drastically, both with the fall in employment and because of competition from the UDM. In December 1983 there had been 187,000 men on colliery books; this was down to 85,000 in early 1989. By the end of 1985, UDM membership was 25,000–30,000 (Gibbon and Bromley 1990: 78). In short, "The national union's standing and bargaining power were indeed shattered . . ." (Gibbon and Bromley 1990: 60). The financial effects of the strike in conjunction with such a drastic loss of membership – which given government policy toward closures could only be anticipated to worsen – were also severe, and three years after its defeat, the NUM opened talks with the TGWU for a merger (Aston, Morris, and Willman 1990).

CONCLUSIONS

Industrial relations, manpower policy, and the organization of labor and management in the Japanese and British coal industries exhibit numerous visible differences, information on which has been presented in this chapter. Despite these differences, pit closures in both countries resulted in massive industrial action, action that occurred in Japan in 1959–60 and in Britain in 1984–85. Equally puzzling, British interactions over pit closures had previously proceeded for decades with a high degree of cooperation between organized labor and management. In the next chapter I offer an interpretation of these various outcomes.

6

SEEKING ALLIES: HOW OTHER ACTORS AFFECT INTERACTIONS OVER JOB LOSS

During the 1950s the coal industry faced dramatic and global changes in the competitive position of its product. As the decade progressed, industrial economies increasingly turned to oil rather than coal as a major source of fuel. In Japan miners at the Miike mines battled pit closures in the 1950s with greater aggressiveness than miners anywhere else in the world (McCormick 1979: 172). But after winning an apparently historic victory in the middle of the decade, at the end of the 1950s they went down to defeat after an even longer strike. In Britain, by contrast, widespread pit closures after 1957 proceeded virtually uncontested. Even as redundancies in the industry increased in the latter part of the 1960s, the National Union of Mineworkers accommodated the contraction of the British coal industry. Only in the mid-1980s did the NUM battle closures, in a dramatic and protracted dispute that the union eventually lost.

This chapter analyzes these three disputes in detail. Using the game-theoretic models developed in Chapter 2, I argue that all three strikes were aimed at organizational survival. In each case, the union involved believed that the future of its organization was at stake. The precise dynamics underlying the three conflicts were somewhat different, however.

In the case of the 1953 strike at Miike, organizational survival for the local union was largely a matter of defending activists. Like the Fiat strike in 1980 and the BL dispute in 1956, the 1953 Miike dispute was provoked when management inadvertently targeted too many shopfloor union representatives for the union to tolerate. The firm was forced to make concessions to labor in the end because, I contend, ironically management apparently overestimated the external subsidies it would receive from other firms in the industry in the event of conflict.

In the second Miike strike as well as in the British mineworkers' strike of 1984–85, the impact of exogenous actors on the calculations of payoffs is even more visible and more important. These two disputes illustrate the second of the four propositions advanced in Chapter 1 (see page 20): namely, that a dispute over job loss may occur when both parties know that some outside actor will help subsidize the costs of the dispute. For the two protagonists, this lowers the costs of conflict, thereby altering the payoffs.

The second Miike strike, I argue, occurred because Japan's national employers' federation, Nikkeiren, was determined to subsidize the strike for the Mitsui firm in order to break the development of industrial trade unionism, a development embodied by the national Japanese coal union, and symbolized by developments at Miike. At the same time, the national miners' union, Tanrō, and the country's major labor confederation, Sōhyō, were also interested in subsidizing the Miike dispute in an ultimately unsuccessful effort to defend the rights of national union organizations to play a role in collective bargaining. With national allies on both sides prepared to help shoulder the costs of conflict, the Miike union and Mitsui's management were virtually pushed into confrontation.

The British miners' strike of 1984–85 illustrates similar properties. The strike was instigated by the national NUM and the Thatcher government, each of which was prepared to pay the price of conflict. A strike could and would not have occurred solely through the interactions between organized labor at those pits actually threatened with closure and the NCB. The goal of the NUM nationally, I argue, was to topple the Thatcher government in order to usher in a Labour government, an administration that the union believed would be more sympathetic to the coal industry. A continuation of Thatcherism, data show, threatened the NUM with such a drastic loss of membership in the foreseeable future as to plausibly cause the disappearance of the union altogether, perhaps through a merger with a larger organization. For this reason, the national union was prepared to subsidize the costs of a strike to those relatively few areas and pits under immediate threat of closure. At the same time, the government was prepared to subsidize the costs of a strike to the NCB in order to effect a more general transformation of British industrial relations, to free the nationalized industries (coal in particular) of militant trade unionism, and as part of a genuine effort to shift British energy use away from coal.

This chapter proceeds in three parts. The first details the interpretations I sketched previously of the two Japanese strikes; the second, the changing course of behavior by the NUM in relation to pit closures and the eventual year-long action there. The third section considers some implications of the analysis of the second Miike strike and the British miners' strike for our understanding of labor politics and industrial relations in these two countries.

INTERPRETING THE JAPANESE
COAL DISPUTES

The two disputes at the Miike mines illustrate different theoretical propositions. The 1953 conflict is an instance of the first of the four propositions
advanced in Chapter 1, a proposition concerning the targeting of excessive
union activists. Hence its causes were similar to those in play at Fiat in
1980, a case reviewed in Chapter 4. The second Miike dispute, by contrast,
illustrates the second of the four propositions presented in Chapter 1, a
proposition concerning subsidies from external allies.

THE 1953 STRIKE

Although less information is available on it than on the later strike, the
first Miike dispute corroborates that when institutions fail to protect union
activists on the shopfloor, informational imperfections of various kinds may
make for an explosive combination that provokes conflict. The causes of
the strike itself, I argue, lie with the firm's lack of information about union
thresholds; its eventual outcome, by contrast, lies with the firm's lack of
information about exogenous sources of subsidy.

As the account in the last chapter showed, evidence demonstrates that
in 1953 the Miike union was reacting specifically to the threat to its activists
and not to personnel reductions per se. The strike was deemed a victory
not because jobs were saved – they were not – but because of the subsequent
guarantee of future protection for union activists in the event of workforce
reductions. The most plausible explanation for what triggered the strike is
thus that the firm inadvertently overshot the union's threshold, targeting
too many activists for discharge. This was, as we shall see, easy to do in
that period since the institutional protection of activists afforded by "lifetime
employment" was not yet in place. In addition, the influence of exogenous
actors changed the payoffs for the firm, making the strike considerably
more costly than originally anticipated. In particular, the company's loss
of markets to its competitors made the strike more expensive than may
have been initially calculated. The eventual concession made to the union
may well have been a result of the high costs of the strike, costs that were
the product of the extensive fragmentation of the industry and the relatively
poor ability of Japan's numerous coal companies to coordinate their activities
at the time. In other industries, firms reportedly were more able to coordinate
their actions in dealing with trade unionism and thereby avoided making
such concessions.

Ironically, the impact of competition among employers may even have worked to encourage the strike in the first place. Writing of competition in the industry in the early 1950s, Laura Hein notes:

> [B]y periodically striking, the union cut production for the mine owners, eliminating the need for the owners to do this themselves. Temporarily, the actions of the union benefited the operators and buttressed their strategy of creating artificial scarcity to propel coal prices back up. (Hein 1990: 243)

This suggests that in 1953, management at Mitsui may have calculated the costs of potential conflict as relatively low and may therefore initially have been somewhat indifferent toward the prospect of industrial action on the part of organized labor. Although conflict threatened the company by allowing competitors into its markets, it also reduced the supply of coal, thereby allowing prices to rise. At least initially, when it may not have been clear that the dispute would be as lengthy as proved to be the case or that Mitsui's competitors would be as successful in raiding its markets as they subsequently proved to be, the company could have targeted activists for dismissal without attending greatly to whether it was selecting more than the union could bear or whether doing so would trigger a strike. That is, the company may have underestimated the probable costs of industrial action, devaluing the importance of assessing with care the union's trigger point. Once the strike was underway, competition from within the industry itself made the costs of conflict higher than anticipated, and Mitsui was forced to concede that it would refrain from targeting activists in the future.

THE 1959–60 STRIKE

This second dispute is better documented in the literature but theoretically more complex. Whereas in the first case it is not implausible to argue that management triggered industrial action inadvertently by targeting too many union activists for dismissal, a similar line of argument is highly implausible for the second case. By the time the company drew up the lists of those to be discharged, it had clear and unequivocal evidence that by targeting 300 activists it would provoke a strike. Indeed, conflicts among management groups turned on the very issue of whether to provoke a strike or not. The empirical evidence supports the interpretation that the conflict, when it came, was thus deliberately instigated by the firm. Informational imperfections hardly seem relevant.

Instead, by 1959 much of Mitsui's management, especially that responsible for the Miike mine, had become determined to vitiate its post-1953 strike agreement with organized labor. *The Oriental Economist* hazards the following interpretation for this hardening of attitude:

> The Mitsui Mining management has long been known for its soft touches to the unions. It has granted almost all of its unions' demands before. The red-ink figures for the past three terms running (upwards of ¥5 billion in the books alone), however, seems to have roused the management to the crux of the whole matter. (*Oriental Economist* 1959b: 707)

This suggests that the firm was under growing financial pressure (from creditors, for instance) to undertake a major realignment of its industrial relations and that thanks to assurances of external support, the estimated costs of conflict may have paled next to the estimated costs of continuing to allow organized labor its extensive pit-level powers. Indeed, it seems that the conflict between management groups was won by the hardliners primarily due to exogenous pressures from Nikkeiren and the company's banks. Ikuo Kume (1993: 167) reports, for instance, without ascribing causality, that "Nikkeiren mobilized business nationwide, while Sōhyō mobilized labor support," while a history of the Mitsui company also notes that, "Attempts at a compromise failed, partly because the company was adhering to a policy reached at the highest levels of government, and partly because the Central Labor Relations Council arbitrating the dispute merely echoed proposals made by the government and management" (Roberts 1989: 449). The genesis of the strike engaged national actors on both sides.

We can only speculate on the reasons. Nikkeiren had long played a major role in coordinating Japanese companies in their dealings with trade unions, and it is likely that the existing arrangements at Miike struck the federation as repugnant and a potential threat to the type of industrial relations system it was encouraging nationally. Described by two experts as "militantly ideological," in the 1950s Nikkeiren "vigorously encouraged employers to confront, rather than cooperate with, the leftist labor movement" (Shinkawa and Pempel forthcoming: 25). In particular, the English-language literature suggests that Nikkeiren was strongly committed to the principle that firms recognize only their own employees as legitimate bargaining agents, a principle that became one of the strike's major issues as Mitsui fired union officials and then subsequently refused to allow them to negotiate on behalf of their mines. Previously, of course, Tanrō's officials had been entrusted with the authority to engage in "diagonal" bargaining for any of its affiliates. By the end of the strike, this was no longer the case. Thus, by winning the strike at Miike, Nikkeiren won the right to repel industrial unionism, thereby setting the Japanese union movement firmly on the course of enterprise unionism.

The impact of exogenous actors on the payoffs of the firm thus seems to have played a major part in encouraging Mitsui to provoke a dispute with organized labor. On labor's side, institutional, informational, and exogenous variables all seem to have been important, although in somewhat different ways for each actor – the Miike Union, Tanrō, and Sōhyō. I analyze each in turn.

The responses of the Miike Coal Miners' Union were theoretically and comparatively unexceptional. As I have argued is inevitably the case, a trade union will resist workforce reductions if too many shopfloor activists are singled out for redundancy. A report in *The Oriental Economist* corroborates the importance of the protection of activists for the Miike union:

> What makes the first unionists so stubborn, then? One of the most important reasons is that, among the 1,200 workers picked by the management for discharge, there are included some 300 "active" union workers. In labor's line of thinking, if the workers are to be discharged simply because of their union activities, there would finally be no one who would take on the union jobs and this will constitute a major obstacle in Japan's union movement. (*Oriental Economist* 1960d: 263)

John Roberts's (1989: 449) history of the company seconds this interpretation, arguing that "One reason for the intransigence of the miners was that the company was using 'rationalization' as a pretext for discharging seven hundred of the most militant union organizers." Given the preexisting 1955 agreement, the Miike Coal Miners' Union had every reason to believe that protection of activists was a concession the company would be prepared to make. Indeed, had Nikkeiren not intervened, this may well have proven to be the case. But by itself, the Miike union could hardly have held out for a year, or made the strike one of the most important in Japan's postwar history; indeed, without guarantees of external support it seems implausible that the Miike local would have dared strike in the first place. The subsidies that Tanrō and Sōhyō were prepared to offer proved crucial, especially once the strike was repudiated by Sankōren, the enterprise federation of Mitsui unions.

Tanrō, too, hoped to get the 1,200 names rescinded, protect Miike's 300 militants, and come to some agreement over whom to let go. Yet Miike miners constituted only a fraction of Tanrō's members. If even Sankōren eventually sided with its five other mines against its Miike affiliate in the dispute, it is unlikely that Tanrō's continued commitment to the Miike union was engendered solely by its commitment to Miike's activists. More likely, Tanrō was motivated by the desire to protect its existing organizational structure and its own role in the collective bargaining of its affiliates, the vehicle for which was the diagonal bargaining then in effect. The intervention of Nikkeiren in the dispute may well have signaled to Tanrō that the very existence of the national miners' federation as a legitimate bargaining actor was at stake. Corroborating this, Roberts (1989: 450) notes that the Miike struggle was regarded as the last stand of the holdouts defending the principle of industry-wide unionism, and for that reason received financial backing by Tanrō and Sōhyō. In addition, both the Miike union and Tanrō seem to have underestimated how quickly a second union would form and to have overestimated the Miike union's ability to mobilize its own rank and file. As we saw in the last chapter, various secondary reports from the period note that the Miike union was surprised at the difficulties it so quickly experienced in preventing the formation of the second union. Both the Miike Coal Miners' Union and Tanrō, in other words, seem to have underestimated the costs of conflict and the extent of external subsidies that would eventually prove necessary to sustain the dispute.

Sōhyō, finally, also exhibited a relatively low trigger point for the firing of activists in the coal industry. The president of the confederation, Kaoru Ota, indicated one reason for this in remarks made at an extraordinary convention of Tanrō in October 1962. Speaking to Tanrō delegates he claimed, "The Japanese labor movement in the past decade was headed by miners. Sōhyō will support you and fight with you" (quoted in *Sōhyō News* 1962a: 4). Tanrō is regularly reported to be "the most powerful union of all the Sōhyō affiliates" (*JFEA News* 1960b: 4). If the dismissal of miners at Miike threatened the continued vitality of Tanrō, this in turn threatened the continued vitality of Sōhyō itself.

This threat was not merely quantitative, of course. As a national confederation, Sōhyō, like Tanrō, had an interest in promoting the recognition and bargaining role of national union officers. This was the issue at stake in the Miike dispute and this inspired the national unions to intervene on the side of the Miike local.

INTERPRETING THE BRITISH MINERS' STRIKE OF 1984–85

The British mining industry has witnessed secular decline since World War I, when the industry employed more than one million men (Fine 1990: xi). On the whole, this decline has been accommodated by organized labor. The strike of 1984–85 proved a dramatic exception to this pattern.

As in the Miike strike of 1959–60, the strike in the British mining industry in 1984–85 was largely the product of exogenous actors affecting the expected payoffs for different courses of action. More precisely, the NUM's leadership appeared to believe that the union's own future was at stake under continued Tory governance, subscribing to the view that its own organizational survival required a dramatic change of national policy that could only be achieved under a Labour cabinet. Even this latter outcome was far from certain since in the past, "The contraction [of the mining industry] had shown little party allegiance. . ." (Winterton and Winterton 1989: 22). But it was, evidence shows, the union's only hope. At the same time, the Conservative government also exhibited a willingness to subsidize the costs of the strike, thereby encouraging the NCB to engage in conflict.

In the best study to date of the British coal industry and the strike, Jonathan Winterton and Ruth Winterton (1989) present data projecting the fate of the industry under three different political scenarios: continued Conservative governance, a Labour government committed to the 1974 Plan for Coal, and a Labour government committed to a "socialist" energy policy. The projections show that "the effective destruction of the British coal industry will be largely completed in the next decade if Conservative policies continue" (Winterton and Winterton 1989: 50).[1] By the year 2010, the study claims, total employment in the industry under continued Conservative rule would be a mere 7,700 persons; under Labour, by contrast, it would stand at 53,000. Whatever the minimum size required for the NUM to exist as an independent entity, 7,700 is indisputably well under it. In other words, the NUM faced – within the lifetime of its current president[2] – its own extinction unless a change in the partisan composition of government were to occur.

Even before the strike, research groups close to the NUM's national leadership were publishing studies projecting that automation alone would in the foreseeable future generate a 75 percent reduction of the current workforce, even if the demand for coal were to remain constant (Burns et al. 1983: 17). While such an estimate has been contested by other scholars (Edwards and Heery 1989: 5–6), its political importance is that it came from a group working under the authorization of the NUM, and therefore – whether true or not – was likely to be believed by the union's national leadership.

At the same time, the NUM's leadership – Arthur Scargill in particular – had considerable prior experience in using the union movement to push the Labour Party to the left. Under Scargill's presidency, the Yorkshire NUM had successfully taken control of the Constituency Labour Party in an increasingly assertive attempt to get leftwing candidates selected to stand for Parliament in the district (see Taylor 1984a). The history of the left in the NUM, therefore, was intertwined with political activism; and the union's national leadership, politically sophisticated and aware (e.g. Scargill 1975), would naturally have considered the potential partisan effects of its actions.

Area organization, too, was equally sensitive to the vital importance of government policy for the rate of future closures. A study commissioned by the Notts Area NUM in the early 1980s noted, for instance:

> At the end of the debate on coal, it will be the decisions of Central Government that will matter. This observation is not in any way to be interpreted as a cry of despair. Even Governments with entrenched stances cannot totally ignore plain common sense and public opinion. At least not in a democracy. . . . (NUM 1983: 7)

Others in the labor movement report that, "The hard left actually talks of the miners bringing down the Thatcher government" (Reid 1985: 92), indicating that this outcome was both desired and widely believed to be possible. Many believed that coal's problems were merely an artifact of Tory government and would evaporate once Labour was elected to office (this view is expressed in Towers 1985: 23).

Indirect evidence in support of the view that the NUM was intent on bringing down the government rather than negotiating a settlement on the ostensible issues of the strike comes from the fact that the NUM consistently refused to underwrite a settlement, even one relatively favorable to its position, as is noted, for instance, by Peter Gibbon (1988: 148). An interpretation along these lines is also advanced in the careful journalistic account by Martin Adeney and John Lloyd (1986), who argue that the NUM deliberately provoked the strike in an ultimately unsuccessful attempt to bring down the government.[3] Others argue, by contrast, that the strike was intended above all to protect jobs and was not, in that sense, fundamentally political (e.g. Howell 1987: 388–93). This contrast, the argument advanced here shows, is unnecessary. The attempt to bring down the government *was* an attempt to save jobs, since the latter was predicated on the belief that only the election of a Labour government could reorient national policy toward the coal industry. Ultimately, however, both the attempt to topple the government and the attempt to save jobs were functions of a desperate and, as it turns out, unsuccessful attempt to preserve the National Union of Mineworkers itself.

On what basis did the NUM believe that it could topple the Thatcher government? Various pieces of evidence suggest that the NUM had good reason to believe that the strike would prove substantially more disruptive than was the case and that national officials seriously overestimated the extent to which ordinary citizens would be exposed to the strike's effects. First, the police effort in restricting picketing was massive and unprecedented. Kahn (1987: 70) notes that, "in the first crucial twenty-seven weeks of the strike, 164,508 'presumed pickets' were prevented from entering Nottinghamshire, and similar roadblocks were established as far away as Kent. . . ." As a result, as Adeney and Lloyd (1986: 101) argue, "it was only the police which prevented the miners' leadership from achieving its objective of halting all coal fields by picketing."[4] The NUM in turn lacked full information on the reorganization of the police preceding the strike, and because of this, overestimated its own ability to roll the strike across the whole of the British coalfield. Had the union been able to picket Nottinghamshire, coal stocks would have fallen much faster than was the case – after all, coal from Notts and other working areas continued to provide the Central Energy Generating Board (CEGB) with 30 percent of its energy requirements during the dispute (Edwards and Heery 1989: 212) – and the government would possibly have had to have ordered blackouts, as had occurred in the 1972 and 1974 miners' strikes. Blackouts would have humiliated the Thatcher government, and the NUM could well have imagined that the Prime Minister, if not the entire government, would have then been forced out of office. Lack of up-to-date information on police tactics, therefore, was probably a critical part of the NUM's belief that the union could drive the government from office.

At the same time, the NUM seems to have been either unaware or ill-informed of the changes in operation of Britain's electricity industry that had taken place over the previous decade. Whereas the CEGB had been entirely dependent on domestic coal for electricity during the strikes of 1972 and 1974, by 1984 changes in production processes meant that the CEBG was in a position to switch from coal to imported oil during the strike (Edwards and Heery 1989: 210), thereby deliberately avoiding blackouts.

Finally, given that the government had backed down in its attempts to launch an accelerated pit closure program in 1981, it is possible that the NUM calculated that government authorities might have lacked the stomach for a lengthy and costly dispute. For all these reasons, then, the NUM reasonably overestimated the likelihood of bringing down the Thatcher government during the strike.

On the other side, the right wing of the Conservative party had already indicated its intent to subsidize a potential coal strike with the Ridley Report (see Chapter 5, page 88). Many have commented that Thatcher believed that for the economic revitalization of the British economy to occur, the place of organized labor had to be redefined; and she intended that reducing the power of the NUM would serve as an object lesson to other unions. Even level-headed observers like Winterton and Winterton argue that

> it would be wrong to expect simple economic rationality of employer behavior, particularly where a state-owned industry is concerned. From a political perspective, the Government would have paid any price to defeat the miners. . . . in order to further the interests of capitalism by inflicting damage upon the labour movement. (Winterton and Winterton 1989: 185)

But it is doubtful that the government would have devoted the enormous national resources to breaking the strike that it did had not strong economic motives also been in play.

In that regard, there is considerable debate in the literature about how competitive British coal actually was in the 1970s and 1980s. The NUM maintained that it was Europe's most competitive producer; the NCB, by contrast, that large numbers of pits were highly uneconomic and had to go. In any case, the financial pressures on the industry were not only political but also derived from international market pressures. The CBGB had been pressing to be allowed to move to imported coking coal since the late 1970s, and as a result "the NCB was being squeezed by the international coking market" (Beynon, Hudson, and Sadler 1991: 12). Moreover, the government's estimates of future energy use – summarized in the 1974 "Plan for Coal" and the 1977 "Coal for the Future" – proved to be wildly off base, as energy consumption nose-dived after the second oil shock. By 1980 energy consumption in the United Kingdom was actually below that of 1973 (Beynon et al. 1991: 31). Even a Labour government would have had a difficult time reestablishing policy on the basis of projections that were so far off.

For both economic and political reasons, then, the government had strong incentives to subsidize a dispute between the NCB and the miners. The NCB, in turn, appears to have been informed in advance that government support would be forthcoming in the event of a direct confrontation with the NUM. One analysis of the aftermath of the strike notes that, "Most interpretations . . . argue that its central cause was the 'anti-corporatist offensive' of the Conservative Government of Margaret Thatcher" (Gibbon and Bromley 1990: 56) and goes on to explain:

> If MacGregor defined his job as 'recovering the right to manage the industry' and essentially provoked the 1984/5 strike as a means of doing just that, it was because his experience at BL and BSC showed that such a stance was a guarantee of Conservative support. (Gibbon and Bromley 1990: 60).

THE RANK AND FILE

To what extent is the interpretation advanced here corroborated at pit level? Did the rank-and-file miner acknowledge that the dispute was less about saving particular pits than it was an attempt to rework Britain's political landscape so as to allow the very industry to exist at all? Support for the strike was, we have seen, highly variable, with some regions nearly entirely behind it and others largely at work. Overall, about one-third of British miners kept working throughout the strike. Of course, views of the strike differed enormously among the men. But the issues of political change and with it of the organizational survival of the NUM itself were hardly foreign to the dispute, even at pit level.

The region in which antistrike behavior was most marked was Nottinghamshire, long known in the mining industry for its unusual industrial and political history. For instance, after the General Strike of 1926, Nottinghamshire was marked by "Spencerism," a movement named for George Spence, founder of a breakaway trade union that lasted a decade until eventually rejoining the Mineworkers' Federation of Great Britain in 1937. The industrial organization of mining in the area also seems to have exhibited some special characteristics (see Krieger 1983; Waller 1983). For various reasons, the strike failed in Notts, which instead became the heartland for the newly established UDM.

There is, however, some evidence that those who supported the strike understood that it was above all a matter of organizational survival. Drawing on extensive field work in a South Yorkshire mining village, Gibbon (1988: 151; emphasis in the original) contends that "it was defence of the *Union* which motivated the majority of male activists in the strike. . . ." In discussing the causes of the strike, one activist argued:

> Maggie vowed that she was going to get us. She's been practicing for it since 1979. She'd got the bonus and incentives schemes which weren't wanted, she'd built stocks up and she'd got the police trained and equipped with all this riot gear. That was the main issue, getting rid of the union. It's surprising how many men at that time (March '84) talked about it like that. (Quoted in *People of Thurcroft* 1986: 45)

Evidence for this view is not entirely satisfactory since it is based on data drawn from a nonrandom population sample. Another study of the aftermath of the strike only partially corroborates Gibbon's view. These data show that, at least in the Doncaster village studied (in the Yorkshire Area) where strike support was extremely high, 17 of 60 men surveyed said they struck to save jobs and pits, 11 out a sense of tradition and history, and 8 because of loyalty to the NUM (Waddington, Wykes, and Critcher 1991: 190, table 3.4). As both studies clearly indicate, asking participants why they engaged in strike activity is likely to elicit an extremely broad range of responses, which are in turn difficult to interpret. In any event, the theme of the NUM's organizational survival was interwoven from the start into the strike and appears to have been one factor motivating the participation in the dispute by a majority of British miners.

IMPLICATIONS AND EXTENSIONS

Rather than formally consider alternative explanations for the three disputes analyzed in this chapter, in this section I instead reevaluate relevant empirical propositions in light of the interpretations offered here. By and large, the literature concurs that both the 1959–60 Miike strike and the 1984–85 NUM strike were fundamentally political, both in the sense of deeply implicating the two governments then in power and in the sense of reworking the role of labor in the polity more generally in the aftermath of the conflicts. Although the interpretation offered here places this view in a more precise theoretical framework – one represented by the games explored in Chapters 1 and 2 – it endorses this general perspective.

Nonetheless, thanks to the theoretical propositions advanced in Chapter 1 and especially to the argument that in both disputes each side was prepared to undertake conflict because of external subsidies from other actors, other aspects of the two cases and of the two industrial relations systems more generally come into sharper focus. I now look in particular at three: the implications of this analysis for cultural interpretations of Japanese management and industrial relations, the implications for understanding the particular causal role of enterprise unionism in Japan and, finally, the implications for interpretations of the NUM strike that focus on the personality and leadership of Arthur Scargill.

CULTURAL FACTORS AND THE JAPANESE CASE

It is common to read that cultural factors are especially important in Japanese industrial relations and, more generally, that such factors play a vital role in accounting for postwar Japanese economic success. According to this view, the Japanese firm is characterized by unusually cooperative and quiescent relations between employees and managers, relations that are in turn rooted in certain features of traditional Japanese culture (see Abegglen 1958).

The evidence presented here suggests by contrast that Japanese unions and employers behave in predictable ways not fundamentally different than those characterizing unions and employers elsewhere. When circumstances warrant, relations between labor and capital may become extremely conflictual and bitter even to the point of open violence. In particular, when their activists are unduly threatened, Japanese unions, like their counterparts elsewhere, react with industrial conflict. This pattern of behavior was repeated time and again during the 1940s and 1950s in Japan. Unless we are prepared to believe that Japanese culture underwent a temporary and radical transformation during those two decades, it seems more convincing to ascribe the extent of cooperation between unions and firms in Japan to the same factors in play elsewhere, factors best explored using economic analysis (see Aoki 1988 for an example).

Moreover, the theory advanced here suggests that there is a direct causal relationship between the current low level of Japanese industrial disputes over job loss and the emergence and eventual consolidation of the system after 1960 of "lifetime employment" for the regular employees of large firms. We saw in Figure 1.1 that strikes over workforce reductions dropped in Japan very substantially after 1960. This, I would argue, was largely the result of the increasingly widespread adoption by large firms of lifetime employment, a practice that had the effect of preventing the targeting of union activists despite continued recourse to workforce reductions on the part of the firm. With lifetime employment, firms simply never resort to involuntary expulsions of union members, concentrating job loss instead on "temporary" and part-time employees, who are usually not unionized. Like the seniority system found in the United States (see Chapter 7), lifetime employment substantially reduces industrial disputes over layoffs and workforce reductions since such reductions, even as they continue to occur, no longer threaten union members, union activists, or trade union organization. Thus, the interpretation advanced here corroborates the growing number of studies of Japanese political economy that focus not on cultural peculiarities but on organizational incentives.

ENTERPRISE UNIONISM IN JAPAN

In contrast to the cultural approach just discussed, institutional interpretations of Japanese industrial relations and trade unionism have focused on three factors: enterprise unionism, seniority wages, and lifetime employment (Ōkōchi 1965; Sumiya 1974). These are conventionally considered the three pillars of Japanese industrial relations and are generally believed to be mutually reinforcing (Milgrom and Roberts 1992: 349–52). For institutionalists, they together account for the relatively high degree of commitment to the firm exhibited by Japanese employees – white-collar and blue-collar alike – for the unusual extent of labor – management cooperation at firm level, and for Japan's success in achieving relatively high productivity growth in the decades since World War II.

At the same time, however, scholars contend that because they are enterprise unions with their membership drawn exclusively from the firms' (permanent) workforce, Japanese unions are especially sensitive to workforce reductions involving permanent employees. Observers have often noted that most major industrial disputes since World War II have centered on job security and workforce reductions (Cole 1971: 118; Hanami 1972: 99; Levine 1958: 118), and that disputes over discharges have been especially bitter and protracted (Shirai 1968: 329).[5]

Detailing this line of argument, Tadashi Hanami argues that large-scale dismissals

> threaten the very foundation of the enterprise union's existence. This threat is due to the fact that these unions recruit their members exclusively from among the employees of a particular enterprise and, as a rule, employees who are laid off lose their membership. The unions, therefore, have no other way of fighting mass dismissals than by "total opposition." They often resort to desperate means, which they label "honorable defeat," that are reminiscent of the Kamikaze tactics used by the Japanese army during World War II. (Hanami 1979: 62)

The interpretation offered here only partially corroborates this line of argument. According to the theory advanced here, the enterprise union itself should have a relatively high threshold for the dismissal of activists. Acting alone, that is, the enterprise union should be impervious to expulsion of all but a relatively large proportion of its officials. The reason is that in most cases permanent employees are required to join the union; thus, unionization at the level of the enterprise is high and stable. The union has a relatively large and secure pool of prospective activists from which to draw, even if some are targeted for dismissal. I have argued in earlier chapters that in these circumstances, unions can tolerate the discharge of some activists without having to engage in a costly industrial dispute.

Instead, the critical factor making Japanese unions so sensitive to the discharge of enterprise union officers is that the enterprise generally will engage in collective bargaining *only with its own employees*. This aspect of the enterprise union system in Japan should be distinguished from the fact that trade unions there typically organize only the employees of a single enterprise. There are two consequences of the refusal by firms to negotiate with any but their own employees. First, it probably lowers the enterprise union's threshold for the expulsion of activists. It is true that in a union shop the union has many other members it can turn to when it needs to replace collective bargaining agents. But the skills and experiences of enterprise union officers are difficult to pass on to their own replacements, especially if the most able of them have just been forced out of the firm. Because these men cannot continue to act in a collective bargaining capacity, thereby training their replacements even after leaving the enterprise, Japanese enterprise unions tend to face succession problems for their officers that are substantially worse than those experienced elsewhere. In other countries, even when union activists are discharged, they may continue to play a role in the collective bargaining for the firm, if only because in most countries, bargaining is not exclusively conducted at enterprise level. So while a British shop steward who has been discharged may not be able to reenter the factory premises and engage in day-to-day bargaining over deployment on the assembly line, for instance, he may reappear as a district official of his union, and his signature on certain kinds of agreements may thus become mandatory. The experiences and abilities of shop stewards are not lost to the union organization in this context as they are in Japan.

Second, when firms refuse to negotiate with any one but employees of the enterprise, they effectively deny any bargaining role to supraenterprise union organizations. The officials of federations of enterprise unions and of national confederations are in these circumstances prohibited from engaging in collective bargaining. This renders such national organizations virtually powerless in the bargaining process in Japan (for comparative data, see Golden and Wallerstein 1996). To the extent, however, that the targeting of activists involves the issue of the legitimacy of supraenterprise officers to negotiate at the enterprise level, these latter organizations have particularly strong incentives to subsidize enterprise disputes over targeting. In the 1950s when there was still some collective bargaining in Japan that involved union officials from outside the firm – as was the case with the diagonal bargaining that characterized the coal industry – national organizations had compelling incentives to subsidize any dispute in which this right appeared in question. By subsidizing the costs of conflict, national organizations helped engender disputes that were especially protracted.

Finally, the issue of the formation of second unions is relevant in determining the threshold of enterprise unions in Japan. Hiroshuke Kawanishi (1992) has recently stressed the importance of dual unionism in Japan: the deliberate fostering on the part of the firm of a second union to compete with the original enterprise organization. Although 80 percent of Japanese collective agreements require a union shop, the union shop is "soft," meaning that employers are not compelled to discharge employees who leave the union. This loophole in Japanese contracts allows the formation of second unions (Ishikawa 1963: 462). These were regularly and deliberately created by employers in the 1950s in conjunction with the targeting of activists from the existing union, as the events in the Miike mines in 1959–60 illustrate. This context, too, has the effect of lowering the original union's threshold for the targeting of activists.

For these reasons, Japanese enterprise unions often tend to exhibit relatively low thresholds for the dismissal of union activists, while national unions appear especially likely to subsidize local disputes over targeting. While the two explanatory factors that I have identified – the refusal by firms to negotiate with anyone other than their own employees and the deliberate creation of second, rival unions – are linked to the phenomenon of enterprise unionism, they are not identical to it. The theory advanced here thus allows for a more precise understanding than is usually the case of the impact of enterprise unionism on trade union reactions to workforce reductions involving union members and the concomitant targeting that so often accompanies it in Japan.

PERSONALITY FACTORS IN THE BRITISH CASE

The personality of Arthur Scargill figures overwhelmingly in the reporting on the 1984–85 miners' strike in Britain, and many believe that had he not been NUM President, the strike might not have occurred. As two analysts note, "The strike has been described as being not a true miners' strike, but 'Scargill's Strike' . . ." (Campbell and Warner 1985b: 6). Whether the strike would have occurred in his absence is an impossible question to answer. However, it certainly can be argued that once the strike began, it continued for reasons largely having to do with factors other than Arthur Scargill's personality. The main evidence for this is that Scargill did not run the NUM alone. The union had two other elected national officials – a Vice-President and a Secretary – and a 26-person National Executive, which comprised representatives of all of the organization's geographic and occupational divisions and which, as we have seen, heavily overrepresented small rightwing areas while underrepresenting the central coalfield, including Yorkshire (McCormick 1979: 65). Nonetheless, *all* the union's major decisions during the strike had the unanimous public support of the NUM's two other elected officials (Goodman 1985: 54); likewise, the National Executive voted repeatedly, and usually unanimously, to support Scargill's motions, even unanimously endorsing the final decision to reject any written agreement to end the strike. It seems doubtful that Scargill would have been able to manipulate the NEC so conclusively had there been real opposition to the conduct of the strike (Allen 1985: 136).[6]

The analysis presented here suggests instead that the NUM as a national organization had good reason to subsidize disputes involving pit closures under the Thatcher government: namely, that over the long run, were the Tories to remain in office, closures were likely to be extensive enough to threaten the union's very survival. That Scargill convincingly postured as an irrational ideologue could only be said to have been in the interests of the NUM since its effect was to convince the government (and the public at large) that the union was prepared to disrupt the workings of the national economy, engender widespread blackouts, and not surrender until the government entirely capitulated or collapsed.

CONCLUSIONS

I have argued in this chapter that both the Miike dispute of 1959–60 and the British miners' strike of 1984–85 were triggered when offers to subsidize the conflicts by national actors proved forthcoming on both sides of the disputes. In both cases, the national union organizations involved were motivated by concerns related to organizational survival. In the Japanese case these had to do with the right to engage in collective bargaining, without which the national union feared the effective loss of any role or authority in the labor movement. In the British case survival was more concrete since the union faced such a catastrophic loss of membership as to endanger its very future.

On the other side, motivations seem to have been both market-driven and more broadly political. Both the NCB and the Mitsui company faced severe financial pressures, the first from the government and the second from its creditors. Both also faced serious market pressures from competitors, pressures that meant both companies would have to reduce costs. Taken alone, however, these factors seem inadequate to account for the behavior of the two companies. Instead, it was the offer – insistence even – of external subsidies that pushed the companies to adopt increasingly confrontational postures in their dealings with organized labor. These came from the government in the British case and from Nikkeiren in the Japanese case. Both had strong views regarding the proper place of organized labor in a well-functioning market economy. Accordingly, both were driven by considerations of long-term economic efficiency. But these considerations acquired more general political overtones. For Nikkeiren, the future growth and prosperity of the Japanese economy required stripping Sōhyō of its aspirations to establish a national industrial union movement along continental European lines. For the Thatcher government, the future growth and prosperity of the British economy required radically reducing the powers of the country's largest most militant trade unions. For both, economic and political goals were so deeply intermixed as to be inseparable.

7

CONCLUSIONS

In the preceding chapters, we have seen that disputes over large-scale personnel reductions are neither inevitable nor unpredictable. Rather, they occur under circumstances that can be specified theoretically. These circumstances are of two types. First, a firm may inadvertently target too many union activists during the course of downsizing for its trade union to tolerate. This was the case at the Fiat works in 1980, at British Leyland in 1956, and at the Miike mines in 1953. Second, industrial action may occur if offers from outside actors (such as a national business association or a national trade union) to subsidize the costs of conflict lower the costs so as to incite both sides to conflict; in this case, each side prefers conflict over nonengagement because conflict becomes relatively cheap. This was the case at Miike in 1959 and in the British mining industry in 1984.

In this chapter I consider three issues relevant to the main argument developed in this book. I first seek to resolve a puzzle presented in the opening pages of this study about why disputes over workforce reductions so often seem irrational. I then examine two extensions of the major argument presented in this book, extensions that, if shown to be true, would increase our confidence in the argument developed here. If my analysis is correct and Fiat's management did not intend to provoke industrial action, whereas Nikkeiren and the Thatcher government did, different consequences for the various industrial relations systems should obtain. I review the evidence to see whether this is so. A second extension of the interpretation proposed has to do with the origins of seniority systems for layoffs. If my argument is correct, unions should favor seniority-based layoffs because of the institutional protections this procedure carries with it. To assess this argument and also to speculate more broadly on the origins of seniority, I look at the origins of seniority layoffs in the United States, where they are most commonly used. The third and final issue that I investigate in this chapter is the extent to which the rational choice approach adopted throughout this study has been able to answer fully the problem at hand.

HEROIC DEFEATS, RATIONALITY, AND JOB LOSS

Disputes over workforce reductions often seem marked by a kind of irrationality, as though the actors involved had to realize their efforts were doomed from the outset. This is true, for instance, both for the 1980 Fiat strike and for the 1984–85 strike of British mineworkers, and to a somewhat lesser extent for the 1959–60 Miike strike. The appearance of irrationality attached to these events is a function of the union's ostensible primary goal during the disputes – namely, achieving the withdrawal of the threat to discharge large numbers of employees. Were this the principal motivation of the strikes in question, the union leaders involved would indeed be pursuing doomed efforts. In all of the strikes investigated in this study, union leaders seemed to know from the outset that workforce reductions, even if only temporary, were inevitable. In *none* of the disputes examined were personnel reductions avoided (although sometimes the number of employees affected was reduced). This is hardly surprising. In any market economy job loss is inevitable in some circumstances. Unions must acquiesce to changes in employment requirements, even if acquiescing to workforce reductions does not necessarily entail accepting the original terms and conditions established by management. In the United States, for instance, where layoffs are common, negotiations between labor and management regularize the conditions under which workforce reductions occur. Often unions are able to improve the outcome in both quantitative and qualitative terms. Nonetheless, job loss is endemic to modern market systems.

Despite this, the unions involved in the disputes studied in this book usually articulated the public goal of preventing workforce reductions altogether. The interpretation advanced in this study argues that such a goal was not actually the primary objective behind the union's behavior. Instead, these disputes are better understood as aimed at issues of organizational maintenance – more precisely, the protection of shop stewards in most cases. With this as their goal, these strikes can be reinterpreted as instrumentally rational courses of action. The fact that in some of the cases considered in this study the union officials involved lost the battle to protect their own organizations does not mean that defeat was inevitable. Instead, union decision makers underestimated their chances of success.

In both the Fiat strike and the British miners' dispute of 1984–85 the rhetoric of conflict focused primarily on the attempt to save jobs. "No firings!" was the FLM's slogan in the Fiat case; "No pit closures except through exhaustion," the NUM's. Workers were mobilized largely around the goal of preserving jobs. In Japan too the Miike union in 1959–60 was typically depicted as clinging to an unrealistic understanding of the workings of the market economy. Its reaction to the threat of workforce reductions was usually understood as an attempt to prevent manpower reductions entirely. The Japan Federation of Employers' Associations, for instance, argued that, "the strike was brought to a head as a result of the Union's failure to recognize ever-changing conditions in the structure of the economy" (JFEA News 1960c: 3).

Nonetheless, comparative evidence shows that the desire to preserve jobs, however deeply felt among employees and among union officials, is not enough to spur a union organization to undertake a costly industrial dispute. In Britain, for instance, even as the NUM mobilized the country's miners against pit closures, thousands of employees in the manufacturing industries were losing their jobs through large-scale restructuring. In the case of British Leyland, which we have examined in some detail, thousands of men were threatened with job loss, much of it concentrated in regions already marked by relatively high unemployment. Yet the unions organizing BL's autoworkers failed to undertake concerted industrial action to try to prevent workforce reductions.

Nor can it be said that the economic threat facing British mineworkers was substantially worse than that confronting their counterparts in the automobile industry – if anything, the reverse was true. In neither case were forced redundancies at stake. The National Coal Board had repeatedly promised that no miner would be subjected to involuntary job loss even with widespread pit closures. At British Leyland, too, large-scale workforce reductions were effected virtually without any forced dismissals. Finally, the financial compensations attached to workforce reductions were actually greater for mineworkers than autoworkers. The threat of job loss was not experienced more severely by miners than by autoworkers and the potential hardships for those let go were not more serious for the former than for the latter. Yet only the former trade union engaged in industrial action ostensibly aimed at preventing job loss.

British evidence thus shows that the extent and intensity of the threat of job loss is a poor predictor of union reactions within a single country. The same is true across countries. In Figure 1.1 we observed a relatively low number of strikes in the postwar era around issues of redundancies and layoffs in the United States. Yet comparative research reveals that workforce reductions are much more common in the United States than in Europe or Japan (e.g. Moy and Sorrentino 1981). The frequency of workforce reductions is thus also a poor predictor of union responses.

Throughout this study I have argued that strikes in situations of mass workforce reductions are not triggered by the threat of job loss per se but instead by the threat such situations may pose to the union organization. The extent of the latter is not well captured by measures of potential job loss. Thousands of workers may be thrown out of work, yet the union representing them may experience virtually no organizational disruption. Thanks to seniority systems for layoffs this is commonly the case in the United States, for instance. Conversely, relatively few workers may be slotted for expulsion from the firm, and yet their union may be subject to acute threat if, for instance, all the employees listed for expulsion are union representatives.

If organizational maintenance triggers industrial disputes over job loss, then the ostensible goal of protecting jobs is often merely a convenient fiction meant largely to mobilize workers. This is not to say that industrial action around the explicit goal of protecting the union organization itself never occurs. In both the 1956 dispute at the British Motor Corporation and the 1953 Miike strike, organizational issues appear to have figured prominently and publicly. In some situations workers will sacrifice pay and undertake risky industrial action to protect their union organization. But it seems that union leaders judge these situations to be rare, since they often resort to slogans about job protection rather than union protection. It is more common for unions to attempt to mobilize their constituents around the attempt to prevent job loss per se than around the goal of defending the union organization.

It is the appearance of attempting to prevent job loss altogether that lends disputes in situations of workforce reductions the veneer of irrationality.[1] For on this issue defeat is certain, particularly once events reach the point of open confrontation. Perhaps the firm will close fewer plants than originally announced; perhaps fewer workers will lose their jobs. But if the firm does not back down before industrial action begins, there is certainly no reason for it to do so once a strike is underway. By this point the union's course of action has become self-defeating. By engaging in a costly dispute when workforce reductions cannot actually be halted, the union will end up losing more than it can win. While the desire to protect jobs is noble and the strikes that revolve around job protection are often heroic, they are ultimately doomed.

Once we reinterpret disputes that occur in situations of workforce reduction as aimed at issues of organizational maintenance and not at preventing job loss, these disputes no longer appear instrumentally irrational. In two cases that we examined – the 1953 Miike strike and the 1956 dispute at the British Motor Corporation – the unions involved secured written agreements protecting their organizations in the event of future workforce reductions. Thus, it is feasible to achieve such a goal. Even though in both cases large-scale workforce reductions were carried out as planned, these strikes were victories for the organizations involved.

In the three other cases we have examined in detail – the 1959–60 Miike strike, the 1980 Fiat strike, and the 1984–85 NUM strike – the unions failed to secure the organizational protections they sought. At Miike, the activists originally slotted for expulsion were all forced out of the firm; a second union was established and the original union largely was displaced by it. At Fiat, workforce reductions were carried out on the basis of lists drawn up exclusively by the firm instead of using rotations as the union, the FLM, had insisted. In the NUM case, finally, government policy toward the coal industry remained largely unaltered, hundreds more pits were closed, and the union's membership drastically reduced. The likelihood of the NUM merging with a larger body became extremely high as a result of the organizational shrinkage that it endured.

In all three cases, however, there is good evidence that the union organizations involved lacked critical information necessary to evaluate accurately the likelihood of success of industrial action – success, that is, in relation to securing organizational protections, not preventing job loss. It was the absence of full information that engendered defeat once these strikes were underway.[2] In the Miike case, we have seen that the union underestimated the speed with which the Mitsui company would be able to establish a rival second trade union and underestimated as well the appeal that the new organization would exercise among Miike miners. At the same time, the union may have been unaware that the company would successfully secure agreements from its competitors not to take over its markets during the course of the dispute. For all these reasons, the unions involved underestimated the ability of the firm to hold out during the strike. Had the financial and organizational pressures on the firm been greater, it is possible that Mitsui would have had to capitulate on the issue of firing union activists, as it seemed the firm was prepared to do initially. Had that occurred, organized labor could have won the strike – not in the sense of preventing workforce reductions, but in the sense of preserving their own organizations.

In the case of the British miners in the mid-1980s, organized labor also lacked critical information that would have indicated that its chances of success were poor. In Chapter 6 I argued that the NUM underestimated the likelihood of blackouts during the dispute because of an absence of current information on the requirements for coal by the electricity industry. In addition, the union underestimated the police preparation that had been undertaken prior to the dispute, thereby overestimating the likelihood that the union could roll the strike through Nottinghamshire and keep many more miners from working than was the case. For both these reasons, the NUM seriously exaggerated the effects the strike would have on the British economy generally, effects that could plausibly have led public opinion to force the government to call new elections, as had occurred in 1974. Had this transpired and had new elections taken place, it is possible that a Labour government would have been elected which would then have altered Britain's energy policy and possibly reduced substantially the number of pit closures over the subsequent decade.

The 1980 Fiat case is the most difficult to evaluate. As we have seen in Chapter 3 the union knew of the firm's productivity problems and knew too of the firm's commitment to reduce costs. The union also had information regarding the likely reactions of the rank and file to a strike and especially the kinds of divisions that would probably surface. For these reasons, the union should have anticipated defeat. But even though the FLM had good information on the feelings of the Fiat rank and file about industrial action, union leaders seem to have radically underestimated the extent to which a noticeable segment of Fiat's employees would actively oppose industrial action. Public displays of antiunion sympathy were at the time virtually unknown in Italy. The FLM was thus completely unprepared for the display of antiunion and antistrike sentiment among Fiat employees that occurred with the march of the 40,000 who rallied against the strike. It was at this point that the union quickly capitulated, relinquishing any hope of securing protections for its militants in the course of mass workforce reductions. Until the march of the 40,000 the FLM continued to believe that it could secure an agreement that would offer some protection to its own organization. Again, the absence of full and accurate information – in this case, information on the reactions of employees who did not support the strike – explains why the union lost its attempt to protect its own organization during workforce reductions.

On the basis of this evidence, I would argue that the goals of all three strikes were realistically conceived and industrial action was an appropriate course of action with which to pursue them. These goals involved securing protections for union militants and activists. The decisions involved occurred on the basis of the best information available. Yet, this proved inadequate. In these three cases an absence of critical information meant that the unions involved exaggerated their own capacities to secure agreements protecting their own activists. On this issue they were defeated.

If, however, in ostensibly resisting job loss the unions involved were pursuing reasonable courses of action – aimed in fact at protecting their own organizations – what about the mass of ordinary workers who supported them? A strike in defense of one's union organization is, I have argued, an instrumentally rational action since success is not precluded from the outset. The same cannot be said for strikes aimed at reversing the threat of workforce reductions. If unions successfully mobilize workers around the hopeless goal of preventing job loss, are workers irrational in their decisions to participate in such strikes?

There is almost no empirical information available on why workers participate in strikes around issues of job loss.[3] In the absence of much data, I can only offer a little informed speculation. First, union officials in general apparently believe that workers are not able to evaluate accurately the various courses of action available once the threat of workforce reductions exists. The evidence for this is that union leaders often deliberately mobilize workers around slogans that are at least to some extent disingenuous. The British miners' strike is a classic example. The demand that no pits ever close except because of geological exhaustion is patently unrealistic, both because pits inevitably close well before complete exhaustion is reached and because even the NUM had long admitted the legitimacy of doing so.

Does this mean that union leaders are correct and workers are irrational, in the sense of unable to evaluate accurately the probabilities associated with various courses of action? Workers may instead suffer from a debilitating lack of information regarding the likely outcomes associated with different courses of action. Often, for instance, secret or closed talks are taking place (or have already occurred) involving union leaders and the firm, talks to which the rank and file has no access but in which crucial information is communicated between the parties. At the same time, the union's efforts to mobilize its constituents may well involve unrealistic or inaccurate presentations of the probabilities associated with different strategies. Union leaders are not very likely to show up at a strike meeting to inform the rank and file that the chances of preventing job loss are remote, for instance; such events are meant to increase enthusiasm, not dampen it. Of course, workers have access to other, presumably less biased sources of information, including the national press, which may cover events in detail during major disputes. But once strike action is underway, it may well become difficult to evaluate the information found there too; as public opinion becomes more polarized, mirroring the polarization of elite positions, information becomes more difficult to evaluate. In short, the evidence supporting the claim that workers involved in disputes over workforce reductions behave irrationally is far from complete; it is more plausible that they behave rationally but with considerably less information than their leaders.

IMPLICATIONS AND EXTENSIONS OF THE ARGUMENT

The theory presented in this study has some indirect implications that we can examine. To the extent that we find that they corroborate the interpretation advanced here, our confidence in this book's argument increases. The implications and extensions of the argument that I examine are two. First, if management's intentions were as different as I argue was the case for the strikes at Fiat on the one hand and British coal and the Japanese mines in 1959–60 on the other, different outcomes for the various industrial relations systems should follow. I examine the historical record to see whether this is true. Second, if I am correct that seniority-based layoffs protect shop stewards during workforce reductions, unions should have been aware of this early on and if given the opportunity, actively sought seniority. I review the history of seniority in the United States, where it is most widely used and evaluate various interpretations of its causes.

STRIKE ORIGINS AND SUBSEQUENT INDUSTRIAL RELATIONS

I have argued that the 1980 strike in the Italian Fiat works was provoked more or less by "mistake" – a term, I should note, not used in this sense in game theory but which conveys a commonsense view of the situation.[4] The firm lacked information about how many rank-and-file activists it could fire without provoking a union response, and it fired more than the union could bear. The firm's goal was a reduction in the size of the workforce; it did not deliberately engineer industrial strife.

The 1959–60 strike in Japanese mining and the 1984–85 strike in British mining have quite different origins. In these cases, national actors *did* intend to provoke industrial conflict and they did so in order to reorganize industrial relations nationally. Whereas enterprise management in neither case would have provoked industrial action on its own, prodding from creditors and support from other national allies engendered a different outcome.

If these arguments are correct, we should expect different outcomes over the long term for the industrial relations systems in question. Where management engendered a dispute inadvertently, the industrial relations system as a whole should remain relatively intact. Where, by contrast, a national business association or the government deliberately provoked conflict, victory should carry with it a major restructuring of the country's industrial relations system overall. Do these hypothesized consequences obtain in the cases at hand?

In Italy the Fiat strike was at first considered by many the opening blow in a major reorganization of the country's industrial relations system. Many analysts believed that the firm had deliberately provoked the strike precisely to restructure industrial relations as a whole. Only with time has it become evident that no such restructuring has occurred.

Evidence for the relative integrity and resilience of Italian organized labor and its industrial relations system in the years following the Fiat dispute appears in various forms. First, wage setting continued to occur at all levels of the system and enterprise bargaining remained significant (Ferner and Hyman 1992). Firms continued to recognize shop stewards as legitimate bargaining agents. Relatedly, no fundamental reorganization of authority relations within the labor movement has occurred. Central confederations, industrial unions, and enterprise bodies have, albeit with some fluctuations, continued with the tasks and responsibilities each assumed in the 1960s (Golden and Wallerstein 1996). Third, while union density declined during the 1980s the decline was relatively modest and membership levels remained well above where they had been in the 1960s, comparable to the rates that had obtained in the period following World War II (Golden and Wallerstein 1996: table A1).

Commenting directly on the issue at hand, Anthony Ferner and Richard Hyman (1992: 585) contend, "Fiat was in many ways a special case," explaining that "Even when managerial assertiveness was at its height, from the defeat of the 1980 strike until the middle of the decade, there was no sweeping rejection of the unions." The company's behavior proved not to represent a larger managerial strategy aimed at taking on organized labor in Italy. Instead, events at Fiat seem best considered an isolated incident, an inadvertent act by the company's managers. They were not part of a broader, concerted, or coordinated strategy on the part of the Italian business community.

The same is decidedly not the case for Japan after 1960. There, as we have seen, industrial relations and collective bargaining were fundamentally altered. One important measure of this is the refusal of firms after about 1960 to bargain with anyone other than their own employees, thereby undercutting the bargaining activities of national trade unions. This consolidated the system of enterprise trade unionism distinctive to Japan. Again and again, commentators stress that the defeat at Miike was part of a broader and ultimately successful attempt on the part of the Japanese business community under Nikkeiren's leadership to restructure industrial relations. Indeed, this interpretation is standard.

The British case, finally, has been the subject of some controversy on the issue at hand: namely, the extent to which the industrial relations system has undergone fundamental reorganization in the 1980s and 1990s. Initially, defenders of the position that trade unions had not been seriously undermined despite the Thatcher government's attempts could point to a variety of indicators of labor resiliency. Most also could be used to indicate a more general resiliency to the industrial relations systems as a whole (e.g. Batstone 1984; Batstone and Gourlay 1986). More recently, however, it appears that the consequences of Thatcherism and especially of changes in the legislation regulating industrial relations and industrial conflict have caught up with the British labor movement. Recent reviews (e.g. Howell 1995; Edwards et al. 1992; Purcell 1995) are unanimous in the view that British industrial relations have been fundamentally altered during the 1980s and 1990s and the union movement profoundly weakened. The argument that the Thatcher government's attempt to reorganize British labor politics – a multifaceted attempt that included provoking the miners' strike in 1984 – has become increasingly well grounded.

That British and Japanese industrial relations were restructured following the disputes we have studied in detail, whereas Italian labor relations were not, provides indirect confirmation of the argument advanced in this study about the causes of these various disputes. The Japanese and British miners' strikes were events in larger strategies by national actors to reorganize collective bargaining, trade unionism, and industrial relations. The Italian Fiat strike, by contrast, was not. Thus, it is not surprising that Italian industrial relations remain relatively intact whereas neither British nor Japanese did.

THE ORIGINS OF SENIORITY IN THE UNITED STATES

In this study I have identified the presence of a seniority system as an institutional condition that prevents industrial action in situations of mass workforce reductions by protecting union organization. Given this, one might think that unions would generally favor seniority-based layoffs and that in many circumstances firms would too. Yet seniority systems for layoffs are characteristic primarily of the Anglo-American industrial relations systems – namely, the United States, Great Britain, and Canada (see Yemin

1982). They are much less widely used – if used at all – on continental Europe and in Japan.[5] Why did seniority-based layoffs emerge in some countries but not others? Do their origins reflect the consequences that I have argued they carry with them?

The case I examine is the United States, where seniority is the main factor determining the order of layoffs. I detail the history of seniority in the United States, and review explanations for why American unions have been such strong supporters of seniority. If I am correct that seniority entails a reduction of industrial conflict over workforce reductions and greater institutional protections for trade unions, this should be evident in the reasons unions gave initially for favoring it. I then speculate more broadly on the reasons why seniority dominates in the United States so much more so than in other OECD countries.

Although seniority is only one of a number of different systems in use for the allocation of job loss, in the United States it is far and away the most common device for identifying those to be laid off. In this country, "in over 80 percent of private sector nonagricultural, nonconstruction employment," unionized and nonunionized, "senior workers enjoy substantial protection against losing their jobs" (Abraham and Medoff 1984: 96). In the early 1970s fully 95 percent of major collective bargaining agreements featured seniority provisions (reported in Abraham and Medoff 1984: 90). Even in nonunion settings seniority almost always serves as the sole or principal determinant for layoffs. There is agreement in the literature that seniority-based selection criteria for layoffs are almost universal in the contemporary United States (along with Abraham and Medoff 1984, see Addison 1986; Rees 1989). They are thus much more widespread than in other OECD countries.

The History of Seniority in the United States

Collectively bargained seniority provisions were first established in the rail industry after the Civil War. The first known written collective agreement in the industry was dated 1875 and included a seniority provision. So far as is known, every union in the industry – engineers, firemen, blacksmiths, and so forth – incorporated seniority provisions into its first written agreement during the formative period of the railway unions in the 1880s (Mater 1940: 392–94). The universal incorporation of seniority into the first written agreements in the industry has generated speculation that seniority may very well have predated unionization (Meyers 1965: 195), or that unions themselves even may have been brought into existence in part as reactions to unsatisfactory observation of custom-based seniority practices (Mater 1940: 393).

Typographers were another group that established seniority through collective bargaining as early as the nineteenth century. Formal procedures for seniority-based layoffs in industry only became widespread, however, in the 1920s and 1930s. The 1935 Wagner Act facilitated union recognition and offered some statutory protection and indirectly encouraged the spread of seniority procedures (Gersuny 1982b: 521; Gersuny and Kaufman 1985). During the Great Depression, however, seniority still did not serve as the sole mechanism for allocating job loss. Worksharing was commonly used, though often in conjunction with seniority (Jacoby 1985: 212–15; Slichter 1941: 103 and 122), perhaps tempered by evaluations of need (marital and family status) and merit (Slichter 1941: 116). (For an enumeration of the categories used here, see Chapter 4, page 70). Worksharing meant that all employees suffered a reduction in working hours (for an equivalent reduction in pay) prior to resorting to layoffs at all. Only if worksharing proved inadequate were layoffs used; these in turn were increasingly ordered according to seniority.

The automobile industry is a case in point. Even in the early interwar period, newly established personnel departments increasingly had recourse to seniority as a basis on which to undertake temporary layoffs during downturns and model changeovers (Lichtenstein 1988: 67). Unionization of the industry extended and codified the role of seniority without, however, making it the sole determinant of job loss for many decades. In a key 1937 agreement between General Motors and the United Automobile Workers, seniority occupied a central position. The agreement stated that temporary reductions of output were to be accomplished without layoffs by a reduction of working hours. Longer reductions of output were to use seniority as the selection criterion for layoffs, modified in cases of men with dependents; in addition, seniority lists were segregated by gender (Gersuny and Kaufman 1985: 467–68).

This combination of egalitarian (worksharing), age-related (seniority), and status-derived (family status and sex) principles is probably typical of the regulation of U.S. labor markets in the interwar era (cf. Jacoby 1985: 247). The electrical industry also used combinations of worksharing, seniority-based, and status-related layoffs from the first decade of the twentieth century until after World War II. Only then did seniority effectively become the sole criterion used to select individuals for layoff, transfer, and recall. As in the automobile industry, seniority-based layoffs in the electrical industry were initially introduced by management during the nonunion era of the 1920s. They were extended after union recognition was granted in the 1930s but still used in conjunction with criteria of need and merit until after World War II (Schatz 1983: 19–20, 105, and 109–14).

Worksharing had become increasingly less common in the United States by the 1960s, however. Indeed, in union firms it was displaced almost entirely by seniority-based layoffs (Jacoby 1985: 246). Needs-based criteria, which typically meant that women were laid off before men, married women before single women, and men with children before men without, were also increasingly less used, although the interaction of seniority principles with affirmative action policies in the 1970s and 1980s to some extent reintroduced status considerations (Gersuny 1982a). Merit and ability, finally, although technically often criteria to which management makes reference, have become less important as "straight" seniority has in practice come to predominate over seniority "modified" by other factors.

Most of this is as true for nonunion as for union settings. For instance, a 1950 study found that even then 95 percent of nonunion firms surveyed reported that seniority played a clear role in selecting employees for permanent or temporary layoff (Spead and Bambrick 1950: 4). Even though most of these companies formally ranked factors other than seniority first, "the practical layoff experience of many of these nonunionized companies has shown them that these qualifying factors, unless they are definitely outstanding, do not outweigh length of service" (Spead and Bambrick 1950: i; see also the recent case studies in Romm 1994). According to Sanford Jacoby (1985: 246), the only salient distinction remaining between union and nonunion firms by the mid-1950s was that the latter were still more likely to establish worksharing before resorting to layoffs in the event of a downturn.

Explaining American Union Commitment to Seniority

Literature on American trade unionism and industrial relations commonly asserts that seniority developed thanks to trade union pressure. This, as I shall argue in greater detail, cannot be the whole story. If it were, then seniority-based layoffs would not also be the device of choice even in nonunionized firms in the United States. Nevertheless, unions have generally been considered important to the establishment of seniority in the United States, and a number of different approaches has been used to explain why American unions favor age-related criteria in the selection of those slotted for job loss. These may be classed as the median voter model, the rent maximization model, and the organizational model. I review and evaluate each in turn.

Perhaps the most common explanation offered for why trade unions in the United States have so often favored the adoption of seniority for layoffs is what is called the median voter model, associated particularly with the work of Richard Freeman and James Medoff (especially 1984). Freeman and Medoff posit a marked distinction between unionized and nonunion settings. In nonunion settings, according to this view, firms respond to the demands of the marginal employee: the person on the margin of entry to or exit from the firm. Such an employee is usually young, mobile, and marketable. The firm can largely ignore the preferences of older, less marketable employees, whose plant-specific skills render them less mobile (Freeman and Medoff 1984: 10).

The presence of trade unions, by contrast, is said to alter fundamentally the operation of the labor market. As democratic institutions, trade unions transmit the preferences of the average, rather than the marginal, member. An average member calculus, in turn, is said to allow the preferences of relatively more senior workers to dominate since the average worker is older. Moreover, such workers are inframarginal; unlikely, in other words, to be on the verge of entering or exiting the firm (Medoff 1979: 393). Quit rates, for instance, fall with seniority, independently of any benefits the firm may offer to tenure, and once seniority is established, it further reduces job movement among older employees. Hence, older workers are likely to keep the jobs they have (Hall 1982). Senior workers, in turn, prefer to distribute job loss on their junior fellows in order to protect their own incomes. Senior workers are believed to favor seniority-based layoffs rather than worksharing or other allocative devices in all but the most catastrophic cases threatening their own jobs (Mitchell 1982).

The median voter model thus posits that democratic unions represent their members by adopting seniority policies. Although Freeman and Medoff (1984: 20) assert that seniority provisions are "desired by workers," they provide no empirical evidence to support this claim. In this regard, their work is not unusual. Industrial and labor historians as well as sociologists also usually assume that workers favor seniority. Some have even contended that seniority constitutes part of the "moral economy" of the American working class (Gersuny and Kaufman 1985). Few, however, provide evidence regarding employee attitudes.

The little information I have been able to locate on the attitudes of American workers to seniority-based layoffs offers little corroboration of the view that unions represent the median worker pursuing seniority. A study of employee attitudes in two manufacturing plants carried out in the late 1930s – just as seniority-based layoffs were coming into widespread use in these settings – reports that a large proportion of workers thought that seniority should receive the greatest weight among criteria used for ordering workforce reductions. However, employees by no means favored the exclusive and rigid reliance on seniority that unions pursued and which eventually came to predominate. Instead, nearly all (97 percent) favored some worksharing before resorting to layoffs; and if layoffs were still deemed necessary, half favored "a policy of deciding each case on its own merits" according to seniority, need, and the merit of the individual employee (Maclaurin 1939: 53).

A study of employee attitudes in both unionized and nonunionized firms conducted two decades later found that a majority of employees (63 percent) did *not* favor seniority-based layoffs (Selznick and Vollmer 1962: 101, table 1). The minority that supported such procedures tended to be older, more senior union members, and those employed in firms in which seniority-based layoffs were regulated by collective agreements. The authors interpret their data as showing an independent impact of union membership, arguing that employee attitudes are "an effect reflecting trade union doctrine" (Selznick and Vollmer 1962: 102). Seniority, they conclude, has proven a useful device with which to enhance American union power but fails to reflect the "enduring aspirations" (Selznick and Vollmer 1962: 116) of American workers.

Not surprisingly, American employees exhibit divided views about the ordering by which workforce reductions should occur. The universal prevalence of seniority in the United States cannot easily be ascribed directly to workers' preferences. These data suggest that if trade unions support seniority procedures for workforce reductions, they do so for their own reasons. This undermines the median voter model of seniority.

A second argument for why unions would favor seniority is a rent maximization model. This is a somewhat unusual approach. According to this argument, unions seek to maximize the rents they can extract from firms. By forcing firms to hire better paid (i.e. more senior) workers before their less well paid (i.e. more junior) counterparts, the union extracts higher rents (Kuhn and Robert 1989). An implication of this model, one not associated with the other two under review here, is that seniority cannot be in the interests of both employers and unions. Instead, what unions gain, firms lose.

This model exhibits two major weaknesses. First, it fails to provide adequate justification for the assumption that unions seek to maximize the rents they can extract from firms. Rents are not necessarily identical to the incomes that union members receive, at least not since the advent of unemployment insurance. Considerations of average member income may or may not favor seniority-based layoffs, depending on the nature of the unemployment insurance regime in place. Second, and more damaging, this approach fails to accord with the historical record regarding the origins of seniority in the United States. As the historical record just reviewed suggests and I shall discuss in more detail shortly, although unions in the

United States may favor seniority, it was often a firm-initiated development. If firms voluntarily and even spontaneously established seniority-based procedures for regulating workforce reductions, it is unlikely that such procedures were simply a price firms had to pay for peaceable labor relations. Instead, firms must have had their own interests in establishing seniority-based layoffs. A central feature of the rent maximization model, however, is that, by assumption, seniority cannot be in the interests of both labor and capital.

A third line of argument for why unions favor seniority-based layoffs concerns the requisites of organizational maintenance for the trade union.[6] According to this approach, trade unions do not seek to transmit the preferences of their (unweighted) average member, as the median voter model would have it. Instead, they seek to transmit the preferences of their activists (a weighted average) in order to retain organizational viability on the shopfloor. Activists are, in turn, likely to enjoy considerable seniority. This is generally true as we have seen earlier, and empirical evidence shows that it holds in the United States as well. Several surveys of union members in the United States carried out under the auspices of the University of Michigan Survey Research Center have found that the strongest correlate of participation in union affairs (attending meetings, voting in union elections, filing a grievance, etc.) is seniority, with employees of more than twenty years standing much more likely to attend meetings and vote in union elections than their younger colleagues (reported in Freeman and Medoff 1984: 208–9).

This line of argument suggests that unions may seek to establish seniority procedures for layoffs where workforce reductions are deliberately manipulated to eject activists from the factory. Available evidence on the development of seniority in the United States lends this view considerable plausibility.[7] Empirical studies universally report that American unions were originally motivated to favor seniority procedures in their efforts to curb the discrimination and favoritism regularly practiced by foremen in their selection of the redundant. "One of the initiating forces behind seniority," John Addison (1984: 91) writes, summing up conventional wisdom, "is said to be a union desire to avoid the arbitrary exercise of authority by managers;" (see also Gersuny 1982a: 113–15; Gersuny 1982b: 519; Gersuny and Kaufman 1985: 465; Lichtenstein 1988: 68; Maclaurin 1939: 52–54; Mater 1940: 399–401; Spead and Bambrick 1950: 5; Reder 1960: 354; Rees 1989: 141; Schatz 1983: 107; Selznick and Vollmer 1962). "Seniority," as another has put it, "is usually attributed to union pressure, and the reasons for the development of that pressure are commonly given as the elimination of favoritism in treatment of workers in significant aspects . . . " (Meyers 1965: 195).

If favoritism annoys workers, it may be literally fatal to unions. Speaking directly to the issue of organizational maintenance, Sumner Slichter (1941: 98) argues: "If the union has no closed shop, restrictions on the employer's freedom to lay off may be a matter of self-preservation, because if union members are always the first to be dropped, the men will not remain in the organization." In the preseniority era, union activists were usually singled out by antiunion foremen, thereby engendering considerable union hostility to foremen. Moreover, the discretion exercised by foremen was typically perceived by workers as discriminatory. In the American literature this is universally reported even by observers not especially sympathetic to such a claim. One study carried out in the late 1930s concluded that "from the workers' standpoint the advantage of a rigid seniority rule is that it is not subject to interpretation and therefore provides protection against favoritism and discrimination" (Maclaurin 1939: 57). The study found that, "there was a widespread feeling . . . that the foreman did not judge ability fairly and if given much latitude would use ability ratings to play favorites" (Maclaurin 1939: 54), even though the writer himself judged this would be unlikely.

Allowing foremen discretion in the selection of those to be laid off may have something of a negative multiplier effect. As we shall see in a moment, the foremen may pick individuals to be laid off who are wrong from the firm's perspective because of their high productivity. To the degree that their selections are seen as discriminatory by other employees, discretionary-based layoffs may also depress the morale and, with it, average productivity of those workers who remain (Slichter 1941: 99), perhaps even engendering industrial conflict. This may drive highly productive employees, who know full well their own value on the labor market, to seek employment elsewhere in an effort to exit from a work situation dominated by uncertainty and arbitrariness. The foreman-centered hypothesis thus illuminates the importance of seniority as an automatic, nondiscretionary device.

Historical evidence thus largely supports the view that American unions favored seniority-based layoff because such a procedure protected their members and activists. This view also explains why many collective agreements (perhaps something on the order of a fifth) provide what is called "superseniority" to union committeemen or stewards, guaranteeing that they will head seniority lists regardless of when they were hired (Slichter 1941: 10). As I suggested initially in Chapter 1, rules such as seniority develop endogenously: that is, they develop out of the need to provide institutional protections for trade unions in a context where picking off union organizers is endemic. This brief review shows that American unions seized on the idea of seniority because of the protections it offered their growing shopfloor organization. Moreover, to the extent that seniority appeals to workers –

which it does, although not universally – this appeal seems based mainly on the way that seniority automates and regularizes decisions that had previously been made arbitrarily.

With seniority thus nearly universal in the United States, workforce reductions are usually managed smoothly and without engendering major industrial disputes, even though workforce reductions are more common in the United States than in Europe. This is not to say that American unions are powerless in the face of economic downturns. But because they do not need to protect their own organizations in such situations, they are free to pursue concessions on behalf of their members. Thus, in the 1970s and 1980s instead of dramatic and violent confrontations over the protection of union representatives during the course of job loss, American unions negotiated the terms of job loss for the members subjected to it, often trading concessions in the wages and benefits of those retained for smaller workforce reductions and better terms of severance.

At the same time, union pressure for seniority cannot entirely explain the origins of seniority in the United States. Two aspects remained unaccounted for. First, why did American unions develop such a strong preference for seniority whereas their counterparts elsewhere often did not? Second, why do all firms in the United States – not only firms in which managers confront trade unions – usually use seniority as the main criterion for selecting those for layoff? My answers to these questions will necessarily be somewhat speculative due to an absence of historical and comparative data.

Cross-national Variations in Union Attitudes toward Seniority

Whereas American unions have been almost uniformly supportive of instituting and then deepening the use of seniority-based layoffs, this has often not been the case elsewhere. Italian unions have generally been hostile to seniority, favoring worksharing instead. It would take extensive historical research to know fully why this was the case (or even whether it had always been true). For the moment, all we can say is that the hostility Italian unions exhibit to seniority and in favor of worksharing is part of a broader and unusually deep commitment to egalitarianism (Accornero 1981, 1992).

British unions, finally, have been deeply divided on seniority-based layoffs over the course of the twentieth century.[8] Although in this case too we suffer from an absence of systematic historical research, the long-standing importance of craft unions in Britain may account for union resistance to seniority there. A comparative study of unions and job loss that includes Britain quotes a telling letter from the files of "a large British union" as follows:

I must point out that this District has never agreed with "last in-first out." We consider such a policy would be a retrograde step because it results in some poor individuals, in particular the activist trade unionist, always being pushed out of a job. The man who has worked in a number of establishments has given equal service to the industry and the needs of the community as the man who has remained in one workshop all his life. Furthermore, membership of the Union should be a better criterion for a job than service with a particular firm. The man with the longest service in a firm may have the shortest membership in the Union, whilst the man who was last to start may have the longest Union membership. (Quoted in Meyers 1964: 36)

This revealing documentation corroborates one of the main implications of my major argument in this study: namely, unions seek (or in this case, oppose) seniority-based layoffs because of the institutional protections (or in this case, threat) they offer the union activist and hence union organization generally. In craft unions, unlike industrial unions, membership and job tenure are not synonymous. Members of craft unions may move jobs frequently and union activism does not therefore necessarily appear more among those with more job seniority than the median. In this labor market context the usual relationship between activism and job tenure does not hold. Hence, the effect of seniority on the union organization would not be the usual ones of offering greater institutional protection. It is thus not surprising that many British unions have historically opposed seniority, although it would take considerable historical research to document this hypothesis.

Why Firms Favor or Oppose Seniority

Despite its benefits for unions, seniority in the United States was in the first instance driven by the benefits it offered firms. Unions came to favor seniority only when firms had already initiated its development. For firms, seniority-based layoffs were part of the broader development of what are called internal labor markets, that is, labor markets within the firm (Doeringer and Piore 1971; also Milgrom and Roberts 1992: ch. 11). Internal labor markets, in turn, appear to have developed in response to two changes in industrial organization. First, in the early twentieth century new technologies became available that gave firms a larger incentive to retain the skilled and even semiskilled employees they had increasingly trained themselves. Second, where these changes in industrial organization coincided with chronic labor shortages – principally in the New World, which unlike the old had to import labor – firms had even stronger reason to provide new forms of training, security, and internal mobility for many classes of workers in order to retain a scarce labor force. At the same time, with the development of large, mass-production industries, unions came to share an interest in internal labor markets, including seniority systems. Above all, seniority protected union organization by protecting activists, thereby facilitating union growth.

Seniority interferes with absolute managerial discretion (i.e. "the market") in the assignment of benefits and duties to employees. It does so by identifying employees automatically and on the basis of a characteristic – organizational age – not obviously or necessarily related to market criteria. For most employees, especially manual industrial employees, productivity is probably a parabolic function, rising with age until some threshold is reached, after which decline sets in. Seniority protects older employees whose incomes, if assigned strictly on the basis of productivity, would decline possibly to zero (i.e. they would be expelled from the firm). But because other considerations enter a firm's efficiency calculations, including the loss of efficiency associated with labor turnover, especially of qualified and experienced employees, the economic effects of seniority are far broader than those associated with the rigidity it may impose on the composition of the labor force.

The literature explaining the commitment of American employers to seniority-based layoffs offers a number of complementary approaches, including those drawn from work on human capital and those deriving from principal–agent material. The latter, in turn, can be divided into two groups: those concerned with principal–agent relations with the firm as principal and workers as agents and those in which the firm is principal and foremen and supervisors are the agents. These views all concur that seniority developed as part of the larger emergence of internal labor markets, which can in turn be seen as attempts to tie employees to the firm and induce greater loyalty on their part. That industrial conflict over workforce reductions would thereby fall was probably a happy by-product for most firms.

The human capital approach argues that because a firm may under some circumstances invest in training an employee, it will seek to ensure that the person remain with the firm (see Becker 1975). To this end, it offers a series of inducements – possibly including a pension plan, fringe benefits and so forth – that make it disadvantageous for the individual to quit because doing so would cause the employee to lose such benefits. Seniority-based layoffs are a form of job protection for more senior workers and thus are often considered one of the benefits devised by employers as part of the development of internal labor markets.

Internal labor markets are, in turn, believed to have developed in much of U.S. manufacturing partly in order to reduce the costs associated with the extremely high turnover rates characteristic of a highly mobile and abundant immigrant labor force in the early part of the twentieth century (Jacoby 1985: 276). Excessive turnover was apparently a chronic problem for employers, and the goal of securing a more stable workforce is often mentioned as a motivation for the adoption of seniority-based layoffs. In particular, many firms manifested an increased interest in seniority provisions as well as other progressive personnel practices in the 1920s, as immigration declined and labor became increasingly scarce just as the labor requirements of industry were expanding (Ross 1958: 911). Moreover, much empirical evidence shows that seniority provisions reduce the quit rate (on both points, see Addison 1984: 91; Freeman and Medoff 1984: 20; Gersuny 1982a: 112; Mater 1940: 403; Medoff 1979: 387; Rees 1989: 145; Schatz 1983: 17; Slichter 1941: 151; but see the criticism by Ross 1958).

A second and complementary approach for why firms establish seniority systems for layoffs argues that seniority-based layoffs solve a principal–agent problem. Employers contract with employees to perform certain duties; but employees may shirk, performing less than employers believe they are paying for. To reduce shirking, employers seek to monitor and to sanction the work effort of their employees. Such disciplinary efforts tend to be ineffective when employees can just walk away from their jobs. By making exit costs high firms empower their own disciplinary devices with clout (Goldberg 1980: 263–69; more generally see Milgrom and Roberts 1992: ch. 6).

Much like the human capital argument, this argument implies that modern large-scale firms develop internal labor markets and the security devices associated with them as part of a broader effort to discipline a recalcitrant (and highly mobile) workforce. Both hypotheses are useful for comparative reflection, because they suggest that where workers are not highly mobile, firms will not need to enact seniority protection. Labor mobility, in turn, is largely a function of whether labor is a scarce or abundant resource; we have already seen that labor scarcity was a particular problem in the United States, as the development of the large corporation coincided with a period of increasing political restrictions on new immigration.

Observation of the various countries investigated in this study corroborate such a hypothesis. Only in the United States was labor chronically scarce during the growth of modern manufacturing, and only here did firms establish widespread seniority provisions. Italy, a country of historic outmigration, has always had abundant labor, and seniority provisions have not been established there. Britain has at times found labor scarce, at other times, abundant, and considerable variation has existed for craft versus semiskilled workers. Seniority provisions there have been partially established and are used by some firms on some occasions but are by no means universal. In Japan, finally, labor shortages have appeared episodically over the course of the twentieth century and internal labor markets have, as in the United States, also developed extensively (Jacoby 1975) apparently as a response to labor shortages (Taira 1970). In Japan, for reasons that remain analytically unexplored, these circumstances took the functionally equivalent form of segmented labor markets and lifetime employment rather than seniority-based layoff procedures.

Effort is more or less directly observable, and monitoring and punishment more or less easily accomplished depending on a series of technical features of production. Once assembly line production replaces craft work, for instance, it becomes difficult to assess the effort of individual employees on the line. In any event, employers do not themselves directly monitor the effort of their employees; instead, they hire other employees to do so for them. Assessing the skill and reliability of these intermediate employees – foremen and first-line supervisors – may itself become a problem for the employer. Some have suggested that firms have an efficiency incentive to automate the selection of persons for layoff through the adoption of seniority-based selection criteria in order to strip foremen of discretionary influence in the selection of those to be laid off. This motivation is, in turn, a function of the absence of adequate career incentives guaranteeing that foremen will act as perfect agents for the firm (Rees 1989: 142).

When firms lay off workers, foremen and first-line supervisors provide the information to management on which to make selection decisions. If management wishes to lay off the least productive, foremen are entrusted with the assessment of productivity. Management does not necessarily have any way of knowing whether the information conveyed is accurate.

Historically, the foreman's knowledge of the work process was often not adequate to permit proper evaluation. Additionally, the foreman's goals were not completely coincident with those of the owners; foremen themselves required supervision lest they pursue their own interests at the expense of the firm. Moreover, the foreman's power to fire workers and to mete out discipline without review by higher authorities within the firm created problems of social control. The firm had to absorb the costs arising from workers' displeasure with what was perceived as arbitrary treatment, for example, strikes, sabotage, and high turnover (Goldberg 1980: 256). As Albert Rees (1989: 141) notes, "Workers' stories of the preunion period stress over and over again that one had to do favors for the foreman to hold a job – flatter him, buy him drinks, even paint his porch." Foremen, in short, may arbitrarily mix favoritism, discrimination, and nepotism in with the other efficiency-oriented criteria they use to select persons for layoff.

Seniority provisions dilute the importance of foremen in the process of selecting individuals for layoff by radically reducing the discretionary influence foremen wield. Employers may decide that organizational age is on average a better proxy for productivity than whatever personalistic and arbitrary criteria their own foremen have been using. Thus, although the principle of seniority appears to conflict with efficiency considerations, this conflict may be less than superficially appears to be the case. Rees has argued that seniority-based layoffs are less inefficient than they appear both because experience correlates broadly with productivity (making seniority a broad-gauged proxy for worker productivity) and because, in the selection of persons for layoff, efficiency criteria were not actually being applied by foremen anyway (Rees 1989: 143).

For all these reasons, then, American firms in particular had strong reason to develop internal labor markets and especially seniority-based layoff procedures during the course of the twentieth century. In continental Europe, by contrast, the development of the large firm generally lagged that of the United States and labor remained abundant for most of the century. For both reasons, internal labor markets developed more slowly and less thoroughly there. So while seniority systems have gradually emerged in some European countries (see Elster 1992), they have done so far more recently than in the United States and seniority is still often mixed with other criteria, in particular needs-based criteria (for details on the German case, see Hartmann 1994 and Schmidt 1990; on the Norwegian, see Engelstad 1994).

CONCLUSIONS: THE LIMITS OF RATIONAL CHOICE ANALYSIS

This study has employed what is in the field of comparative politics still a new and perhaps controversial method of analysis, commonly referred to as rational choice. The hallmarks of this method are that it is a brand of intentional analysis, as Jon Elster (1983) has put it, meaning that outcomes are analyzed as the results of strategic interactions among instrumental and goal-seeking agents. Outcomes, in this view, depend fundamentally on two things: the preferences (or goals) of the agents involved and the choices confronting them. This latter feature, in turn, is typically established by the institutional framework in which agents find themselves.

How well has this method served us for the problem at hand? Perhaps most important, it has allowed us to identify critical institutional differences that generate different outcomes across cases of mass workforce reductions. I have assumed that the fundamental preferences of local unions and of local employers are the same regardless of national, industrial, or temporal context. Firms want to use situations of mass workforce reductions to target union activists, in order to break the union as an organization on the shopfloor, whereas unions seek to defend their activists and their organizations. In this sense, all the cases examined here – British autoworkers in the 1950s, their Italian counterparts in the 1980s, Japanese miners in the 1950s – are fundamentally similar. Yet outcomes differ among these cases. In some, industrial conflict ensued, whereas in others, it did not. I have shown that one major reason for these different outcomes is institutional. Where rules exist that prevent the targeting of union activists and representatives during the course of workforce reductions, industrial conflict is unlikely to occur.[9] Such rules include seniority provisions or other methods for selecting those to be expelled from the workplace that protect the union organizations involved.[10]

The success of rational choice in teasing out the effects of apparently small institutional differences is well known, and this has undoubtedly been its major contribution to the study of American politics. Equally well known, however, is its major limitation, namely that it must take preferences as given. To what extent has this affected the present study?

That the approach adopted throughout this book takes preferences as given is particularly evident in the second set of cases explored in this study, those involving the coal disputes at Miike in Japan in 1959–60 and in Britain in 1984–85. In these cases, otherwise unexpected outcomes occurred when exogenous actors changed the payoffs for the local agents. These exogenous actors were variously found to be national trade unions, national business organizations, and governments. They all lowered the costs of conflict for the local trade unions and firms by offering to subsidize industrial disputes over workforce reductions. They thereby helped catalyze such disputes.

In this study, I have discussed the possible motivations of these outside actors. I contend that national unions, like their local counterparts, pursued goals related to organizational maintenance. In both the second Miike strike and the British coal strike, national unions found their roles and authority – and even their very existence – under severe threat. Business and the government, by contrast, pursued what we may think of as macrovariants on the microphenomenon of the targeting of activists: that is, they were aggressively attempting to reshape the labor organizations and industrial relations systems with which they dealt.

Nonetheless, the sudden intrusion of outside actors into local interactions, and the dramatic effects such incursions may have, lend a certain randomness or unpredictability to situations of workforce reductions. This study has done little to identify the factors making such adventures more or less likely. That is, I have taken the preferences of national actors as empirically given in these cases and have not sought to argue (as I did for their local counterparts) that *all* business associations or governments share similar preferences. Indeed, the literatures describing the preferences of Nikkeiren in the 1950s and the Thatcher government in the 1980s tend to portray both as unusually committed to radical antilabor agendas. In both cases, the preferences of these national actors were extreme.

We can speculate on the circumstances under which business associations and governments adopt such radical strategies. First, radical attacks on the existing industrial relations system were probably unnecessary until the middle of the twentieth century in most OECD countries, or at least until the laws against unjust dismissal were fully in place. Before then, firms wishing to expel union activists, thereby undercutting the capacities of workers to engage in collective bargaining, could do so at their discretion. They did not need to await the excuse provided by large-scale personnel reductions. Even if firms did not use their discretion to fire union activists, the absence of legal protections for trade union representatives would have made the latter more likely to concede wage reductions when requested. For this reason, trade unionism was also less of a threat in some respects.

Only with the widespread establishment of laws against unjust dismissal did unions as organizations acquire strong foundations in the enterprise. The institutional effects of trade unionism, including increased wage rigidity, emerged as a consequence. With laws against unjust dismissal in place, union busting in a single enterprise was no longer a viable course of action for a firm, and attacks on single union organizations occurred only inadvertently. Confronting higher costs and increased international competition, a massive restructuring of the entire industrial relations system became almost the only way to break an established union movement and try to bring down labor costs. This, however, required collective action on the part of business; that is, it required an organized effort by a cohesive national business association or by an antilabor government or both.

Trade unions, then, are especially vulnerable during periods of high unemployment. But the reason is not mainly that high unemployment instills fear in ordinary workers, thereby depressing rank-and-file loyalty and inducing labor quiescence, although all that may be the case. Rather, high unemployment may make management especially aggressive in attacking trade unionism. In some circumstances, this aggression will take the form of attempting to alter fundamentally the industrial relations system and with it labor's place in a nation's political economy.

Why firms and governments do this is still an open question. More than a half-century ago, the economist Michael Kalecki reflected on the reasons business was initially so opposed to Keynesian policies to reduce unemployment. The use of government policies to smooth out the business cycle, he argued, would have the following consequences over time:

> under a regime of permanent full employment, "the sack" would cease to play its role as a disciplinary measure. The social position of the boss would be undermined and the self assurance and class consciousness of the working class would grow. Strikes for wage increases and improvements in conditions of work would create political tensions. It is true that profits would be higher under a regime of full employment. . . . But "discipline in the factories" and "political stability" are more appreciated by business leaders than profits. (Kalecki 1943: 326)

In this radical questioning of the commitment by firms to the profit motive, Kalecki introduces the possibility that firms may exhibit other, more complicated political preferences in some circumstances. This study concurs with Kalecki's observation that firms may exhibit unusual preferences, particularly when they band together for political purposes. The reasons remain to be investigated.

NOTES

NOTES TO CHAPTER 1

1 Note that this is *not* the conventional usage of the concept of rationality. Normally, rationality involves the use of appropriate means for given goals. Here, I am suggesting that the goals involved may themselves be of questionable rationality, in the sense of being patently unattainable. For a justification of this latter usage, see Elster (1985). For a clarification of the issues involved, see the discussion in Chapter 7 of the present book.
2 The extent of such regulations has been one of the reasons the OECD has repeatedly called for greater flexibility in the use of labor (OECD 1986a, b).
3 In addition, recent work demonstrates that a strike may result even if both parties are fully rational and fully informed (Fernandez and Glazer 1991; Haller and Holden 1990). These models, although conceptually important, are not very fruitful empirically because they generate possibility theorems and an infinity of equilibria. It is therefore difficult to derive falsifiable propositions from them.
4 For a review, see Kennan and Wilson 1989.
5 Most models using incomplete information are either general bargaining models, broadly applicable to bargaining situations generally, or, to the extent that they incorporate features specific to industrial relations, are designed to analyze wage bargaining. Models of wage bargaining are not easily transferred to situations of workforce reductions, however, since in the former labor moves first, whereas in the latter the firm opens the game. In wage bargaining, industrial action never occurs if the firm moves first (Kennan 1986: 1105).
6 The importance of active manpower policies in keeping unemployment low in the 1980s has been noted by Layard, Nickell, and Jackman 1991: 62–64 and 472–73.
7 For a comparative study of the extent of wage rigidity in different countries in the era following the oil shock, see Alogoskoufis and Manning 1988.

8 Good introductions to game theory include Fudenberg and Tirole 1991; Gibbons 1992; Kreps 1990: part III; and Myerson 1991. For a text with extensive political science applications, see Ordeshook 1992.

9 Later each assumption is relaxed.

10 Relaxing these assumptions subsequently, I consider situations where organized labor is strike-prone and the firm is trigger-happy; that is, where there are no costs (or low costs) to industrial action.

11 So-called wildcat strikes may occur even in the absence of trade unionism. But these are unlikely to be frequent, protracted, or even very compact. Regular, cohesive, and protracted industrial action requires organization.

12 One must be careful to avoid fallacious reasoning here. Inferring from the existence of protective legislation in most countries that all firms actually want to union bust is akin to arguing that because all countries have legislation against theft, everyone actually wants to engage in the activity. Yet theft would probably be more common than it is without legal protection against it. The historical record suggests that union busting would too.

13 A good recent example is Sweden, once heralded as representing Western Europe's most notable case of pacific class compromise. After 1983 Sweden's peak business association began disassembling the collective bargaining system so favored by labor, eventually causing a collapse of centralized bargaining and a concomitant widening of wage differentials (see Hibbs and Locking 1995 on the latter; Pontusson and Swenson 1996 on the former). In the early 1980s the Conservative-led coalition government attempted (unsuccessfully, as it turned out) to dismantle Sweden's so-called Ghent system for the distribution of unemployment insurance, which unions administer and which is a critical component for Sweden's exceptionally high unionization levels (see Rothstein 1992). If even Swedish employers can turn so aggressive, so can employers anywhere.

14 In studies of trade unionism, setting a maximand for organized labor remains an unresolved issue. The classic debate between Arthur Ross (1948) and John Dunlop (1944) turned on the maximization issue, with the former unwilling to identify a maximand. Whereas Ross contended that a focus on the political processes of trade unions, and especially on the importance of organizational survival for the leadership, was essential, Dunlop – and with him most later economists – was more concerned with specifying an objective function for the union. As Henry Farber (1986) suggests, however, it may be possible both to attend to the political processes of unions and to specify a clear objective function. By identifying the maximization of shopfloor activists as the goal of the organization, I seek to do just this.

15 Farber (1986: 1079–80) discusses the difficulties in devising a satisfactory theory of the objectives of union leadership. Maximization of membership is sometimes used, but this is generally operationalized as maximization of employment because of an implicit closed-shop assumption; that is, it is assumed that all employees in any specific workplace automatically become union members. This assumption is inappropriate in most European countries, however. Maximizing the number of shopfloor activists seems a way to cover both closed and open shop situations. Where there is no closed shop, recruitment depends critically on activists; thus, the leadership may be assumed to maximize the

number of activists in order to maximize members. Where there is a closed shop, the leadership may be assumed to maximize activists in order to maintain a wage advantage over nonunion settings adequate to retain the inframarginal worker.

16 Some information on these surveys is reported in Robinson 1996, one of the only studies to make use of these surveys.

17 Unfortunately, the survey question appears to be badly phrased. The codebook reports that survey respondents were asked to look at a list of voluntary organizations and activities and say (a) which, if any, they belonged to and (b) which, if any, they were currently doing unpaid volunteer work for (World Values Study Group 1994: 15). Organizations that were listed included churches, political parties, environmental groups, sports groups, trade unions, and so forth. While "unpaid volunteer work" may be a good way to characterize activism in religious or environmental organizations, it is not a phrase generally used for union activism. For this reason, the reliability of the survey instrument is problematic, and the results should be considered somewhat questionable.

18 It is difficult to know how to interpret the Italian finding, which is surprisingly high. The only plausible explanation is that respondents interpreted the question as including strike participation. This would account for the unusually large proportion of them claiming to undertake "unpaid volunteer work" for their union.

19 This does not mean that unions do not want to make the conditions as good as possible for ordinary members subject to workforce reductions. Where their own organization is not under threat, unions consistently try to reduce the number of workers slated for dismissal and to improve the terms and conditions of expulsion. But where their own organization is subject to threat, the union strives to protect itself first.

20 Later, I relax this assumption and investigate what happens when the union uses industrial action to defend its organization.

21 Standard measures of industrial disputes are the number of strikes, the number of participants, and the number of hours lost. While these data are generally available for the four countries, for Japan the only strike data that are regularly disaggregated by cause are for the number of disputes. It is therefore not possible to analyze other aspects of industrial action over workforce reductions in Japan. For this reason, I restrict the analysis to an examination of the number of strikes over workforce reductions as a proportion of all strikes in each of the four countries.

22 Italian data on strikes by cause are available only since 1956.

23 Data on strikes by cause are not available for the United States after 1981. However, even in the 1970s the proportion of disputes concerning job loss remained consistently less than 5 percent.

24 Data on the cause of industrial disputes for the United Kingdom are available only since 1966.

NOTES TO CHAPTER 2

1 Subsequently I show that the union can "win" such a dispute only if it never occurs in the first place.

2 This assumes that the union comprises only employees of a single firm.

3 This result is empirically useful. It suggests that union movements will generally have an easier time maintaining a reputation for toughness where they are highly centralized; that is, where national confederations enjoy considerable authority and resources (especially financial resources, including control over strike funds). Where national confederations enjoy great authority and resources, single firms will fear their intervention into local disputes in the event that the firm targets union representatives. Corroborating this, it is generally the case that postwar strike rates have been low in those countries classed as "corporatist," or where central labor organizations maintain greatest resources. Some evidence is available in Cameron 1984; but see also Tsebelis and Lange 1995, who show that there has been a recent change in the relationship between corporatism and low strike activity. At the same time, of course, the model also predicts low strike rates where national confederations are unlikely ever to subsidize local disputes, since in these cases, firms target and unions acquiesce.

NOTES TO CHAPTER 3

1 The precise question was, "What do you think of collaboration between workers and bosses?" Responses were as follows: "It is necessary because to everyone's advantage" (44 percent); "It is possible but should be collectively bargained" (29 percent); "It is impossible because they have opposed interests" (26 percent). Remaining responses were invalid. Reported in Accornero et al. 1980: 10, table 12.

2 It was not until participation on the picket lines began to fall over the following two weeks that another 30 percent of participants realized they were likely to lose the dispute, while the remaining 18 percent claimed to be surprised at the outcome even as the final agreement was being signed (Bonazzi 1984: 36).

3 Interviews were conducted by Bonazzi and Carmignani in 1983. They included 35 in-depth interviews with union officials and officials from the PCI as well as an open-ended survey of 138 of the most visible strike participants.

4 Given the absence of strike funds, the more usual pattern is to articulate strikes by rotating striking workers in and out of a plant in small groups or to call very short (e.g. four-hour) demonstrative strikes.

5 Apparently, Edwardes himself generally found the AUEW more cooperative than the TGWU (Edwardes 1983). The literature generally concurs that the TGWU was more opposed to contraction of the company and more inclined to support Robinson's opposition but was isolated by the other unions active in BL (Marsden et al. 1985: 151).

6 The figures are not strictly comparable. The proportion of unionized workers in the CIG in 1981 should be measured relative to the proportion of unionized workers in the plant prior to the layoffs (that is, in 1980). Since unionization began to fall after the strike, we may infer that the data reported in Table 3.2 slightly overstate the degree to which union members were disproportionately laid off.

7 Data on Mirafiori reveal a similar ratio. In October 1980, 115 shop stewards from Mirafiori were laid off (reported in Bessone et al. 1983: 117). At the time, Mirafiori employed 73,250 persons and had 766 shop stewards in all

(reported in Golden 1988: 240, table 30 and 234, table 29). This amounts to one steward for every 96 employees.

NOTES TO CHAPTER 4

1 One empirical difficulty of this hypothesis is that the union has a strategic interest in exploiting the firm's incomplete information. In particular, in order to forestall targeting, union leaders may try to get the firm to believe that the union's threshold is lower than may actually be the case (i.e. that a strike will ensue if x activists are expelled, whereas actually the union intends to strike only if $x + a$ representatives are let go). For this reason, using statements from union leaders as evidence in these situations is likely to be unsatisfactory, as the discussion of research procedures in Chapter 1 already indicated.
2 Elster also discusses mixed systems, which use elements from various categories and are empirically most common of all.
3 Unfortunately, data on the extent of seniority are not available for most European countries.
4 Interpreting the differences between the AUEW and the TGWU is tricky. The TGWU indicated that it was prepared to undertake sustained industrial action in support of the dismissed steward and against workforce reductions but was prevented from carrying out such a threat by the maneuvering of the AUEW. This assumes that the TGWU was sincerely committed to militant resistance. Equally plausibly, however, the TGWU was able to engage in populist position-taking precisely because officials knew that, thanks to the AUEW, they would not be called upon to follow through on their threats. There is no way to discriminate empirically between these two interpretations, because insincere (i.e. strategic) union officials are unlikely to confess publicly.
5 Unfortunately, evidence regarding recruitment patterns of stewards by union organization within BL appears unavailable.

NOTES TO CHAPTER 5

1 Cross-national analyses of aggregate strike rates (e.g. Hibbs 1978; Korpi and Shalev 1980) have produced inconsistent results. Moreover, there are few studies of cross-national variations in the strike rates of specific industries and almost none of whether these conform to more general national patterns.
2 Voting in the NUM occurs at the pit head using the single transferable vote. Elections tend to be contested, usually closely so, in part because the union is heavily factionalized (see McCormick 1979: 63–64), and turnout tends to be high.
3 Data are not yet available on employment reductions in the 1990s, but these look to be quite substantial, as Japan faces its worst recession since the war.
4 Hiwatari (1993) details the 1978 case of Nippon Steel, when the company decided to terminate production at one plant. The union there announced it would "risk the fate of the union in the struggle to make the company repeal [its plan]" (quoted in Hiwatari 1993: 8). However, the plant union was isolated by the company union, which "engineered a near consensus among plant unions" (Hiwatari 1993: 8), and persuaded the rank and file to accept the shutdown

of the roll mill. Affected workers were ultimately transferred to other factories. The case illustrates the argument developed in the next chapter concerning the importance of external (national) actors in offering subsidies to plant unions for strikes to occur in situations of mass workforce reductions.

5 This argument is somewhat controversial. A good presentation of evidence supporting the view that Japanese firms are more resistant to shedding labor than firms in other OECD countries is Tachibanaki 1987; see also Shirai 1968. But even Tachibanaki (1987: 652–53) notes that in Japan, with enough fall in output, workforce reductions occur; the threshold, he argues, is higher than in the United States or Western Europe. Moreover, despite his attentiveness to special features of Japanese employment rates, Tachibanaki (1987: 670) too concludes that "it is unreasonable to emphasize the importance of lifetime jobs in interpreting the working of the Japanese labor market."

6 A large debate concerns the origins of permanent employment, especially the extent to which it may be a product of unique features of Japanese culture. The debate was initiated by Abegglen (1958), who offered a culturalist interpretation of Japanese management and labor relations. Interpretation has shifted over time, however, so that today the most persuasive interpretation of the development of lifetime employment is that in Japan, as in the other advanced capitalist nations, postwar job security for a minority of midcareer male employees emerged as part of the development of internal labor markets. Empirical work by Koike has been especially important in demonstrating that economic rationality, not cultural distinctiveness, offers an adequate handle on Japanese labor relations and personnel management (see Koike 1983a, b, 1987, and especially 1988; for a summary of the terms of debate, see Jacoby 1979). Theoretical work by Aoki (1984; see also 1988) makes a similar point.

7 One study quotes Richard Crossman's account of a July 1967 meeting of the Cabinet Committee on pit closures, where the latter confessed to "the appalling fact that after three years the Labour Government had evolved neither an instrument for assessing the social impact of its actions nor an instrument for ameliorating that impact upon the community" (from *The Crossman Diaries,* quoted in Krieger 1979: 229).

8 It is common in Japan that firms list employees for "voluntary" retirement to reduce the size of their workforce. As one study notes, however, in a discussion of various disputes over job loss around 1960: "Those who were hostile to the company usually were discriminated against and, rather than suffer a loss of face as a result of discharge, they would choose 'voluntary retirement.' . . . Thus, there had developed a peculiar personnel management system in which the employer could make arbitrary and discriminatory decisions" (Fujita 1974: 335).

9 It is worth stressing that the discharges announced in 1953 were nonetheless carried out. Some secondary analyses erroneously report that the union's victory consisted of a reversal of the original discharges and that the firm backed down in workforce reductions. This is not true. Instead, the union won the right to participate in the selection of those to be dismissed in future discharges.

10 Of course, in Britain unions gained protection through a seniority provision, whereas in Japan management agreed simply not to designate individuals without the union's agreement.

11 The only five pits in Britain without any strikebreakers during the strike were also located in South Wales, however, illustrating the regional diversity and historical complexity of the strike (Francis 1985: 268; see also the account by Howells 1985).

NOTES TO CHAPTER 6

1 This forecast has largely been confirmed. By fiscal year 1991–92 British Coal's industrial workforce in the collieries numbered 44,000 (of a total workforce of 58,000), down from 231,000 in 1980–81 (British Coal Corporation 1991–92: 30–31). Winterton and Winterton had projected that NCB employment would be 50,000 in 1990 were the Conservatives to remain in power.

2 Under union rules, the President remains in office for life. In fact, Scargill voluntarily submitted to a new election in 1988, which he won with 53.8 percent of the vote (Leadbeater 1988: 10).

3 Adeney and Lloyd, however, tend to lay considerable blame at the feet of Scargill's supposed syndicalism (see their pp. 22ff). Nonetheless, the view that the NUM's national leadership aimed at toppling the Thatcher government with the dispute is perhaps the most common interpretation of the union's motive (see e.g. Hyman 1986: 342).

4 This assumes, of course, that the national leadership deliberately intended to undertake strike action in the absence of a national vote, using flying pickets instead. This is not an untenable proposition. Writing of the years prior to the strike, Vic Allen (1981: 302) notes that the NUM's national leadership under Scargill was keenly aware that pit closures were an inherently divisive issue. The NUM thus could have planned from the outset to operate the strike on the assumption that winning a national strike vote would be impossible. Many apparently believed, especially in light of majority rejections by the national membership of strike votes earlier in the 1980s, that "Notts and the Midlands . . . would *never* support threatened miners in South Wales, Scotland and the North East" (Beynon 1985: 11; emphasis in the original).

5 Some have concluded from this that Japanese workers are mainly concerned with employment security not wage increases (Shirai 1974: 289), although such a conclusion is obviously unwarranted in the absence of direct evidence regarding employee attitudes. How unions respond to discharges may or may not reflect the preferences of a majority of union members.

6 This is not to say that no manipulation occurred at all. Kahn (1987: 69) reports that in April, Scargill successfully used his agenda control to prevent the NEC from ordering a national strike ballot.

NOTES TO CHAPTER 7

1 I have already noted (see Chapter 1, n1) that this formulation breaches the technical meaning of the term "rationality." Rationality has to do with applying efficient means to predetermined goals. It is unconventional to contend that a particular goal is substantively irrational, although there may be grounds for doing so. In *The Protestant Ethic and the Spirit of Capitalism,* for instance, Max

Weber condemns Calvinism as "irrational from the standpoint of purely eudæ-monistic self-interest" (Weber 1958: 78), despite his more usual claim that there are no grounds on which to evaluate substantive rationality (e.g. Weber 1968: I, 85ff).

2 Recall that in Chapter 4 I argued that incomplete information on the part of the firm about the type of union it confronted could cause conflict to occur in the first place. Here I argue that once conflict is underway, incomplete informa-tion on the part of the union could cause it to lose on the issue of protecting activists (not preventing job loss, on which it inevitably loses in any case).

3 Of all the strikes examined here, information on why workers participated is available for the 1984–85 miners' dispute (see Chapter 6, The Rank and File). However, the data were collected after the fact in restricted localities and are difficult to interpret.

4 Technically, the firm did not make a mistake in the sense of doing something it would correct if it had to do it over again. It simply ended up on the wrong side of a probability distribution.

5 Elster (1992: 150) claims that seniority is "widespread" both in Europe and the United States. Although it is true that seniority is used frequently in some European countries, including Germany, Norway, Sweden, and Britain, it is much less universally used than in the United States and it is not used much at all in other European countries, such as Italy. Systematic cross-national data are not available on the use of seniority-based procedures for workforce reduc-tions.

6 This argument has not been formally developed as have the preceding two, but informally underlies much empirically based reasoning on unions and seniority in the United States.

7 The British evidence on the development of seniority-based layoffs in the automobile industry in the 1950s (see Chapter 3) also corroborates the connec-tion between union pressures for seniority and attempts to stabilize shopfloor organization and protect activists.

8 I have not been able to locate any information on the attitudes of Japanese unions to seniority-based layoffs. I thus exclude the case from consideration here.

9 It will only occur when exogenous agents, for their own reasons, are nonetheless determined to subsidize a dispute. This, however, is most likely to occur if the union organization is under severe threat, and this threat is likely to be simultaneously local and more general. So even if targeting is not involved – it was not, for instance, in the case of the British coal mines in 1984 – indicators of organizational threat should be evident.

10 For instance, if union representatives are themselves party to the selection process (as occurs indirectly in Germany, for instance), the union is also likely to remain well protected despite job loss.

REFERENCES

Abegglen, James C. 1958. *The Japanese Factory: Aspects of its Social Organization.* Glencoe, IL.: Free Press.

Abraham, Katherine G., and James L. Medoff. 1984. "Length of Service and Lay-offs in Union and Nonunion Work Groups." *Industrial and Labor Relations Review,* 38, no. 1 (Oct.): 87–97.

Accornero, Aris. 1981. "Sindacato e rivoluzione sociale." *Laboratorio Politico,* 1, no. 4 (July–Aug.): 5–34.

   1992. *La parabola del sindacato: ascesa e declino di una cultura.* Bologna: Il Mulino.

Accornero, Aris; Baldissera, Alberto; and Scamuzzi, Sergio. 1980. "Ricerca di massa sulla condizione operaia alla Fiat: primi risultati." *Congiuntura Sociale,* no. 2 (Feb.): 1–22.

Accornero, Aris; Carmignani, Fabrizio; and Nino Magna. 1985. "I tre 'tipi' di operai della Fiat." *Politica ed Economia,* 16, no. 5 (May): 33–47.

Addison, John T. 1984. "Trade Unions and Restrictive Practices." In *The Economics of Trade Unions: New Directions,* ed. Jean-Jacques Rosa. Boston: Kluwer-Nijhoff.

   1986. "Job Security in the United States: Law, Collective Bargaining, Policy, and Practice." *British Journal of Industrial Relations,* 24, no. 3 (Nov.): 381–418.

Adeney, Martin, and John Lloyd. 1986. *The Miners' Strike 1984–5: Loss without Limit.* London: Routledge and Kegan Paul.

Agnelli, Umberto. 1980. "È giunta l'ora di licenziare." Interview with Giuseppe Turani. *La Repubblica,* June 21: 1.

Akerlof, George A., and Janet L. Yellen, eds. 1986. *Efficiency Wage Models of the Labor Market.* Cambridge: Cambridge University Press.

Allen, V[ic] L. 1981. *The Militancy of British Miners.* Shipley: Moor Press.
   1985. "Miners' Man." *New Society,* Jan. 24: 136–37.

Alogoskoufis, George S., and Alan Manning. 1988. "On the Persistence of Unemployment." *Economic Policy,* 7 (Oct.): 427–69.

Altshuler, Alan, et al. 1984. *The Future of the Automobile: The Report of MIT's International Automobile Program.* Cambridge, Mass.: MIT Press.

Amalgamated Union of Engineering Workers-TASS (AUEW-TASS). N.d. [c. 1978]. *British Leyland Cars. Collapse or Growth. An Alternative to Edwardes.* Pamphlet; Modern Records Center, Warwick, MSS. 202B/B/7.

Amendola, Giorgio. 1979. "Interrogativi sul 'caso' Fiat." *Rinascita,* Nov. 9: 13–15.

Anderson, John C. 1979. "Local Union Participation: A Re-examination." *Industrial Relations,* 18, no. 1 (Winter): 18–31.

Aoki, Masahiko. 1984. *The Co-operative Game Theory of the Firm.* Oxford: Clarendon Press.

———. 1988. *Information, Incentives, and Bargaining in the Japanese Economy.* Cambridge: Cambridge University Press.

Ashworth, William. 1986. *1946–1982: The Nationalized Industry.* Volume 5 of *The History of the British Coal Industry.* Oxford: Clarendon Press.

Aston, Beverly; Morris, Tim; and Paul Willman. 1990. "Still Balancing the Books: The NUM and the 1984–85 Strike." *Industrial Relations,* 21, no. 3 (Autumn): 173–84.

Ayusawa, Iwao. 1960. "Japanese Labor in 1959." *Oriental Economist,* 28, no. 591 (Jan.): 29–32.

———. 1962a. *Postwar Developments in Organized Labor, 1945–1952.* Part I of *Organized Labor in Japan.* Tokyo: Foreign Affairs Association of Japan.

———. 1962b. *Organized Labor in Present-Day Japan, 1953–1961.* Part II of *Organized Labor in Japan.* Tokyo: Foreign Affairs Association of Japan.

———. 1966. *A History of Labor in Modern Japan.* Honolulu: East-West Center.

Bagnasco, Arnaldo. 1986. *Torino. Un profilo sociologico.* Turin: Einaudi.

Baldissera, Alberto. 1984. "Alle origini della politica della disuguaglianza nell'Italia degli anni '80: la marcia dei quarantamila." *Quaderni di Sociologia,* 31, no. 1: 1–78.

Baldwin, George B. 1953. "Structural Reform in the British Miners' Union." *Quarterly Journal of Economics,* 67, no. 4 (Nov.): 576–97.

Baroncini, Paola. 1985. "Crisi operai tra taylorismo e automazione. Condizione di vita e di lavoro della popolazione operaia della Fiat di Piedimonte San Germano." *Ispequaderni,* nos. 34–35 (June): entire issue.

Batstone, Eric. 1984. *Working Order.* Oxford: Basil Blackwell.

Batstone, Eric, and Stephen Gourlay. 1986. *Unions, Employment and Innovation.* Oxford: Basil Blackwell.

Batstone, Eric; Boraston, Ian; and Stephen Frenkel. 1977. *Shop Stewards in Action: The Organization of Workplace Conflict and Accommodation.* Oxford: Basil Blackwell.

Bean, Charles R. 1994. "European Unemployment: A Survey." *Journal of Economic Literature,* 32, no. 2 (June): 573–619.

Becchi Collidà, Ada, and Serafino Negrelli. 1986. *La transizione nell'industria e nelle relazioni industriali: l'auto e il caso Fiat.* Milan: Franco Angeli.

Becker, Gary. 1975. *Human Capital: A Theoretical and Empirical Analysis, with Special Reference to Education.* 2nd ed.; New York: National Bureau of Economic Research.

Belforte, S[ilvia], and M[artino] Ciatti. 1980. *Il fondo del barile. Riorganizzazione del ciclo produttivo e composizione operaia alla Fiat dopo le nuove assunzioni.* Milan: La Salamandra.

Bessone, Mario, et al. 1983. "Dossier Fiat Auto: il prezzo dei profitti." *Azimut,* 2, no. 5 (May–June): 104–22.

Beynon, Huw. 1985. "Introduction." In *Digging Deeper: Issues in the Miners' Strike,* ed. Huw Beynon. London: Verso.

Beynon, Huw; Hudson, Ray; and David Sadler. 1991. *A Tale of Two Industries: The Contraction of Coal and Steel in the North East of England.* Milton Keynes: Open University Press.

Boltho, Andrea. 1975. *Japan: An Economic Survey 1953–1973.* Oxford: Oxford University Press.

Bonazzi, Giuseppe. 1984. "La lotta dei 35 giorni alla Fiat: un'analisi sociologica." *Politica ed Economia,* 15, no. 11 (Nov.): 33–43.

——— 1987. "Contrattare alla Fiat." *Prospettiva Sindacale,* 18, no. 64 (June): 76–82.

——— 1988. "La sociologia e il gioco della produzione." *Politica ed Economia,* 19, no. 1 (Jan.): 3–6.

Bonazzi, Giuseppe et al. 1987. "L'espulsione tutelata. Processi di reconversione socio-lavorativa degli ex-dipendenti delle grandi fabbriche." Istituto Ricerche Economico-Sociali del Piemonte (IRES). *Quaderni di Ricerca,* no. 48 (Dec.): entire issue.

Booth, Allison L. 1987. "Extra-statutory Redundancy Payments in Britain." *British Journal of Industrial Relations,* 25, no. 3 (Nov.): 401–18.

Briggs, Asa. 1961. "The Welfare State in Historical Perspective." *Archives Européennes de Sociologie,* 2, no. 2: 221–58.

British Coal Corporation. 1991/92. *Report and Accounts 1991/92.* London: British Coal Corporation.

British Leyland (BL) Cars. 1980. "Final Draft of Proposed Agreement on Bargaining, Pay, Employee Benefits and Productivity, Covering Hourly Rated Employees in BL Cars." Newsheet distributed to manual employees.

British Motor Corporation (BMC). 1956. "Press statement." Typescript dated July 19.

Bulmer, M.I.A. 1971. "Mining Redundancy: A Case Study of the Workings of the Redundancy Payments Act in the Durham Coalfield." *Industrial Relations Journal,* 2, no. 4 (Winter): 3–21.

Buran, Paolo. 1982. "La classe ostile: forme di conflitto e forme di soggettività operaia a Torino negli anni '70," *Laboratorio Politico,* 2, no. 1 (Jan.–Feb.): 154–74.

Burns, Alan; Newby, Martin; and Jonathan Winterton. 1985. "The Restructuring of the British Coal Industry." *Cambridge Journal of Economics,* 9, no. 1 (March): 93–110.

Burns, Alan; Feickert, Dave; Newby, Martin; and Jonathan Winterton. 1983. "The Miners and New Technology." *Industrial Relations Journal,* 14, no. 4 (Winter): 7–22.

Calmfors, Lars, and John Driffill. 1988. "Bargaining Structure, Corporatism and Macroeconomic Performance." *Economic Policy,* 3, no. 1 (April): 13–61.

Cameron, David. 1984. "Social Democracy, Corporatism, Labour Quiescence, and the Representation of Economic Interest in Advanced Capitalist Society." In *Order and Conflict in Contemporary Capitalism: Studies in the Political Economy of Western European Nations,* ed. John H. Goldthorpe. New York: Oxford University Press.

Campbell, Adrian, and Malcolm Warner. 1985a. "Changes in the Balance of Power in the British Mineworkers' Union: an Analysis of National Top-office Elections, 1974–84." *British Journal of Industrial Relations,* 23, no. 1 (March): 1–24.

1985b. "Leadership in the Miners' Union: Arthur Scargill's Rise to Power." *Journal of General Management,* 10, no 3 (Spring): 4–22.

Carmignani, Fabrizio. 1984. "Il 'sindacato di classe' nella lotta dei 35 giorni alla Fiat." *Politica ed Economia,* 15, no. 11 (Nov.): 43–48.

Centre for Policy Studies. 1983. "BL: Changing Gear." London: Centre for Policy Studies.

Clegg, Hugh Armstrong. 1979. *The Changing System of Industrial Relations in Great Britain.* Oxford: Basil Blackwell.

Cole, Robert E. 1971. *Japanese Blue Collar: The Changing Tradition.* Berkeley: University of California Press.

1972. "Permanent Employment in Japan: Facts and Fantasies." *Industrial and Labor Relations Review,* 26, no. 1 (Oct.): 615–30.

Comito, Vincenzo. 1982. *La Fiat tra crisi e ristrutturazione.* Rome: Editori Riuniti.

Cook, Alice H. 1966. *An Introduction to Japanese Trade Unionism.* Ithaca, N.Y.: New York State School of Industrial and Labor Relations.

1967. "Political Action and Trade Unions: A Case Study of the Coal Miners in Japan." *Monumenta Nipponica,* 22, nos. 1–2: 103–21.

Cooper, David, and Trevor Hopper, eds. 1988. *Debating Coal Closures: Economic Calculation in the Coal Dispute 1984–5.* Cambridge: Cambridge University Press.

Crawcour, Sydney. 1978. "The Japanese Employment System." *Journal of Japanese Studies,* 4, no. 2 (Summer): 225–45.

Crick, Michael. 1985. *Scargill and the Miners.* New ed. Harmondsworth: Penguin.

Dealessandri, Tom, and Maurizio Magnabosco. 1987. *Contrattare alla Fiat. Quindici anni di relazioni sindacali.* Ed. Carlo Degiacomi. Rome: Edizioni Lavoro.

Della Rocca, Giuseppe. 1977. "L'offensiva politica degli imprenditori nelle fabbriche." In *Problemi del movimento sindacale in Italia 1943–1973,* Aris Accornero, ed. 2nd ed. Milan: Feltrinelli.

Dina, Angelo. 1981. "Fiat: i '35 giorni' e dopo." *Classe,* 12, no. 19 (June): 5–36.

Doeringer, Peter, and Michael Piore. 1971. *Internal Labor Markets and Manpower Analysis.* Lexington, Mass.: D.C. Heath.

Dore, Ronald P. 1973. *British Factory – Japanese Factory: The Origins of National Diversity in Industrial Relations.* Berkeley: University of California Press.

1986. *Flexible Rigidities: Industrial Policy and Structural Adjustment in the Japanese Economy 1970–80.* Stanford, Calif.: Stanford University Press.

Dunlop, John T. 1944. *Wage Determination under Trade Unions.* New York: Macmillan.

The Economist. 1958. "Signs of Panic," 186, no. 5978 (March 22): 1060.

    1959a. "Agonising Reappraisal for Coal," 193, no. 6061 (Oct. 17): 300.

    1959b. "Can Coal Compete?" 191, no. 6040 (May 30): 861–63.

    1959c. "Sacrificing the Mines," 190, no. 6021 (Jan. 10): 151.

    1960a. "Coal at the Bottom?" 194, no. 6073 (Jan. 16): 223–24.

    1960b. "The Disappearing Energy Gap," 194, no. 6076 (Feb. 6): 529.

    1960c. "Miners Militant?" 194, no. 6115 (Oct. 29): 439.

    1978. "Appomattox or Civil War?" 267, no. 7030 (May 27): 21–22.

Edwardes, Michael. 1983. *Back from the Brink: An Apocalyptic Experience.* London: Pan.

Edwards, Christine. 1983. "Power and Decision Making in the Workplace: A Study in the Coal Mining Industry." *Industrial Relations Journal,* 14, no. 1 (Spring): 50–69.

Edwards, Christine, and Edmund Heery. 1989. *Management Control and Union Power: A Study of Labour Relations in Coal-mining.* Oxford: Clarendon Press.

Edwards, Paul, and Hugh Scullion. 1982. "The Local Organisation of a National Dispute: The British 1979 Engineering Strike." *Industrial Relations Journal,* 13, no. 1 (Spring): 57–63.

Edwards, Paul et al. 1992. "Great Britain: Still Muddling Through." In *Industrial Relations in the New Europe,* ed. Anthony Ferner and Richard Hyman. Oxford: Basil Blackwell.

Elster, Jon. 1983. *Explaining Technical Change: A Case Study in the Philosophy of Science.* Cambridge: Cambridge University Press.

    1985. "The Nature and Scope of Rational-Choice Explanation." In *Actions and Events: Perspectives on the Philosophy of Donald Davidson,* ed. Ernest Le Pore and Brian P. McLaughlin. Oxford: Basil Blackwell.

    1989. *The Cement of Society: A Study of Social Order.* Cambridge: Cambridge University Press.

    1992. *Local Justice: How Institutions Allocate Scarce Goods and Necessary Burdens.* New York: Russel Sage Foundation.

Engelstad, Fredrik. 1994. "The Emergence of the Seniority Criterion by [sic] Work Force Reductions in Norway." In *Layoffs and Local Justice,* ed. Fredrik Engelstad. Oslo: Institute for Social Research.

Farber, Henry S. 1986. "The Analysis of Union Behavior." In *Handbook of Labor Economics,* ed. Orley Ashenfelter and Richard Layard. Vol. 2; Amsterdam: North Holland.

Federazione CGIL-CISL-UIL Piemonte. 1980. "Fiat storia di una lotta." *Bollettino Mensile di Documentazione,* no. 36 (Dec.): special issue.

Federazione Lavoratori Metalmeccanici (FLM) Fiat Rivalta. 1982. "Ricerca del consiglio di fabbrica sulla produttività, anni 1987/80/81/82." Internal document (typescript).

    N.d. [c. 1980]. "Memoria storica delle lotte Fiat." Internal document (typescript).

Fernandez, Raquel, and Jacob Glazer. 1991. "Striking for a Bargain between Two Completely Informed Agents." *American Economic Review,* 81, no. 1 (March): 240–52.

Ferner, Anthony, and Richard Hyman. 1992. "Italy: Between Political Exchange and Micro-Corporatism." In *Industrial Relations in the New Europe,* ed. Anthony Ferner and Richard Hyman. Oxford: Basil Blackwell.

Fine, Ben. 1990. *The Coal Question: Political Economy and Industrial Change from the Nineteenth Century to the Present Day.* London: Routledge.

Flanders, Allan. 1973. "Measured Daywork and Collective Bargaining." *British Journal of Industrial Relations,* 11, no. 3 (Nov.): 368–92.

Flmese. 1980. No. 2 (April–May): 16.

Francis, Hywel. 1985. "The Law, Oral Tradition and the Mining Community." *Journal of Law and Society,* 12, no. 3 (Winter): 267–71.

Frantz, George. 1984. "Government and Declining Industry: The Japanese Coal Mining Industry." Unpublished paper, Department of Government, Cornell University.

Freeman, Richard B., and James L. Medoff. 1984. *What Do Unions Do?* New York: Basic Books.

Fruin, W. Mark. 1975. "The Japanese Company Controversy." *Journal of Japanese Studies,* 4, no. 2 (Summer): 267–300.

Fryer, Bob. 1985. "Trade Unionism in Crisis: The Miners' Strike and the Challenge to Union Democracy." In *Digging Deeper: Issues in the Miners' Strike,* ed. Hew Beynon. London: Verso.

Fryer, John. 1979. "The Man Who Stopped Leyland," *The Sunday Times* (London) Nov. 25.

Fryer, Robert H. 1973. "Redundancy, Values and Public Policy," *Industrial Relations Journal,* 4, no. 2 (Summer): 2–19.

Fudenberg, Drew, and Jean Tirole. 1991. *Game Theory.* Cambridge, Mass.: MIT Press.

Fujita, Wakao. 1974. "Labor Disputes." In *Workers and Employers in Japan: The Japanese Employment Relations System,* ed. Kazuo Ōkōchi, Bernard Karsh, and Solomon B. Levine. Tokyo: Princeton University Press and University of Tokyo Press.

Garon, Sheldon. 1987. *The State and Labor in Modern Japan.* Berkeley: University of California Press.

Garraty, John A. 1978. *Unemployment in History: Economic Thought and Public Policy.* New York: Harper & Row.

Gennard, John. 1982. "Great Britain." In *Workforce Reductions in Undertakings: Policies and Measures for the Protection of Redundant Workers in Seven Industrialized Market Economy Countries,* ed. Edward Yemin. Geneva: International Labour Office.

Gersuny, Carl. 1982a. "Employment Seniority: Cases From Iago to Weber." *Journal of Labor Research,* 3, no. 1 (Winter): 111–19.

——— 1982b. "Origins of Seniority Provisions in Collective Bargaining." *Labor Law Journal,* 33, no. 8 (Aug.): 518–24.

Gersuny, Carl, and Gladis Kaufman. 1985. "Seniority and the Moral Economy of U.S. Automobile Workers, 1934–1946." *Journal of Social History,* 18 (Spring): 463–75.

Gibbon, Peter. 1988. "Analysing the British Miners' Strike of 1984–5." *Economy and Society,* 17, no. 2 (May): 139–94.

Gibbon, Peter, and Simon Bromley. 1990. "From an Institution to a Business? Changes in the British Coal Industry 1985–9." *Economy and Society,* 19, no. 1 (Feb.): 56–94.

Gibbons, Robert. 1992. *Game Theory for Applied Economists.* Princeton, N.J.: Princeton University Press.

Glyn, Andrew. 1988a. "Colliery Results and Closures after the 1984–85 Coal Dispute." *Oxford Bulletin of Economics and Statistics,* 50, no. 2 (May): 161–73.

———. 1988b. "The Economic Case against Pit Closures." In *Debating Coal Closures: Economic Calculation in the Coal Dispute 1984–5,* ed. David Cooper and Trevor Hopper. Cambridge: Cambridge University Press.

Goldberg, Victor P. 1980. "Bridges over Contested Terrain: Exploring the Radical Account of the Employment Relationship." *Journal of Economic Behavior and Organization,* 1, no. 3 (Sept.): 249–74.

Golden, Miriam. 1988. *Labor Divided: Austerity and Working-Class Politics in Contemporary Italy.* Ithaca, NY: Cornell University Press.

Golden, Miriam, and Michael Wallerstein. 1996. *Reinterpreting Postwar Industrial Relations: Comparative Data on Advanced Industrial Societies,* MS.

Goodman, Geoffrey. 1985. *The Miners' Strike.* London: Pluto Press.

Gordon, Andrew. 1985. *The Evolution of Labor Relations in Japan: Heavy Industry, 1853–1955.* Cambridge, Mass.: Harvard University Press.

Halberstam, David. 1986. *The Reckoning.* New York: William Morrow.

Hall, Robert E. 1982. "The Importance of Lifetime Jobs in the U.S. Economy." *American Economic Review,* 72, no. 4 (Sept.): 716–24.

Haller, Hans, and Steiner Holden. 1990. "A Letter to the Editor on Wage Bargaining." *Journal of Economic Theory,* 52, no. 1 (Oct.): 232–36.

Hanami Akamatsu, Tadashi. 1972. "Future Industrial Relations: Japan." *International Institute for Labour Studies Bulletin,* no. 10: 85–113.

Hanami, Tadashi. 1979. *Labor Relations in Japan Today.* Tokyo: Kodansha International.

———. 1984. "Conflict Resolution in Industrial Relations." In *Industrial Conflict Resolution in Market Economies: A Study of Australia, the Federal Republic of Germany, Italy, Japan and the USA,* ed. Tadashi Hanami and Roger Blanpain. Deventer: Kluwer.

Harris, José. 1972. *Unemployment and Politics: A Study in English Social Policy 1886–1914.* Oxford: Clarendon Press.

Hartley, Jean; Kelly, John; and Nigel Nicholson. 1983. *Steel Strike: A Case Study in Industrial Relations.* London: Batsford Academic and Educational.

Hartmann, Brigitte. 1994. "Workforce Reductions in Germany." In *Layoffs and Local Justice,* ed. Fredrik Engelstad. Oslo: Institute for Social Research.

Hayes, Beth. 1984. "Unions and Strikes with Asymmetric Information." *Journal of Labor Economics,* 2, no. 1 (Jan.): 57–83.

Hein, Laura E. 1990. *Fueling Growth: The Energy Revolution and Economic Policy in Postwar Japan.* Cambridge, Mass.: Harvard University Press.

Hibbs, Douglas A. Jr. 1978. "On the Political Economy of Long-Run Trends in Strike Activity." *British Journal of Political Science,* 8, part 2 (April): 153–77.

Hibbs, Douglas A., Jr., and Håkan Locking. 1995. "Wage Dispersion and Pro-
    ductive Efficiency: Evidence for Sweden." FIEF Working Paper no.
    128, Stockholm.
Hicks, J[ohn] R. 1966. *The Theory of Wages.* 2nd ed. New York: St. Martin's.
Hirai, Yōichi. 1991. "Mitsui Miike sōgi (1960 nen) – Jin'in seiri no 'shitsu' to
    Sankōren ridatsu mondai" (Mitsui Miike Labor Dispute (1960) – 'Qual-
    ity' of Personnel Reduction and Withdrawal of *Sankōren*). In *Nihon no
    rōdō sôgi (1945–1980 nen) (Labor Disputes in Japan from 1945 to 1980*),
    ed. Rōdō Sōgi-shi Kenkyūkai (Study-Group for the History of Labor
    Disputes). Tokyo: Tokyo Daigaku Shuppankai (University of Tokyo
    Press).
Hiwatari, Nobuhiro. 1993. "The Political Economy of Enterprise Unionism and
    Industrial Collaboration in Japan: Explaining Union Strategies to Cope
    with Economic Stagnation and Aging Work Force." Unpublished pa-
    per, Institute of Social Sciences, University of Tokyo.
Horvath, Francis W. 1987. "The Pulse of Economic Change: Displaced Workers
    of 1981–85." *Monthly Labor Review,* 110, no. 6 (June): 3–11.
Houseman, Susan N. 1991. *Industrial Restructuring with Job Security: The Case of
    European Steel.* Cambridge, Mass.: Harvard University Press.
Howell, Chris. 1995. "Trade Unions and the State: A Critique of British Indus-
    trial Relations." *Politics & Society,* 23, no. 2 (June): 149–83.
Howell, David. 1987. "Goodbye To All That?: A Review of the Literature on
    the 1984/5 Miners' Strike." *Work, Employment and Society,* 1, no. 3
    (Sept.): 388–404.
Howells, Kim. 1985. "Stopping Out: The Birth of a New Kind of Politics." In
    Digging Deeper: Issues in the Miners' Strike, ed. Hew Beynon. London:
    Verso.
Hudson, Ray, and David Sadler. 1985. "Cole and Dole: Employment Policies in
    the Coalfields." In *Digging Deeper: Issues in the Miners' Strike,* ed. Hew
    Beynon. London: Verso.
Huszczo, Gregory E. 1983. "Attitudinal and Behavioral Variables Related to Par-
    ticipation in Union Activities." *Journal of Labor Research,* 4, no. 3 (Sum-
    mer): 289–97.
Hyman, Richard. 1986. "Reflections on the Mining Strike." *Socialist Register
    1985/86,* ed. Ralph Miliband, John Saville, Marcel Liebman, and Leo
    Panitch. London: Merlin Press.
Ichiyo, Muto. 1984. "Class Struggle on the Shopfloor – the Japanese Case
    (1945–84)." *Japan-Asia Quarterly Review,* 16, no. 3: 38–49.
Ishikawa, Kichiemon. 1963. "The Regulation of the Employer-Employee Rela-
    tionship: Japanese Labor-Relations Law." In *Law in Japan: The Legal Or-
    der in a Changing Society,* ed. Arthur Taylor von Mehren. Cambridge,
    Mass.: Harvard University Press.
Istituto per lo Sviluppo della Formazione Professionale dei Lavoratori (ISFOL) –
    Regione Piemonte, in collaboration with the cooperative Matraia.
    1983. "Caratteristiche e comportamenti degli operai Fiat in mobilità."
    Quaderni di Formazione, no. 3/83 (May–June): entire issue.
Jacoby, Sanford [M.] 1979. "The Origins of Internal Labor Markets in Japan."
    Industrial Relations, 18, no. 2 (Spring): 184–96.

1985. *Employing Bureaucracy: Managers, Unions, and the Transformation of Work in American Industry, 1900–1945.* New York: Columbia University Press.

Japan Coal Miners' Union (Tanrō). 1961. *For a Deeper Understanding of the Struggle of the Miike Coal Miners.* Japan Coal Miners' Union: Tokyo.

JFEA News. 1960a. "The Coal Mining Industry in Japan and its Unemployment Problem," no. 3 (Jan.): 1–3.

——— 1960b. "Miike Coal Dispute and its Salient Problems," no. 4 (April): 3–5.

——— 1960c. "The End of the Miike Labor Dispute and the Problems Hereafter," no. 6 (Oct.): 2–4.

Japan Labor Bulletin, 1963a. "Coal Industry Disputes," new series, 2, no. 2 (Feb.): 2.

——— 1963b. "The Japan Coalmining Employers' Council Cancel [sic] the Restriction on Output," new series, 2, no. 11 (Nov.): 3.

——— 1964a. "Coal Industry Labor Shortage," new series, 3, no. 6 (June): 2.

——— 1964b. "Coal Mine Labor Numbers Less than 120,000," new series, 3, no. 8 (Aug.): 2.

Japan Quarterly. 1960. "Crisis in the Coal Industry," 7, no. 1 (Jan.–March): 5–6.

Jefferys, Steve. 1988. "The Changing Face of Conflict: Shopfloor Organization at Longbridge, 1939–1980." In *Shopfloor Politics and Job Controls: The Post-War Engineering Industry,* ed. Michael Terry and P. K. Edwards. Oxford: Basil Blackwell.

Jones, D. T., and S. J. Prais. 1978. "Plant-Size and Productivity in the Motor Industry: Some International Comparisons." *Oxford Bulletin of Economics and Statistics,* 40, no. 2 (May): 131–51.

Jones, Daniel T. 1983. "Technology and the UK Automobile Industry." *Lloyds Bank Review,* no. 148 (April): 14–27.

Kahn, Peggy. 1987. "Coal Not Dole: The British Miners' Strike of 1984–85." *Socialist Review,* 17, nos. 3–4 (May–Aug.): 56–88.

——— 1988. "The Dual Crisis of British Coal-Mining in the Mid-1980s." Paper presented at the annual meetings of the North Central Sociological Association, Pittsburgh, April 14–17.

Kalecki, M[ichael]. 1943. "Political Aspects of Full Employment." *Political Quarterly,* 14, no. 4 (Oct.–Dec.): 322–30.

Kawada, Hisashi. 1974. "Workers and Their Organizations." In *Workers and Employers in Japan: The Japanese Employment Relations System,* ed. Kazuo Ōkōchi, Bernard Karsh, and Solomon B. Levine. Tokyo: Princeton University Press and University of Tokyo Press.

Kawanishi, Hirosuke. 1992. *Enterprise Unionism in Japan.* London: Kegan Paul.

Kennan, John. 1986. "The Economics of Strikes." In *Handbook of Labor Economics,* ed. Orley C. Ashenfelter and Richard Layard. Vol. 2; Amsterdam: North Holland.

Kennan, John, and Robert Wilson. 1989. "Strategic Bargaining Models and Interpretation of Strike Data." *Journal of Applied Econometrics,* 4, supplement: S87–S130.

Kerr, Clark, and Abraham Siegel. 1964. "The Interindustry Propensity to Strike – an International Comparison." In *Labor and Management in Industrial Society,* ed. Clark Kerr. Garden City, N.Y.: Anchor Books.

Keyssar, Alexander. 1986. *Out of Work: The First Century of Unemployment in Massachusetts.* Cambridge: Cambridge University Press.

King, Gary; Keohane, Robert O.; and Sidney Verba. 1994. *Designing Social Inquiry: Scientific Inference in Qualitative Research.* Princeton, N.J.: Princeton University Press.

Kiyoshi, Tsuchiya. 1962. "The Coal Industry." *Japan Quarterly,* 9, no. 4 (Oct.–Dec.): 478–83.

Klandermans, Bert. 1986. "Psychology and Trade Union Participation: Joining, Acting, Quitting." *Journal of Occupational Psychology,* 59, no. 3 (Sept.): 189–204.

Koike, Kazuo. 1983a. "Internal Labor Markets: Workers in Large Firms." In *Contemporary Industrial Relations in Japan,* ed. Taishiro Shirai. Madison: University of Wisconsin Press.

———. 1983b. "Workers in Small Firms and Women in Industry." In *Contemporary Industrial Relations in Japan,* ed. Taishiro Shirai. Madison: University of Wisconsin Press.

———. 1987. "Japanese Redundancy: The Impact of Key Labor Market Institutions on the Economic Flexibility of the Japanese Economy." In *Labor Market Adjustments in the Pacific Rim,* ed. Peter T. Chinloy and Ernst W. Stromsdorfer. Boston: Kluwer-Nijhoff.

———. 1988. *Understanding Industrial Relations in Modern Japan.* Houndmills, Basingstoke: Macmillan.

Korpi, Walter, and Michael Shalev. 1980. "Strikes, Power, and Politics in the Western Nations, 1900–1976." In *Political Power and Social Theory,* ed. Maurice Zeitlin. Vol. 1; Greenwich, Conn.: JAI Press.

Koshiro, Kazutochi. 1984. "Lifetime Employment in Japan: Three Models of the Concept." *Monthly Labor Review,* 107, no. 8 (Aug.): 34–35.

Kreps, David M. 1990. *A Course in Microeconomic Theory.* Princeton, N.J.: Princeton University Press.

Krieger, Joel. 1983. *Undermining Capitalism: State Ownership and the Dialectic of Control in the British Coal Industry.* Princeton, N.J.: Princeton University Press.

———. 1979. "British Colliery Closure Programmes in the North East: from Paradox to Contradiction." In *Analysis and Decision in Regional Policy,* ed. I. G. Cullen. London Papers on Regional Science No. 9. London: Pion.

Kuhn, Peter, and Jacques Robert. 1989. "Seniority and Distribution in a Two-Worker Trade Union." *Quarterly Journal of Economics,* 54, no. 3 (Aug.): 485–505.

Kume, Ikuo. 1988. "Changing Relations among the Government, Labor, and Business in Japan After the Oil Crisis." *International Organization,* 42, no. 4 (Autumn): 659–87.

———. 1991. "Institutionalizing Labor Accommodation in Postwar Japan: The Micro-Macro Link of Japan's Postwar Political Economy." Paper presented at the annual meetings of the American Political Science Association, Washington, D.C., Aug. 29–Sept. 1.

———. 1993. "A Tale of Twin Industries: Labor Accommodation in the Private Sector." In *Political Dynamics in Contemporary Japan,* ed. Gary D. Allinson and Yasunori Sone. Ithaca, N.Y.: Cornell University Press.

Law, Christopher M. 1985. "The Geography of Industrial Rationalisation: The British Motor Car Assembly Industry, 1972–1982." *Geography,* 70, part 1 (Jan.): 1–12.

Layard, Richard; Nickell, Stephen; and Richard Jackman. 1991. *Unemployment: Macroeconomic Performance and the Labour Market.* Oxford: Oxford University Press.

Leadbeater, Charles. 1988. "Scargill's Forecast of NUM Unity Rings Hollow." *Financial Times.* Jan. 26: 10.

Lee, Raymond M. 1987. "Introduction." In *Redundancy, Layoffs and Plant Closures: Their Character, Causes and Consequences,* ed. Raymond M. Lee. London: Croom Helm.

Levi, Margaret. 1988. *Of Rule and Revenue.* Berkeley: University of California Press.

Levine, Solomon B. 1958. *Industrial Relations in Postwar Japan.* Urbana: University of Illinois Press.

———. 1984. "Employers Associations in Japan." In *Employers Associations in Industrial Relations: A Comparative Study,* ed. John P. Windmuller and Alan Gladstone. Oxford: Clarendon Press.

Lewchuk, Wayne. 1986. "The Motor Vehicle Industry." In *The Decline of the British Economy,* ed. Bernard Elbaum and William Lazonick. Oxford: Clarendon Press.

Leyland Combine Trade Union Committee. N.d. [c. Nov. 1979]. "British Leyland, The Edwardes Plan and Your Job." Pamphlet distributed to employees.

Lichtenstein, Nelson. 1988. "The Union's Early Days: Shop Stewards and Seniority Rights." In *Choosing Sides: Unions and the Team Concept,* ed. Mike Parker and Jane Slaughter. Boston: South End Press.

Lipset, Seymour Martin. 1981. *Political Man: The Social Bases of Politics.* Baltimore: Johns Hopkins University Press.

Locke, Richard M. 1992. "Industrial Restructuring and Industrial Relations in the Italian Automobile Industry." In *Bargaining for Change: Union Politics in North America and Europe,* ed. Miriam Golden and Jonas Pontusson. Ithaca, NY: Cornell University Press.

Mackney, Paul. 1987. *Birmingham and the Miners' Strike: The Story of a Solidarity Movement.* Birmingham: Birmingham Trade Union Council.

Maclaurin, W. Rupert. 1939. "Workers' Attitudes on Work Sharing and Lay-off Policies in a Manufacturing Firm." *Monthly Labor Review,* 48, no. 1 (Jan.–June): 47–60.

Marsden, David; Morris, Timothy; Willman, Paul; and Stephen Wood. 1985. *The Car Industry: Labour Relations and Industrial Adjustment.* London: Tavistock.

Marsh, A. I., and E. E. Coker. 1963. "Shop Steward Organisation in the Engineering Industry." *British Journal of Industrial Relations,* 1, no. 2 (June): 170–90.

Marsh, Arthur; Hackmann, Maria; and Douglas Miller. 1981. *Workplace Relations in the Engineering Industry in the UK and the Federal Republic of Germany.* London: Anglo-German Foundation for the Study of Industrial Society.

Marsh, Robert M., and Hiroshi Mannari. 1972. "A New Look at 'Lifetime Commitment' in Japanese Industry." *Economic Development and Cultural Change*, 20, no. 4 (July): 611–30.

Martin, Benjamin. 1961. "Japanese Mining Labor: The Miike Strike." *Far Eastern Survey*, 30, no. 2 (Feb.): 26–30.

McCormick, Brian J. 1969. "Strikes in the Yorkshire Coalfield, 1947–1963." *Economic Studies*, 4, nos. 1/2 (Oct.): 171–97.

———. 1979. *Industrial Relations in the Coal Industry.* London: Macmillan.

McDonald, Ian M., and Robert M. Solow. 1981. "Wage Bargaining and Employment." *American Economic Review*, 71, no. 5 (Dec.): 896–908.

Mater, Dan. 1940. "The Development and Operation of the Railroad Seniority System." *Journal of Business*, 13, no. 4 (Oct.): 387–419.

Maxcy, George, and Aubrey Silberston. 1959. *The Motor Industry.* London: George Allen & Unwin.

Medoff, James L. 1979. "Layoffs and Alternatives under Trade Unions in U.S. Manufacturing." *American Economic Review*, 69, no. 3 (June): 380–95.

Melman, Seymour. 1958. *Decision-Making and Productivity.* New York: Wiley.

Metcalf, David. 1986. "Employment Subsidies and Redundancies." In *Unemployment, Search and Labour Supply*, ed. Richard Blundell and Ian Walker. Cambridge: Cambridge University Press.

Meyers, Frederic. 1964. *Ownership of Jobs: A Comparative Study.* Los Angeles: Institute of Industrial Relations Monograph No. 11, University of California-Los Angeles.

———. 1965. "The Analytic Meaning of Seniority." *Industrial Relations Research Association Proceedings* (Winter): 194–202.

Milgrom, Paul, and John Roberts. 1992. *Economics, Organization and Management.* Englewood Cliffs, N.J.: Prentice Hall.

Millward, Neil, and Mark Stevens. 1986. *British Workplace Industrial Relations 1980–1984: The DE/ESRC/PSI/ACAS Surveys.* Aldershot: Gower.

Ministry of Labor, Japan. *Year Book of Labor Statistics.* Tokyo: Ministry of Labor, various years.

Mitchell, Daniel J. B. 1982. "Recent Union Contract Concessions." *Brookings Papers on Economic Activity*, 1: 165–204.

Moy, Joyanna, and Constance Sorrentino. 1981. "Unemployment, Labor Force Trends, and Layoff Practices in 10 Countries." *Monthly Labor Review*, 104, no. 12 (Dec.): 3–13.

Mukherjee, Santosh. 1973. *Through No Fault of Their Own: Systems for Handling Redundancy in Britain, France and Germany.* A PEP Report; London: Macdonald.

Myerson, Roger B. 1991. *Game Theory: Analysis of Conflict.* Cambridge, Mass.: Harvard University Press.

Nakayama, Ichiro. 1964. "The Second Union." *The Role of the "Second Union" in Labor-Management Relations in Japan.* Translation Series No. 3., Occasional Papers of Research Translations, Institute of Advanced Projects, East-West Center, Honolulu.

National Union of Mineworkers (NUM) (Notts Area), Education and Research Department, 1983. "An Appraisal of the British Coalmining Industry and an Examination of the Possible Consequences Following Pit Closures in the N.U.M. (Nottinghamshire Area)." Brinsley, Nottinghamshire: Notts. Area N.U.M.

Oaklander, Harold. 1982. "United States." In *Workforce Reductions in Undertakings: Policies and Measures for the Protection of Redundant Workers in Seven Industrialized Market Economy Countries,* ed. Edward Yemin. Geneva: International Labour Office.

Okamoto, Hideaki. 1974. "Management and Their Organizations." In *Workers and Employers in Japan: The Japanese Employment Relations System,* ed. Kazuo Ōkōchi, Bernard Karsh, and Solomon B. Levine. Tokyo: Princeton University Press and University of Tokyo Press.

Ōkōchi, Kazuo. 1965. "The Characteristics of Labor-Management Relations in Japan." *Journal of Social and Political Ideas in Japan,* 3, no. 3 (Dec.): 44–49.

Olson, Mancur. 1982. *The Rise and Decline of Nations: Economic Growth, Stagflation, and Social Rigidities.* New Haven, Conn.: Yale University Press.

Ordeshook, Peter C. 1992. *A Political Theory Primer.* New York: Routledge.

Organization for Economic Cooperation and Development (OECD). 1977. *The Development of Industrial Relations Systems: Some Implications of Japanese Experience.* Paris: OECD.

　　1983. *Quarterly Labour Force Statistics,* no. 2.

　　1986a. *Flexibility in the Labour Market: The Current Debate.* Paris: OECD.

　　1986b. *Labour Market Flexibility. Report by a High-Level Group of Experts to the Secretary-General.* Paris: OECD.

　　1993. *Quarterly Labour Force Statistics,* no. 2.

The Oriental Economist. 1958. "Safety Personnel Question of Coal Miners [sic] Union," 26, no. 575 (Sept.): 493.

　　1959a. "Rationalization in Coal Mines," 27, no. 589 (Nov.): 654.

　　1959b. "Struggle at Mitsui Mining Flaming [sic]," 27, no. 590 (Dec.): 707.

　　1960a. "Mitsui Mining Dispute Continues," 28, no. 591 (Jan.): 38.

　　1960b. "Miike Mine Lockout," 28, no. 593 (March): 131.

　　1960c. "Labor Dispute at Miike Colliery," 28, no. 595 (May): 226–27.

　　1960d. "Miike Mine Struggle Nearing End," 28, no. 595 (May): 263.

　　1960e. "Miike Dispute Nearing End," 28, no. 599 (Sept.): 509.

Oswald, Andrew J. 1986a. "Is Wage Rigidity Caused by 'Lay-offs by Seniority'?" In *Wage Rigidity and Unemployment,* ed. Wilfred Beckerman. Baltimore: Johns Hopkins University Press.

　　1986b. "Wage Determination and Recession: A Report on Recent Work." *British Journal of Industrial Relations,* 24, no. 2 (July): 181–94.

　　1993. "Efficient Contracts are on the Labour Demand Curve: Theory and Facts." *Labour Economics,* 1, no. 1 (June): 85–113.

Oswald, Andrew J., and Peter J. Turnbull. 1985. "Pay and Employment Determination in Britain: What Are Labour 'Contracts' Really Like?" *Oxford Review of Economic Policy,* 1, no. 2 (Summer): 80–97.

Padoa-Schioppa, Fiorella. 1988. "Underemployment Benefit Effects on Employment and Income Distribution: What We Should Learn from the System of the *Cassa Integrazione Guadagni.*" *Labour,* 2, no. 2 (Autumn): 101–24.

Panitch, Leo. 1976. *Social Democracy and Industrial Militancy: The Labour Party, the Trade Unions, and Incomes Policy, 1945–1974.* New York: Cambridge University Press.

Partito Comunista Italiano (PCI). 1980. Conferenza nazionale dei comunisti sulla Fiat. Torino, 22–24 febbraio. Collection of documents distributed to participants.

Pempel, T. J. 1982. *Policy and Politics in Japan: Creative Conservatism.* Philadelphia: Temple University Press.

Pencavel, John H. 1970. "An Investigation into Industrial Strike Activity in Britain." *Economica,* 37, no. 147 (Aug.): 239–56.

People of Thurcroft. 1986. *Thurcroft: A Village and the Miners' Strike. An Oral History.* Nottingham: Atlantic Highlands.

Perline, Martin, and V. R. Lorenz. 1970. "Factors Influencing Member Participation in Trade Union Activities." *American Journal of Economics and Sociology,* 29, no. 4 (Oct.): 425–38.

Perotti, Pietro, and Marco Revelli. 1986. "Fiat autunno 80. Per non dimenticare. Immagini e documenti di una lotta operaia." *Quaderni del Cric [Centro di Ricerca e Iniziativa Comunista],* supplement to no. 1 (March–June): entire issue.

Pizzorno, Alessandro. 1978. "Political Exchange and Collective Identity." In *Comparative Analyses.* Vol. 2 of *The Resurgence of Class Conflict in Western Europe since 1968,* ed. Colin Crouch and Alessandro Pizzorno. New York: Holmes & Meier.

Pontusson, Jonas, and Peter Swenson. 1996. "Labor Markets, Production Strategies, and Wage Bargaining Institutions: The Swedish Employer Offensive in Comparative Perspective." *Comparative Political Studies,* 29, no. 2 (Spring): 223–50.

Przeworski, Adam and Henry Teune. 1970. *The Logic of Comparative Social Inquiry.* New York: John Wiley & Sons.

Purcell, John. 1995. "Ideology and the End of Institutional Relations: Evidence from the UK." In *Organized Industrial Relations in Europe: What Future?,* ed. Colin Crouch and Franz Traxler. Aldershot: Avebury.

Reder, Melvin W. 1960. "Job Scarcity and the Nature of Union Power." *Industrial and Labor Relations Review,* 13, no. 3 (April): 349–62.

Rees, Albert. 1989. *The Economics of Trade Unions.* 3rd ed. Chicago: University of Chicago Press.

Rees, William M. 1982. "Miners and Redundancy." *Industrial Law Journal,* 11, no. 3 (Sept.): 178–85.

——— 1985. "The Law, Practice and Procedures Concerning Redundancy in the Coal Mining Industry." *Industrial Law Journal,* 14, no. 3 (Sept.): 203–14.

Reid, Jimmy. 1985. "What Scargill Means." *New Society,* Jan. 17: 91–93.

Revelli, Marco. 1989. *Lavorare in Fiat.* Milan: Garzanti.

Rhodes, Martin, and Vincent Wright. 1988. "The European Steel Unions and the Steel Crisis, 1974–84: A Study in the Demise of Traditional Unionism." *British Journal of Political Science,* 18, part 2 (April): 171–95.

Richardson, Ray, and Stephen Wood. 1989. "Productivity Change in the Coal Industry and the New Industrial Relations." *British Journal of Industrial Relations,* 21, no. 1 (March): 33–55.

Riker, William. 1990. "Political Science and Rational Choice." In *Perspectives on Positive Political Economy,* ed. James E. Alt and Kenneth A. Shepsle. Cambridge: Cambridge University Press.

Rimlinger, Gaston V. 1959. "International Difference in the Strike Propensity of Coal Miners: Experience in Four Countries." *Industrial and Labor Relations Review,* 12, no. 3 (April): 389–405.

Roberts, John G. 1989. *Mitsui: Three Centuries of Japanese Business.* 2nd ed. New York: Weatherhill.

Robinson, Ian. 1966. "Re-Thinking Labor Movement Power: From Movement Character to Mobilization Capacity." Presented at the annual meeting of the Comparative Industrial Relations Research and Teaching Society, San Francisco, Jan. 4.

Rogowski, Ronald. 1989. *Commerce and Coalitions: How Trade Affects Domestic Political Alignments.* Princeton, N.J.: Princeton University Press.

Rohlen, Thomas P. 1979. " 'Permanent Employment' Faces Recession, Slow Growth, and an Aging Work Force." *Journal of Japanese Studies,* 5, no. 2 (Summer): 235–72.

Romiti, Cesare. 1988. *Questi anni alla Fiat.* Interview by Giampaolo Pansa. Milan: Rizzoli.

Romm, Stuart. 1994. "Layoff Practices in American Companies: Efficiency, Fairness and Seniority." In *Layoffs and Local Justice,* ed. Fredrik Engelstad. Oslo: Institute for Social Research.

Ross, Arthur M. 1948. *Trade Union Wage Policy.* Berkeley: University of California Press.

———. 1958. "Do We Have a New Industrial Feudalism?" *American Economic Review,* 48, no. 5 (Dec.): 903–20.

Rothstein, Bo. 1992. "Labor-Market Institutions and Working-Class Strength." In *Structuring Politics: Historical Institutionalism in Comparative Analysis,* ed. Sven Steinmo, Kathleen Thelen, and Frank Longstreth. Cambridge: Cambridge University Press.

Rutledge, Ian. 1977–78. "Changes in the Mode of Production and the Growth of 'Mass Militancy' in the British Mining Industry, 1954–1974." *Science and Society,* 41, no. 4 (Winter): 410–29.

Rutledge, Ian, and Phil Wright. 1985. "Coal Worldwide: The International Context of the British Miners' Strike." *Cambridge Journal of Economics,* 9, no. 4 (Dec.): 303–26.

Ryder, Sir Don, a Team of Inquiry led by. 1975. *British Leyland. The Next Decade: An Abridged Version of a Report Presented to the Secretary of State for Industry.* London: HMSO.

Salmon, John, 1983. "Organised Labour in a Market Economy: A Study of Redundancy and Workplace Relations as an Issue of Power-Conflict in the British Motor Industry." Ph.D. dissertation, University of Warwick.

———. 1988. "Wage Strategy, Redundancy and Shop Stewards in the Coventry Motor Industry." In *Shopfloor Politics and Job Controls: The Post-War Engineering Industry,* ed. Michael Terry and P. K. Edwards. Oxford: Basil Blackwell.

Samuels, Richard J. 1987. *The Business of the Japanese State: Energy Markets in Comparative and Historical Perspective.* Ithaca, N.Y.: Cornell University Press.

Scarbrough, Harry. 1982. "The Control of Technological Change in the Motor Industry: A Case Study." 2 vols.; Ph.D. dissertation, Aston University, Birmingham.

——— 1986. "The Politics of Technological Change at British Leyland." In *Technological Change, Rationalisation and Industrial Relations*, ed. Otto Jacobi et al. London: Croom Helm.

Scargill, Arthur. 1975. "The New Unionism." *New Left Review*, no. 92 (June): 3–33.

Schatz, Ronald W. 1983. *The Electrical Workers: A History of Labor at General Electric and Westinghouse 1923–60*. Urbana: University of Illinois Press.

Schmidt, Volker H. 1990. "Local Justice in West Germany: Some Preliminary Findings on Education, Health and Work." Prepared for a conference of the Local Justice project groups, Paris, June 11–13.

Scognamiglio, Renato. 1990. *Diritto del lavoro*. Naples: Jovene.

Scullion, Hugh. 1981. "The Skilled Revolt against General Unionism: The Case of the BL Toolroom Committee." *Industrial Relations Journal*, 12, no. 3 (May–June): 15–27.

Seglow, Peter, and Patricia Wallace. 1984. "Trade Unions and Change in the British Car Industry." *Research Paper 84/2*. London: Policy Studies Institute.

Selznick, Philip, and Howard Vollmer. 1962. "Rule of Law in Industry: Seniority Rights." *Industrial Relations*, 1, no. 3 (May): 97–116.

Shalev, Michael. 1990. "Class Conflict, Corporatism and Comparison: A Japanese Enigma." In *Japanese Models of Conflict Resolution*, ed. S.N. Eisenstadt and Eyal Ben-Ari. London: Kegan Paul.

Shigeru, Haibara. 1960. "The Miike Miners' Struggle." *Sohyo News*, no. 184 (Dec. 25): 2–4.

Shigeyoshi, Tokunaga. 1984. "Some Recent Developments in Japanese Industrial Relations, with Special Reference to Large Private Enterprises." Discussion paper IIVG/dp84-208. Berlin: Wissenschaftszentrum für Sozialforschung.

Shinkawa, Toshimitsu, and T. J. Pempel. Forthcoming. "Occupational Welfare and the Japanese Experience." In *Occupational Welfare and the Welfare State in Comparative Perspective*, ed. Michael Shalev. London: Macmillan.

Shinzō, Shimizu. 1982. "Miike sōgi shōron – 80-nendai kara no sairon" (Short essay on the Mitsui labor dispute – Review from the 1980s). In *Sengo rōdō kumiai undō-shi ron – Kigyō shakai chōkoku no shiza (Essays on the History of Labor Disputes after WWII – from the View Point of Overcoming Industrial Society)*, ed. Shimizu Shinzō. Tokyo: Nihon Hyōronsha.

Shirai, Taishiro. 1968. "Income Patterns and Job Security in Japan." In *Industrial Relations: Contemporary Issues*, ed. B. C. Roberts. First World Congress of the International Industrial Relations Association, Geneva, 4–8 September 1967. London: Macmillan.

——— 1974. "Collective Bargaining." In *Workers and Employers in Japan: The Japanese Employment Relations System*, ed. Kazuo Ōkōchi, Bernard Karsh, and Solomon B. Levine. Tokyo: Princeton University Press and University of Tokyo Press.

Sinclair, Peter. 1987. *Unemployment: Economic Theory and Evidence.* Oxford: Basil Blackwell.

Slaughter, C. 1958. "The Strike of Yorkshire Mineworkers in May, 1955." *Sociological Review,* new series, 6, no. 2 (Dec.): 241–59.

Slichter, Sumner H. 1941. *Union Policies and Industrial Management.* Washington, D.C.: Brookings Institution.

Sōhyō News. 1960. "Confidence in Victory Grows as Strike Enters 150th Day," no. 177 (July 10): 9.

    1962a. "Sōhyō President Ota Greets Coalminers," no. 211 (Nov. 10): 4–5.

    1962b. "Struggle Declaration Jointly Issued by Tanrō, Sōhyō, and the Socialist Party," no. 211 (Nov. 10): 2–3.

    1963. "Mitsui Coalmine [sic] Company Threatens Activists with Dismissal," no. 215 (Feb. 10): 1–2.

Soskice, David, 1990. "Wage Determination: The Changing Role of Institutions in Advanced Industrialized Economies." *Oxford Review of Economic Policy,* 6, no. 4 (Winter): 36–61.

Spead, John J., and James J. Bambrick, Jr. 1950. *Seniority Systems in Nonunionized Companies.* National Industrial Conference Board Report, Studies in Personnel Policy, no. 110.

Spinrad, William. 1960. "Correlates of Trade Union Participation: A Summary of the Literature." *American Sociological Review,* 25, no. 2 (April): 237–44.

Streeck, Wolfgang. 1985. "Introduction: Industrial Relations, Technical Change and Economic Restructuring." In "Industrial Relations and Technical Change in the British, Italian and German Automobile Industry: Three Case Studies," ed. Wolfgang Streeck. Discussion paper IIM/LMP 85-5. Berlin: Wissenschaftszentrum für Sozialforschung.

Sumiya, Mikio. 1966. "The Development of Japanese Labour-Relations." *Developing Economies,* 4, no. 4 (Dec.): 499–515.

    1974. "The Emergence of Modern Japan." In *Workers and Employers in Japan: The Japanese Employment Relations System,* ed. Kazuo Ōkōchi, Bernard Karsh, and Solomon B. Levine. Tokyo: Princeton University Press and University of Tokyo Press.

Tachibanaki, Toshiaki. 1984. "Labor Market Flexibility and Job Tenure." In *The Economic Analysis of the Japanese Firm,* ed. Masahiko Aoki. Amsterdam: North-Holland.

    1987. "Labor Market Flexibility in Japan in Comparison with Europe and the U.S." *European Economic Review,* 31, no. 3 (April): 647–84.

Taira, Koji. 1962. "The Characteristics of Japanese Labor Markets." *Economic Development and Cultural Change,* 10, no. 2, part 1 (Jan.): 150–68.

    1970. *Economic Development and the Labor Market in Japan.* New York: Columbia University Press.

Taylor, Andrew J. 1984a. "The Modern Boroughmongers? The Yorkshire Area (NUM) and Grassroots Politics." *Political Studies,* 32, no. 3 (Sept.): 385–400.

    1984b. *The Politics of the Yorkshire Miners.* London: Croom Helm.

    1988. "Consultation, Conciliation and Politics in the British Coal Industry." *Industrial Relations Journal,* 19, no. 3 (Autumn): 222–33.

Taylor, Stan. 1981. "De-industrialisation and Unemployment in the West Mid-lands." In *Unemployment,* ed. Bernard Crick. London: Methuen.

Thoms, David, and Tom Donnelly. 1985. *The Motor Car Industry in Coventry since the 1890's.* New York: St. Martin's.

Tolliday, Steve. 1987. "The Failure of Mass Production Unionism in the Motor Industry, 1914–39." In *1914–1939.* Vol. II of *A History of British Industrial Relations,* ed. Chris Wrigley. Brighton, Sussex: Harvester Press.

Towers, Brian. 1985. "Posing Larger Questions: The British Miners' Strike of 1984–85." *Industrial Relations Journal,* 16, no. 2 (Summer): 8–25.

Treu, Tiziano. 1982. "Italy." In *Workforce Reductions in Undertakings: Policies and Measures for the Protection of Redundant Workers in Seven Industrialized Market Economy Countries,* ed. Edward Yemin. Geneva: International Labour Office.

Tsebelis, George, and Peter Lange. 1995. "Strikes around the World: A Game Theoretic Approach." In *The Workers of Nations: Industrial Relations in a Global Economy,* ed. Sanford M. Jacoby, New York: Oxford University Press.

Turner, Royce Logan. 1985. "Post-War Pit Closures: The Politics of De-Industrialisation." *Political Quarterly,* 56, no. 2 (April–June): 167–74.

Ujihara, Shojiro. 1974. "The Labor Market." In *Workers and Employers in Japan: The Japanese Employment Relations System,* ed. Kazuo Ōkōchi, Bernard Karsh, and Solomon B. Levine. Tokyo: Princeton University Press and University of Tokyo Press.

Ventura, Luciano. 1990. "Licenziamenti collettivi." *Enciclopedia giuridica treccani.* Vol. 19; Rome: Treccani.

Waddington, David; Wykes, Maggie; and Chas Critcher. 1991. *Split at the Seams? Community, Continuity and Change after the 1984–5 Coal Dispute.* Milton Keynes: Open University Press.

Walker, Bruce. 1987. "Changes in the UK Motor Industry: An Analysis of Some Local Economic Impacts." Motor Industry Local Authority Network in Association with the Institute of Local Government Studies, University of Birmingham.

Waller, Robert. 1983. *The Dukeries Transformed: The Social and Politics Development of a Twentieth Century Coalfield.* Oxford: Clarendon Press.

Wallington, Peter. 1985. "Policing the Miners' Strike." *Industrial Law Journal,* 14, no. 3 (Sept.): 145–59.

Weber, Max. 1958. *The Protestant Ethic and the Spirit of Capitalism.* New York: Charles Scribner's Sons.

——— 1968. *Economy and Society,* ed. Guenther Roth and Claus Wittich. 2 vols.; Berkeley: University of California Press.

White, P. J. 1983. "The Management of Redundancy." *Industrial Relations Journal,* 14, no. 1 (Spring): 32–40.

Wilks, Stephen. 1984. *Industrial Policy and the Motor Industry.* Manchester: Manchester University Press.

Willman, Paul. 1984. "The Reform of Collective Bargaining and Strike Activity in BL Cars 1976–1982." *Industrial Relations Journal,* 15, no. 2 (Summer): 6–17.

Willman, Paul, and Graham Winch. 1985. *Innovation and Management Control: Labour Relations at BL Cars.* Cambridge: Cambridge University Press.

Winterton, Jonathan. 1981. "The Trend of Strikes in Coal Mining 1949–1979." *Industrial Relations Journal,* 12, no. 6 (Nov.–Dec.): 10–19.

——— 1985. "Computerized Coal: New Technology in the Mines." In *Digging Deeper: Issues in the Miners' Strike,* ed. Huw Beynon. London: Verso.

Winterton, Jonathan, and Ruth Winterton. 1989. *Coal, Crisis, and Conflict.* Manchester: Manchester University Press.

Wood, Jonathan. 1988. *Wheels of Misfortune: The Rise and Fall of the British Motor Industry.* London: Sidwick & Jackson.

World Values Study Group. 1994. World Values Survey, 1981–1984 and 1990–1993. Computer file, ICPSR version. Ann Arbor, Mich.: Institute for Social Research producer, 1994. Ann Arbor, Mich. Inter-university Consortium for Political and Social Research distributor.

Yemin, Edward, ed. 1982. *Workforce Reductions in Undertakings: Policies and Measures for the Protection of Redundant Workers in Seven Industrialized Market Economy Countries.* Geneva: International Labour Office.

MAIN JOURNALS AND MAGAZINES CONSULTED

Conquiste del Lavoro, 1979–91
The Economist, 1959–60
JFEA News (Japan Federation of Employers Associations), 1959–60
Japan Labor Bulletin, 1962–68
Japan Quarterly, 1960–62
Journal of Finance and Commerce, 1953–56
The Oriental Economist, 1953–60
Rassegna Sindacale, 1979–81
Sōyhō News, 1960–64
The Times (London), 1979–80

INDEX